The Italian Squad

ALSO BY ANDREW PAUL MELE

"Tearin' Up the Pea Patch":
The Brooklyn Dodgers, 1953 (McFarland, 2015)

A Brooklyn Dodgers Reader
(McFarland, 2005; paperback 2010)

The Italian Squad

*How the NYPD Took
Down the Black Hand
Extortion Racket*

ANDREW PAUL MELE

McFarland & Company, Inc., Publishers
Jefferson, North Carolina

LIBRARY OF CONGRESS CATALOGUING-IN-PUBLICATION DATA

Names: Mele, Andrew Paul, 1938– author.
Title: The Italian squad : how the NYPD took down the
Black Hand extortion racket / Andrew Paul Mele.
Description: Jefferson, North Carolina : McFarland & Company, Inc., Publishers,
2020 | Includes bibliographical references and index.
Identifiers: LCCN 2019057059 |
ISBN 9781476679051 (paperback : acid free paper) ∞
ISBN 9781476638768 (ebook)
Subjects: LCSH: Black Hand (United States) | Immigrants—Crimes
against—New York (State)—New York—History—20th century. | Italian
American criminals—New York (State)—New York—History—20th century. |
Organized crime—New York (State)—New York—History—20th century. |
New York (N.Y.). Police Department—History—20th century. |
Petrosino, Joe, 1860-1909.
Classification: LCC HV652.N72 B5364 2020 | DDC 364.10609747/1—dc23
LC record available at https://lccn.loc.gov/2019057059

BRITISH LIBRARY CATALOGUING DATA ARE AVAILABLE

ISBN (print) 978-1-4766-7905-1
ISBN (ebook) 978-1-4766-3876-8

Front cover: *clockwise from top left* Mulberry Street in Little Italy in
New York City at the turn of the 20th century (Library of Congress);
Detective Michael Mealli (author's collection); Detective Andrew Mealli
(author's collection); Lieutenant Detective Joseph Petrosino
(Library of Congress); cover design by Andrew Paul Mele, Jr.

Printed in the United States of America

*McFarland & Company, Inc., Publishers
Box 611, Jefferson, North Carolina 28640
www.mcfarlandpub.com*

For my dad,
PAUL A. MELE

And my uncle,
ANDREW N. MELE

Two good men who helped make the
NYPD NEW YORK'S FINEST

Table of Contents

Preface

When I was a boy, my grandmother, Mary Mele, told me stories of times Uncle Mike and Aunt Anna got baskets of fruit or flowers or opera tickets delivered to their home. These favors came from the most famous tenor of his day, Enrico Caruso, and they were sent out of gratitude for Uncle Mike's part in capturing the Black Handers who tried to extort the opera star. I enjoyed the stories without knowing the extent of their truth until decades later when I spoke with their daughter, Teresa, then a woman in her eighties. She explained that her dad, Michael Mealli, had been a member of the original Italian Squad of the New York City Police Department. It was in this capacity that he had worked on the Caruso extortion case. She also said that she had many newspaper clippings of her dad's exploits with the NYPD and that I was welcome to visit her at her home at 2040 63rd Street in Brooklyn and peruse her memorabilia.

I was very interested as it pertained to family history, but I had not yet become an author, and my curiosity was somewhat contained. By the time I was engaged in research of my own and the Caruso–Uncle Mike story came into my mind, Teresa had passed away. I then began to conduct my own research, and through old clippings from the *New York Times* and the *Brooklyn Daily Eagle*, I was able to corroborate the events of March 1910. It struck me as curious, however, when I read some accounts that had the head of the Italian Squad, Joseph Petrosino, involved with the Caruso case, even to the point of advising the tenor to talk to the police. There was even a 1960 film called *Pay or Die* that starred Ernest Borgnine as Petrosino. In it, the Caruso case is singled out. Understandably, none of the accounts I read used dates or any documentation of the events since Petrosino had been killed in Palermo, Sicily, in 1909, one year before the events of the Caruso extortion case unfolded.

The story of Italians in America is a profound one in that their contributions to the American way of life have been extraordinary. It begins in the earliest days of European exploration with Columbus, Caboto (Cabot), Verrazzano and Vespucci. It continues through the development of our

1

government as the writings of Filippo Mazzei influenced Madison and Jefferson; in particular, the paraphrasing of Mazzei's words "All men are by nature equally free and independent" to "All men are created equal" by Thomas Jefferson in the Declaration of Independence. It goes on to Constantino Brumidi, the artist who painted the fresco on the dome in the Capitol in Washington, D.C., and who signed his painting of George Washington at Yorktown, which hangs in the dining room of the House of Representatives, "C. Brumidi, artist, citizen of the U.S."

Then there is the Garibaldi Brigade who fought on the Union side during the Civil War. Amadeo P. Giannini started a banking empire which became the Bank of America. Coincidently, Amadeo opened his first financial institution in 1904 in San Francisco, the same year that the Italian Squad came into being in New York City. Individual achievements by Italian Americans are far too numerous to list here but they range from the cowboy Charles Angelo Siringo, who once arrested Billy the Kid, to Mother Cabrini, the first American saint in the Catholic church, canonized in 1946.

In the heavy immigration period between 1880 and 1920 more than four million emigrated from Italy in what has been called one of the greatest mass migrations in world history. More than two million came to the United States and a half million stayed in New York City. Within this deluge of humanity came a small but deadly cancer, the criminal dredges of Italian society. There were thousands of Black Hand criminals free to prey on the unfortunate immigrant. Facing as they did the poverty, language barrier, and the difficulties of assimilating into an alien culture, these new Americans were often utterly powerless to fend off their assailants. The police in New York were rendered virtually helpless in combating these types of crimes because of the aforementioned language and tradition barriers that stood between them and the immigrant population.

One of the few in law enforcement who comprehended the problem was the first Italian American detective in the NYPD, Joseph Petrosino. It was at his insistence that a special unit was formed solely to counteract the criminal element in the Italian community. It was known as the Italian Squad and each and every member put his life on the line in doing his duty.

The genesis of this book actually began some 70 years ago with those stories my grandma told. By the time I started to write it, it was two generations later but I owe a debt of gratitude to my dad and his brothers and sisters as well for the family atmosphere established over the decades, allowing the memories to foster and to aid as a basis for the telling of such a historical drama of which one generation of Meles (Meallis) played such a significant role.

My sister Marylee Kearney and my first cousins Catherine Ferri and Marguerite Hughes contributed their own memories of conversations with parents and aunts and uncles as did the grandsons of Nicholas Mealli and Michael Mealli, Nick Mele and Michael Romersa. Nick recalled conversations with his granddad that helped to re-create events in the transition of the family from Italy to America. Mike contributed family photographs and conversations with his mother.

The material on Joseph Petrosino was plentiful and I studied a number of well-researched volumes on this amazing man and his life and times. They are listed in the bibliography. Material on Michael Mealli was less easy to uncover and for the early research I gratefully express my appreciation to two internet researchers for the history of the NYPD. Pascal Storino, Jr., provided the results of his research, which proved to be a collection of news articles recounting the exploits of detective Michael Mealli. Christopher Beggs added some research of his own as well as his expertise in retouching old photos. There are some reprinted in this volume that are more than 100 years old. I thank Chris for improving the quality so that they can be a part of this record.

Danny Ingellis is retired from the NYPD where he worked as a detective in the Staten Island District Attorney's office. Danny is a photographer as well, and some of his photographs are seen in these pages. He was extremely helpful as an advisor on the inner workings of the NYPD. Once again, I am grateful to Joseph and Debra Coscia for their support, encouragement and valuable assistance in formatting the book. Also to Joe for his proofing the manuscript before submission.

To my daughter Christine Mele-Love for the hours she spent searching the internet for ancestry information and for tracing the cross–Atlantic voyages of Angelo and Annamarie Mele, the parents of Michael and Andrew. To my son Andrew Mele for his creativity. To my granddaughter Alexandra for bridging the generation gap and solving my computer problems.

I cannot fail to acknowledge the men of the NYPD Italian Squad. They possessed courage, dedication, imagination, heart, and pride in their heritage. They were special and deserve to be included on any list of Italian Americans whose contributions to their adopted country were singularly notable.

Chapter One

Arrival, Assimilation, Acceptance

The date was August 30, 1860, the place, the village of Padula in the province of Salerno in the Campania region of Italy. It was the day that Giuseppe Michael Pasquale Petrosino was born. His father, Prospero, was a tailor, and his mother, Maria, died when Giuseppe was a boy. There were two siblings, a younger brother and sister to Giuseppe. Prospero remarried another Padula girl, also named Maria, and they had three more children. Known as *Mezzogiorno*, the people of the southern regions of Italy and Sicily were economically deprived in this period of Italian history and struggled with the land and their lives. Life was in a turmoil for the country, generally, as Giuseppe Garibaldi was leading his army in an effort to unify the Italian peninsula as well as the Kingdom of the Two Sicilies and the Papal States. So in 1873, when the young Petrosino was 13 years old, Prospero took the family and decided to cross the Atlantic for the United States. It would be a journey of 25 days before they arrived in New York City.

At the time that young Giuseppe Petrosino and his family arrived in America, New York and its services departments were in their infancy. The police, having come into being in 1820, was in a very formidable stage. In their in-depth study of the history of the New York Police Department, Lardner and Reppetto wrote about how today's magnificent force developed out of a "raging band of men who, in the mid–nineteenth century, slept in foul-smelling precinct dormitories for a good part of every tour of duty, smoked cigars or chewed tobacco on patrol, got their jobs through local aldermen (and lost them when the tides shifted), and often refused to investigate thefts unless rewards were offered."[1]

As early as 1820, the first days of the police force in New York, there were 123,000 inhabitants concentrated in the lower end of Manhattan Island. Most were native-born Americans and mostly Protestant. There wasn't much in the way of weaponry to disrupt an officer's day. Not until

Immigrants arriving at Ellis Island in New York City, a scene especially prevalent in the years from 1880 to 1920 (Library of Congress).

the 1840s did the Colt .45 gain acceptance, and it was not until 1852 when Henry Deringer developed a pistol in Philadelphia that the danger of firearms come into the relatively peaceful existence of the patrolman on the beat. There were docks and piers and ships in and out of the harbor, which allowed for such vices as prostitution and gambling, and Cornelius Vanderbilt illegally ferrying passengers back and forth across the Hudson River, to keep the police occupied. Most police officers were patrolmen, and their daily routines involved keeping drunks and loiterers off the streets.

There were the usual street gangs, in the Bowery to the north, made up of native-born "Yankees" and Irish-Americans who frequently clashed on the streets of Manhattan. Before the police carried firearms, officers wielded three types of clubs: a 26-inch-long nightstick, a shorter daystick or "billy club," and a ceremonial rosewood baton. The typical system of patrol duty often had an officer begin a patrol at midnight and end at 6 a.m., then go home until 6 a.m. and patrol until midnight. The next morning he might patrol from 8 a.m. until 1 p.m., go on reserve duty until midnight, go back on patrol until 6 a.m., and then go home for 12 hours. Without any means of communication between patrolmen, the system they created involved arm signals from one to another or through a "roundsman," an individual so called because he made the rounds checking on the patrolmen. Because of this system of scheduling, the recruits spent many hours living and sleeping in the section of the station that was a sort of dormitory. Lardner and Reppetto tell us that the conditions were less than ideal. "There were no showers, and a couple of narrow windows supplied what there was in the way of ventilation. It accommodated about forty men in beds spaced about two feet apart."

The Bronx and the northern end of Manhattan were mostly made up of city dumps and goat fields, known as Goatsville. Heading south was the Five Points and the Bowery. From Seventh Avenue on the west to Fourth on the east and through most of the twenties and thirties lie the most lucrative areas, known as the Tenderloin. The area was considered lucrative because it represented the best opportunities for "graft" to be collected by officers.

The changes that occurred in the daily life of the police officer at the onset of the 20th century were for the most part the result of the tremendous wave of immigration, much of it from the southern and poorest regions of the Italian peninsula and Sicily. By 1900 New York was the second largest Italian city—after Naples. Out of a population of two million, more than a half-million were Italian immigrants. They lived cramped in crumbling houses on the Lower East Side and were described as a "human antheap in which suffering, crime, ignorance, and filth were the dominant elements."[2] The environment into which these thousands upon thousands of Italians had immigrated staggers the imagination. How they could have faced the degradations and hardships with any hope of building a new and respectable life for their families is beyond comprehension and yet they persevered. It presented, as Police Commissioner William McAdoo had noted at the time, "an insoluble problem for the police."

Embedded within these masses were gangsters and hoodlums who had criminal records in Italy. Criminal elements like the Mafia and the Black Hand infiltrated the city. Their exit from Italy was made easier by the Italian government through a careless system of passports allowing for that country's undesirables to make it to America and prey upon the immigrant population. Needless to say, these conditions created major problems for police, the vast majority who were Irish- and English-speaking, and therefore unable to communicate in the Italian neighborhoods. An attitude that developed in the law enforcement community was to leave the Italians contained in their own neighborhoods so they could straighten things out for themselves.

There was far-flung corruption in both the political arena and in the police department and distrust in the authorities by the immigrant population. Yet the policemen of the 1880s earned $1,200 a year, about twice the salary of the average worker. There was a retirement benefit after 20 or 25 years (it shifted back and forth) with half pay, while most jobs had no pensions at all. The first civil service rules were enacted in 1884 and applicants had to submit to an examination, then pay $250 to a local politician to secure an appointment, followed by a one-month training period. It involved some criminal law and instructions in rules and general orders and some first aid training. By the 1880s, regardless of anything else, the New York police were being referred to by the term Mayor William Havemeyer and Chief George Matsell had bestowed upon them, "The Finest."

The police use of force was arbitrary. They wielded their clubs as they saw fit and were seldom taken to task. At the scene of a fire in midtown Manhattan one day, the police tried to hold off a crowd of bystanders. An older man with his coat pulled up over his ears and a cigar in his mouth walked toward the scene. Suddenly a policeman grabbed him by the collar, swung him around "and gave him a resounding whack on the back with his club. 'Don't you see the fire line?' the policeman yelled at him. 'Get away from here and be quick about it.'"[3] The man walked away. He turned out to be Ulysses S. Grant, the former president, who had settled in New York. As it turned out there were no repercussions, and apparently the behavior was accepted as normal.

Shortly after the time that Giuseppe Petrosino stepped foot in the big city in America, there was another birth. This one was in New York City. Michael Mealli was born on July 2, 1876. His parents were Angelo Mele and Annamarie (Spilizina). There were four siblings to Michael. Paul died on December 12, 1894, at age 12. Catarina, the oldest and the only girl, was born in 1873. Andrew was born on December 3, 1885, and Nicola was born on January 16, 1889. At the turn of the century immigrants from Italy were about 80 percent male and 80 percent from southern Italy. The Meles simply fit the mold. In Italy the name was "Mele," but as commonly happened at the time, in the transition at Ellis Island, it was phonetically spelled as "Mealli." Catarina married while in her early teens to Chriscenzo Sarlo. The Sarlos were also of the same town in Italy. Both families came to America about the same time and lived in an Italian neighborhood in downtown Brooklyn, the Meallis at 10 Navy Street, the Sarlos just across the street at 11 Navy Street. The origin of the name stems from a town in the north just 13 miles west of Genoa in the region of Liguria. Mele, Italy, is home to 2,687. While part of the family kept the "Mele" name, Michael and Andrew both joined the police force under the new spelling, "Mealli."

Navy Street and the area around the Navy Yard in Brooklyn was the home neighborhood to many hardworking, honest people, many who were Italian immigrants at the turn of the 20th century. There were, however, a share of young men in gangs that turned to criminal activity. In 1907 the "Navy Street Boys" were led by a 19-year-old gang leader who would become noted as Frank Nitti in later years. The gang included three brothers named Capone: Ralph, Salvatore, and the youngest, eight-year-old Alphonse. Michael Mealli was a 31-year-old detective attached to the Italian Squad of the NYPD at the same time and still lived on Navy Street. The Capone family (Caponi) would eventually grow to nine children. Alphonse—Al Capone—was fifth in line. The Capones lived at 95 Navy Street, the Meallis at 10.

It was in this period that more than four million Italians emigrated from Italy in what would be called one of the greatest mass migrations in world history. Italian immigrants entering the U.S. went from 12,354 a year in 1880 to 100,135 in 1900. The steamship companies were making so much money off the steerage traffic that they sent their own agents through the Italian countryside, offering jobs in America. The contracts that these agents offered were made illegal after 1885; however, they drew laborers by the thousands. The average sum carried by Italian immigrants through Ellis Island around 1900 and the immediate years following was $17. The *padrones* (Italian for "boss") recruited young men for work often just as they stepped off the boat. The others had to look for jobs; their $17 would allow them to survive for two or three weeks without work. One teenage boy explained how he was recruited minutes after he stepped off the ferry from Ellis Island. "Bartolo rented a room in a wooden house in Adams Street in Brooklyn. There were fifteen men in the room, a stove in the middle of the room and beds all around the sides.... Most of the men in the room worked at digging a sewer. They paid Bartolo about one quarter of their wages."[4]

Between 1890 and 1900 alone, 655,888 Italian immigrants entered the United States. This great migration had its genesis during the period of unification in the 1860s and 1870s. The greatest flow of immigrants left their homeland between 1880 and 1911. One author's description was succinct: "The land literally hemorrhaged peasants."[5] Eighty percent of the immigrant population was from the south of Italy and Sicily. The poverty and hunger that persisted in these areas had not changed following the unification, and so these laborers thought to benefit from the urgent need for unskilled labor in the western continent.

The long and tumultuous history of the region was ripe with war and colonization. Since the 8th century B.C., Greek city-states sent their fleets out to all corners of the Mediterranean and Black seas and founded their colonies in the most advantageous locations. Odessa, a Russian port, was once a Greek colony, as was Marseilles in France and Naples, or in the Greek *Neapolis* (New City), in Italy. Southern Italy and, in particular, Sicily were strategically placed. The earliest conflict the Greeks encountered was with a tribe called *Itali*, from which the name Italy derives. Sicily, because of its geographical location, was a constant battleground and it became the site for the later Punic wars between Greece and Carthage. The growth of the colonies was principally through trade and agriculture. Ultimately the area came under the rule of the Roman Empire and agricultural estates were run by slave labor: Greeks, Persians, Egyptians, and any other victims of Rome's wars. Rebellion of one sort or another became the tradition for Sicilians and, to a lesser extent, the southern Italians.

One scourge of the Mediterranean that lasted from about 800 A.D. to 1800 was piracy. Saracen pirate fleets numbered hundreds of ships. In time people began to flee inland, abandoning low-lying shore areas and allowing the once-fertile land to deteriorate. Some cities were even left empty in the wave of the pirate terror. The Saracens were in retreat by the 11th century, pushed by a wave of Normans, a warrior race of Scandinavians. They conquered Sicily and fought battles on the Italian mainland. The Normans segued into Frederick II's Holy Roman Empire. A positive influence during his reign, the south of Italy and Sicily declined after Frederick, leaving feudalism and poverty. The causes stemmed from the barbaric Turks who cut trade routes, crucially affecting the economics of the area. Arab and Spanish domination did little to improve conditions from the 16th to the 19th centuries, and emigration soon became the best hope for the people of the area.

In the 19th century, Italians reached out to areas for work and began to establish colonies throughout Europe and the Mediterranean. Amfitheatrof in *Children of Columbus* informs us that they built railroads in Russia and the Balkans, worked on the Suez Canal and helped to construct the first Aswan Dam. As they began to emigrate, many found South America, and Argentina in particular, a desirable place of focus. Many married and settled into their new habitats. They settled in Canada and Brazil, where more than a third of all immigrants were Italian. Their focus now turned to the United States. From about 1880 these migrations commenced. Mostly laborers, they were drawn by the need for their work as the industrial system in this country began to build.

It meant a sea voyage to New York and Ellis Island for processing. About 15 percent of immigrants were detained for medical reasons. In 1878 there were 20,000 Italians in the country. By 1900 out of a population of two million, one-half million were Italians. The majority of immigrants who made the initial journey were male and came without their families. The *padroni* ("boss" in Italian) system provided jobs to some. After time, when they were able to find employment they sent for their families or returned to Italy and came back with families or portions of them. Angelo Mele made several trips and brought his family to New York piecemeal.

Giuseppe Petrosino was 13 when his family landed in New York City. He enrolled in Public School 24 at Bayard and Mulberry streets in Manhattan and began to learn English. There was an ongoing neighborhood conflict between the Irish and Italian kids. The Irish had dominated the area for years and did not like the new additions to their realm. Often the Italian children were victims of attacks after school with fistfights and rock throwing. Joe was described as a quiet boy, and a friend said he was "a big strapping boy, and he was very ambitious."[6] As a result, the other kids looked up to him and turned to him in their battles with the Irish youth, and he never disappointed them. He wanted to be a success as an immigrant in New York. The need to earn money forced Joseph to quit school before entering high school. Neither Joe's father nor his brother, Vincent, were stable enough to earn a decent living, so it remained for the youngest Petrosino male to keep the family afloat. An enterprising young man, Petrosino and a friend, Anthony Marria, started a shoeshine and newspaper business in front of 300 Mulberry Street, headquarters of the New York City Police Department. It was through the nefarious activities of Tammany Hall, the corrupt political machine run by Irish politicians, that Petrosino learned the facts of the street life in New York. Italian bootblacks in 1870s Manhattan were forced to pay money for the right to work a certain corner or location. The youthful Petrosino learned English at night school classes set up by the city for immigrants. Petacco, Petrosino's biographer, tells us he became a citizen through the naturalization process of his father since he was still a minor.

His pride and his ambition led Petrosino to a decision that caused him to abruptly give up the shoeshine business and make an attempt to better himself. He worked for a time for a stockbroker named DeLuca who had an office on Broome Street. He went around seeking employment and tried a number of jobs. At one point he actually applied to the police force but at five foot, three inches, he was four inches too short, too swarthy, had a thick Italian accent and, above all, wasn't Irish. According to author Stephen Talty, "He even toured the country as an itinerant musician, playing his violin in the Deep South before returning to Manhattan."[7] He was 18 when he landed a job as a street cleaner for the city of New York. Oddly enough, at the time, the sanitation department was under the jurisdiction of the police department. He diligently progressed and soon was commanding the scow that towed the garbage out to sea where the cargo was dumped. The laborers from Italy continued to land in New York and the 833 that lived there in 1850 had swelled to half a million by 1910.

Not everyone welcomed these newcomers. To many they were still "wops," "dagos" and "guineas." And through the period of growth and upheaval in the city, Petrosino persevered. He came to the attention of Aleck "Clubber" Williams, a police inspector, who noted Petrosino's commanding presence and show of authority. Williams was thoroughly corrupt in dealings between criminals and Tammany Hall, but also brutal in his dealings with street criminals. Police would not carry arms until 1877. Until then their principal weapon was a nightstick (called a paddy club), and Williams wielded one with deadly force. He joined the police force in the late 1860s, and in one of his early exploits, he beat two gang members unconscious and threw the both of them through a plate-glass window. It is reported that he beat six other members of the gang with his paddy club in the street outside the saloon. In 1871 he was promoted to captain and later to inspector. When he was transferred to the fashionable district below 42nd Street on the West Side, he said, "I've had nothing but chuck steak for a long time, and now I'm going to get a little of the tenderloin."[8] Thus, the name "The Tenderloin" district was born. It was a place where Williams and others were able to partake of the "graft and gravy" which were prevalent there.

An investigation of Clubber Williams in 1894 revealed his enormous income (he was said to be receiving $30,000 a year in protection money from one brothel alone), a 17-room estate in Connecticut, and a 53-foot yacht plus cash and commercial real estate. Shortly afterward Police Commissioner Teddy Roosevelt forced Clubber Williams into retirement.

Williams had prevailed upon Petrosino when he was commander of the garbage scow to join the police force and arranged his appointment even though he was four inches shorter than the required height. Williams had good reason for his selection of the young Italian. The police force was made up of nearly all Irishmen. Someone who could relate to, and help keep in line, the Sicilians and Calabrians on the streets of the city could prove to be a valuable asset. In 1883 Joseph Petrosino became one of the first Italians to join the New York Police Force. There were some German officers, and some Jewish, but the force was overwhelmingly Irish.

Even then, Petrosino was met with opposition, this time among his own people. He was cursed at and received death threats from Italians. Considering the background of southern Italy and Sicily, to these people, anyone wearing a uniform was representing a corrupt and antagonistic enemy. One Sicilian American said that to "join up with the foreigners and volunteer to police your own kind was 'an extreme and deliberate affront' that wasn't easily forgotten."[9] At Williams's suggestion, Petrosino began at the lowest level in the police force, as an informer with the idea of joining the police later. It was a valuable experience that gave him insight into police operations. On October 10, 1883, Petrosino, at 23 years old, officially became a member of the NYPD. He was following in the footsteps of Vincenzo Giudice, also from Padula, who was first Italian to wear the uniform of the New York Police Department.

By 1890, Petrosino had moved on to investigative work within the Italian community. He moved into a small apartment in an Irish section of the city. This necessary move further estranged him from his countrymen, though not from all of them. Many realized that the police were badly needed in the community and understood. Nevertheless, it must have been a trying period of development for the young Italian police officer in late 19th century New York City. He was a loner, keeping to himself for the most part, during the years he was a patrolman on 13th Street. He was kept at arm's length by the Irish and Jewish members of the force. There was never a dereliction of duty on his part. "In every situation he displayed efficiency, courage, shrewdness, and perfect knowledge of departmental regulations."[10]

His first assignments came as a member of the precinct that patrolled the Tenderloin district, from 23rd to 42nd streets and from Fifth to Seventh avenues, the most troublesome and unruly area of the city. In one of his first experiences walking a beat, Petrosino was strolling by the piers at the foot of Canal Street when he heard the cries of a struggle. An African American man named William Farraday was being beaten by four white men. Petrosino waded into the fray with his nightstick flaying, and after a few blows, drove off the attackers. Tough and incorruptible would be the identifying marks from the earliest days of his career as a police officer.

In 1895 Theodore Roosevelt had become head of the New York Board of Police Commissioners and as such dedicated himself to reforming the

Mulberry Street was the main street in Little Italy in New York City at the turn of the 20th century (Library of Congress).

often-corrupt police department. As commissioner, Roosevelt hired cops on the basis of their ability rather than contacts or party affiliations. He shored up the men and their duties. He was aware of the importance of having immigrants to police immigrants and with this in mind, he became aware of Joseph Petrosino. Roosevelt was obviously impressed with the tough, rugged, five-foot-three-inch officer, who worked longer and harder at his job. He infiltrated areas of Little Italy using disguises: a laborer, a Catholic priest, an Orthodox Jew. His reputation grew. He was assigned to any and all crimes that involved Italians. "The brass had only to glimpse the slightest Italian angle to a case, and the cry rang out: 'Send for the dago!'"[11]

Roosevelt was ambitious and saw the role of police commissioner as a stepping stone to a political career. Petrosino was well aware of it also and he never missed an opportunity to publicize his boss. The two became friends and saw each other frequently. In turn Roosevelt named Petrosino, after just two years on the job, the first Italian detective sergeant in the country. This happened on July 20, 1895. From then on he worked only on those cases that were especially assigned to him.

Described as bull-necked and dark-eyed, he often wore all black, a

Prince Albert coat over a black suit and a familiar black derby hat. He was in the middle of one case after another and some, like the Carboni affair, took on an unusual tone. One night in 1897 Angelo Carboni got into an argument in a café with Natale Brogno. During the scuffle that followed Brogno was stabbed in the back. Although Carboni swore he was innocent, he was convicted of murder by a Manhattan jury. A judge sentenced him to death saying that this was a warning to all Italians prone to committing that sort of crime. Petrosino heard on the street that Carboni was a hardworking, respectful man and that there was reason to think that another individual might be responsible for the crime.

He took it upon himself to look into the crime and visited Carboni at Sing Sing prison. Carboni again professed his innocence, saying that he was fighting with Brogno face to face when the man fell with a knife in his back. The detective determined to look further into the case. He learned that Salvatore Ceramello, one of many enemies of Brogno, had been in the café that night, had a history of violence, and had disappeared from Little Italy the next day. He searched diligently for a month for the new suspect and with the date of Carboni's execution in the electric chair approaching, Petrosino located his prey in Baltimore. He arrested him and reported the capture and a full confession to police headquarters. Less than a week before his scheduled execution, Angelo Carboni walked out of Sing Sing. Petrosino proved his mettle. He would be as diligent in aiding the innocent as he was in pursuing the guilty.

In another case, the detective went undercover in the guise of a laborer infiltrating a group of anarchists. His report to Teddy Roosevelt and President McKinley revealed nefarious plans including the assassinations of world leaders, among them President McKinley. His warnings went unheeded and McKinley was assassinated in Buffalo, New York.[12]

A misinterpretation linking the Black Hand and the Mafia is often made. Although extortion and protection and murder and kidnapping were the prevailing themes of both, they differed in interpretation. The actions of the Black Hand remained the motions of individuals or small gangs whose threatening letters were often followed up by criminal activity. The Mafia, on the other hand, was born in western Sicily in the 1860s. Sicilian history is fraught with struggles against authority, which would also come into play when immigrants looked with distrust against the police in America. Secret societies began to spring up to combat the authority of the Bourbon Monarchy, the ruling power of the Kingdom of the Two Sicilies. As they offered protection to the people, in time they evolved into "sects" that offered protection from themselves. The Black

Hand developed independently, allowing for every thug or murderer to create his own criminal empire.

As the Black Hand became stronger, they became bolder, and their brash tactics burst out into the open on a morning in August 1903. A contractor in Brooklyn, Nicolò Cappiello, received a letter threatening to blow up his house if he didn't adhere to their instructions. It was signed *La Mano Nera,* the Black Hand. The Neapolitan had never heard of the Black Hand so he dismissed the letter. Two more letters arrived and then a visit to his house by two men. This time, frightened, he yielded to their threats and paid $1,000. They returned several days later and now demanded $3,000. Cappiello went to the police who made five arrests. All five were convicted and sent to jail.

The Black Hand even developed a "lay-away plan," regular payments with prearranged dates instead of a one-time lump-sum payment. A shop-keeper on Elizabeth Street approached Joe Petrosino to tell him of his hav-ing had three visitors. They knew the shopkeeper had received Black Hand letters but had not responded to them. They offered their protection from any harm from the letter senders. "Just wet our whistles," they told the frightened shopkeeper.[13] The term referred to the Sicilian system by which they provided protection to anyone who wanted to run a business safely. All they had to do was pay regularly. It was the onset of the "protection racket" in this country, and a mainstay to the mobsters' business. The sys-tem had been imported from Sicily by Don Vito Cascio Ferro, the Mafia boss who had returned to Sicily following the famous "barrel murder" in which he had been implicated.

That same month an eight-year-old boy, Antonio Mannino, was kid-napped. The boy's father, Vincenzo, received a letter signed by the Black Hand. Petrosino was assigned to the case. Suddenly the newspapers were filled with stories of this new presence that called itself the Black Hand. The police followed every lead and Petrosino discouraged any payment to the kidnappers, but a week after the boy's disappearance, he was found by a relative walking on the street. The Mannino family refused to speak to the police and Petrosino was convinced they had paid up. The number of cases rose, and there were more kidnappings, a store burning, and a bombing. It was a frightful summer. The next year the crimes continued, and they included a murder. The Italian detective was building a repu-tation among his peers and the immigrant population. One Black Hand victim recalled how he had been kidnapped as a child. He was kept in a room by a man and a woman; the woman came by to feed him. One night as he lay in bed he saw the skylight being lifted and a rope dropped down.

A man climbed down the rope and motioned to the terrified boy not to scream. As he did so he showed him his badge, whispered that he was detective Petrosino, told him not to be afraid and hid the boy under the bed. When the kidnappers came back, he arrested them both.

By the summer of 1904, they were calling it "Black Hand Fever." On August 22, Joseph Graffi was murdered in a New Rochelle apartment, a knife thrust into his heart. A bomb exploded in a grocery store on Elizabeth Street in Manhattan injuring the proprietor's wife. A wealthy Bronx contractor entered his home to find his wife missing. He searched the house and the neighborhood for six days until one night he answered a knock on his door. Two Italians told him they were holding his wife and demanded ransom. He paid them and she was returned. She told her husband that the two Black Handers had knocked on her door one afternoon and dragged her away.

The newspapers called for curbing the number of Sicilians that would be allowed into the country. Petrosino opposed such action but realized something more had to be done and so he formulated a plan and took it to Police Commissioner William McAdoo. The detective wanted to form an "Italian Squad," a group of police officers dedicated solely to solving crimes committed by and against the Italian immigrant community, primarily in Manhattan's Little Italy.

McAdoo was against the plan. He thought the idea of singling out an Italian unit would be counterproductive to other nationalities in the city. Tammany Hall was also in opposition. Protecting Italians who did not readily vote could harm their standings with the Irish immigrants and consequently other nationalities who were entering the country around 1900. Petrosino persevered. He tried to reason with the powers that be by cautioning them of the danger that the Black Hand was generating. He passed his concerns to journalists and tried to unite prospective victims to take action. The continued violence of the Black Hand Society finally turned the decision in Petrosino's favor. On September 14, 1904, Commissioner McAdoo told the detective, "They finally granted your request."[14] There would be an Italian Squad and Petrosino would head it.

Detective Sergeant Joe Petrosino was established as the "Italian Sherlock Holmes." In the years ahead Michael Mealli would also establish a reputation for his diligent police work and the press would refer to him as "The Italian Specialist." When Mealli got his first job working for the city of New York, it was when he was one of twenty new appointees to the New York City Fire Department. His appointment was announced in an article in the *Brooklyn Daily Eagle* dated August 15, 1902, by Fire Commissioner

Sturgis. Mealli was assigned to what is today Engine Company No. 108. Originally Ladder Company #8 when it was established in 1887, it was redesignated as Ladder #58 on October 1, 1899, and was thus identified when Mealli joined. Before the borough of Brooklyn was incorporated into the city of New York on January 1, 1898, the department operated as the Brooklyn Fire Department. In 1913 it became Ladder 108. Michael Mealli reported to 112 Seigel Street in Williamsburg. The company's tenure there lasted 84 years and on August 9, 1971, Ladder #108 moved to a new firehouse at 187 Union Avenue where they remain to this day.

A few months later, on January 30, 1903, Mealli was appointed as a patrolman of the NYPD and assigned shield #3529. Thus began a topsy-turvy, rough-and-tumble career as a police officer and later a detective. There would be some shaky days for Mike in his 16 years as a police officer and the first one came in May of the year he was appointed. Mealli, working out of the 50th Precinct on Fulton Street in Brooklyn, was charged with "conduct unbecoming an officer." Whatever the reasons for the charge, it apparently had little stability, as the complaint was dismissed. Just three months later, however, he was charged with "neglect of duty" and fined one-half days pay. At the time of Mealli's appointment to the force, he was one of only 17 Italian police officers in a force of over 8,000. Joseph Petrosino was the only Italian detective on the force. Petrosino lobbied for additional Italians to be named as detectives and on April 28, 1905, Mealli was transferred to Headquarters Squad, Brooklyn, for duty in the detective bureau.

The Italian Secret Service was created in 1904. Dubbed "The Italian Squad," its stated purpose was to "keep pace with that lawless element which is prevalent to some extent among our rapidly increasing Italian population," as written by Mayor John P. Mitchell.[15] It would be Detective Sgt. Petrosino's duty to recruit officers to work in the squad. For their own safety and that of their families, the identities of the officers assigned was known only to the police commissioner and a small number of the highest-ranking members within the department.

Joseph Petrosino was 17 years older than Michael Mealli, and neither could know upon joining the force that fate would lock them together as future allies in a monumental struggle against a cold, vicious and deadly foe to be known formally as the Society of the Black Hand.

Chapter Two

The Black Hand Society— "La Mano Nera"

It was poverty that drove hundreds of thousands of Italians to the U.S. from their homeland in the south of Italy and Sicily. They wanted the opportunity to work and care for their families and thought they could get that chance in the new country. They settled in areas of New York that the immigrants called "colonies," but were known as "Little Italys" to the non–Italians. Lower Manhattan housed the greatest number of Italian immigrants and grew to be the principle "Little Italy" in the country. But hundreds of Sicilians settled on the East Side between 106th and 116th streets while the Neapolitans gathered around the Mulberry Street area and also in the section near the Navy Yard. The future detective and Italian Squad member Mike Mealli and his siblings grew up in this neighborhood and within this environment. Italians and Jews began to replace the Irish and Germans as the most dominant immigrant group living in the most depressed conditions in the city. When the journalist Jacob Riis published *How the Other Half Lives,* he brought the horrible living conditions of the Italian immigrant to the attention of the public. He described one tenement block near Mulberry Street as 132 rooms containing 1,324 Italian immigrants sleeping in tiers of bunks, ten or more people to a room.

It was a difficult transition for these hardworking immigrants seeking employment, caring for their families and assimilating into a foreign culture. Adding to this was a new threat, a deadly one, and the words, *La Mano Nera* (Black Hand), instilled fear into their otherwise arduous existence.

There is often little or no distinction made between Black Hand and Mafia, but this is a misconception. While the origins of the criminal organization known as the Mafia are subject to speculation, there is evidence that its activities stem from at least the 1860s.

Filippo Antonio Gualterio, prefect of Palermo, used the term in a report in April 1865, which was thought to be the first use of the term.

He described the "so-called Mafia or criminal associations" as organized extortionists and murderers.[1] The Mafia, however, operated in Sicily as early as 1840, but without a formal name. Simply put, Mafia bosses forced farmers to employ their men and pay a portion of their profits for "protection." Those who refused were intimidated, injured or murdered. These associations were often called *La Cosa Nostra*—"Our Thing." Often vendettas grew out of the conflicts between various Cosa Nostra organizations. By 1860, these criminal societies had a strong hold over Sicilian industries, particularly the citrus industry.

These factions reached the United States before the Civil War. It began in New Orleans with brothers Joseph and Raffaele Agnello by 1860. They were natives of Palermo and soon another group sprung up, this one made from immigrants from Messina and led by Joseph Macheca. Conflicts developed, creating Mafia wars and in 1869 violence escalated to the point of several murders of leaders taking place. By April 1872 both Agnello brothers had been slain by the Macheca gang. In the meantime, new Mafia societies developed in San Francisco, St. Louis and Massachusetts, the latter which logged its first Mafia murder in Dedham on November 21, 1889.

The first-known such crimes in New York City occurred on July 21, 1857, when Patrolman Eugene Anderson was shot and killed during a robbery by a known Mafia member, Michaele Cancemi. Sentenced to 20 years, Cancemi served his time and then returned to Italy.

The Black Hand was a type of criminal extortion whose roots can be traced to Sicily and the Kingdom of Naples as early as the 1750s. The name is linked to at least two other groups: One, a group of Spanish anarchists, a secret society that dated back to the days of the Inquisition. The other, a secret military society officially formed on May 9, 1911, by officers in the Army of the Kingdom of Serbia. However, an antecedent was a conspiracy group that assassinated the Serbian royal couple in 1903. Later, as the Black Hand Society, they were responsible for the assassination of Archduke Franz Ferdinand at Sarajevo in 1914, which ultimately led to the outbreak of World War I.

In the mid–1800s, the Black Hand Society had already made its way to the America of Italian immigrants, the first known victim being Francisco Domingo, a Sicilian whose murdered body was found on an embankment of the Mississippi River near New Orleans on January 3, 1855. The proliferation of the criminal actions by the Black Hand built up in the 1880s as the Italian immigrations into the country rose dramatically. Their method was the use of extortion, the unlawful exaction of money or property through intimidation, and they flourished from the 1880s until about 1920. These extortionists preyed on immigrants in the Italian community of Little Italy in New York City, later spreading to other American cities like Chicago, New Orleans and Kansas City.

The newspapers often referred to the Black Hand as a "criminal organization," but NYPD detective Joseph Petrosino continually tried to dissolve that misconception. "I've told you many times before," he said, "that the Black Hand doesn't exist as a functioning organization. It's the newspapers that have built up the myth of an octopus that's supposed to have the whole city of New York in its tentacles. What does actually exist is gangs, mostly very small, and not connected with one another, that have appropriated this name that the anarchists invented to frighten their victims."[2] The nature of the Black Hand crimes and the methods used to intimidate victims indicated an unorganized body with no central leadership and lacking structure. This was in part the reasons why they were difficult to apprehend; they lacked cohesion, except for the letters that made the same threats in virtually all cases. It was found that in almost every case of a Black Hand arrest, the man had been arrested for some crime in Italy. They simply joined the immigrants and entered the country. Deputy Police Commissioner Arthur Woods explained, "The criminals settled amongst their countrymen and proceeded to prey upon them like parasites, fattening off the main body."[3]

The typical tactic of the Black Hand was to send letters to victims, threatening harm if they failed to deliver an amount of money specified. The letters were signed with a hand imprinted with black ink and often accompanied by symbols like daggers, or a hangman's noose. These criminals resorted to arson, bodily harm, and even kidnapping and murder if payments were not forthcoming. On August 3, 1903, a Brooklyn building contractor Nicola Cappiello received a letter that was signed with a black hand and skull and crossbones. It said, "If you don't meet us at Seventy-second Street and Thirteenth Avenue Brooklyn, to-morrow afternoon, your house will be dynamited and your family killed. The same fate awaits you in the event of your betraying our purposes to the police."[4] They demanded $10,000. Cappiello refused to pay and more messages arrived. Several days later three friends arrived at his house with a fourth man and they offered to mediate the demand for $1,000. The contractor agreed. After paying the $1,000, they returned and asked for more. Realizing what he was in for, Cappiello went to the police. The "friends" were arrested, tried and convicted.

Black Hand criminals were relentless—often tracking a victim for weeks and months and over miles. John Bentergna of New York had been part of a Black Hand gang but tried to disassociate himself. When an attempt was made on his life, he fled to Chicago, but the society sought him out. He went to St. Louis, then Omaha, then Denver, always with the Black Hand in pursuit. Finally he got to Los Angeles where he received letters postmarked from New York City threatening him. He was shot at on a Los Angeles street. Having been a barber in New York, he rented a chair in an LA barbershop. One day a man tapped on the window of the shop where Bentergna was working. As he turned a shot was fired through the window, killing him.

Salvatore Spinella, in a letter to the *New York Times* around the turn of the century, explained how he had come to New York from Italy and went to work as a painter. He prospered and bought two buildings, and then the Black Hand sent a letter demanding $7,000. Spinella refused to pay. "I tell them go to hell," he wrote, "and the bandits try to blow up my house. They set off one, two, three, four, five bombs in my houses." Spinella went to the police. His tenants all vacated his buildings out of fear. "From thirty tenants I am down to six. I owe a thousand dollars interest that is due next month and I cannot pay. I am a ruined man. My family lives in fear. My brother Francesco and I do guard duty at the windows with guns night and day. My wife and children have not left the house for weeks. How long can this go on?"[5] In the end Spinella lost everything and was forced to seek work as a laborer. In some ways he was one of the lucky ones.

A candy stand in Brooklyn was burned down killing the owner, Ernest Curci. Twenty people were injured when a bomb exploded on 151st Street. The murder of Joseph Graffi in New Rochelle by a knife thrust into the heart. By 1906, it seemed the society was everywhere. In Hillsville, Pennsylvania, the Black Hand under the Carbon Limestone Company owned large quarries in which immigrants arriving from Italy were sent to work. The entire town, called "Helltown" by inhabitants, was ruled over by Joe Bagnato, the head of the local Black Hand. Every payday the laborers would deposit a portion of their envelope contents with Bagnato. A headline in the *Brooklyn Daily Eagle* on December 17, 1906, announced "Another Black Hand Bomb." Shortly before 10 p.m. the previous night an explosion occurred in the basement of a five-story tenement building at 633 Columbus Avenue in Manhattan. The force of the blast blew the iron doors of the cellar halfway across the avenue. Fire marshals found two zinc cans that had contained powder and iron pieces and to which a fuse had been attached. The Italian grocer living in the building, S. Atlansio commented, "They [the Black Hand] will get me yet."[6]

The Black Hand extended its violence to Little Italys in other areas of America. The fear it instilled was widespread. The mention of the words *La Mano Nera* would cause people to make the sign of the cross in hopes of divine protection. Extortion letters were written in a number of dialects indicating the origins of these criminals, the symbols they used varied greatly. The imprint of a hand dipped in black ink, of course, but they added daggers, bleeding hearts and hands holding a knife. The extortionists preyed on the more well-to-do, but no one was immune from their treachery. Generally unorganized, there was no central leadership. Any thug or gangster could issue a Black Hand letter and commit whatever atrocities they were capable of. Sometimes small groups or gangs contributed as well, though they often worked without knowledge of other Black Handers.

There was the case of a Black Hand victim, Pasquale Pati, a banker at 238–240 Elizabeth Street. The victim of numerous Black Hand letters over a period of 14 years, Pati refused to submit to extortionists demands. When Pasquale refused to submit to an extortion letter several weeks prior, a bomb was tossed into the bank. Depositors, fearful of losing their savings, began to make withdrawals and over a period of several weeks over $400,000 of the $500,000 of capital that the bank owned was withdrawn. Doing business under the name Pasquale Pati & Son, the firm conducted a bank, a post office business and dealt in steamship tickets and real estate. Pati's son-in-law, Louis Cattiere, also worked in the business. Pati, known as the "J. Pierpont Morgan of Little Italy," resided at 144 Ocean Parkway in Brooklyn. He owned real estate in the Bronx, Brooklyn and Manhattan.

Four weeks prior, a bomb was placed under the front window of the bank. The explosion did damage wrecking the front window. Since the bombing, Pati and his son-in-law had kept revolvers handy while in the bank. When, on March 6, 1908, three armed men entered the bank, one of them approached Pati and said, "I am going to kill you, your wife and son."[7] The three of them plus Cattiere were all on the premises at the time. As the man raised his right hand, Pati grabbed his .32-caliber revolver and fired at the man. At about the same time Cattiere also opened fire, firing six times. Italian Squad detectives Archiepoli, DiGilio, Botti, Miceli, and Bonomio were nearby and rushed to the bank. They overpowered one man trying to escape.

Pati told the detectives of threatening letters and also phone calls that he had been receiving, explaining the reasons he proceeded to arm himself. Three shots hit the Black Hander and after being removed to St. Vincent's Hospital, he gave his name as Francesco Pellatro and gave a second name of Giuseppe Sapia. The arrested man was Michaelo D'Augustine. In addition to the bomb four weeks prior, Pati told police that about a year and a half before then, a fire had been set in the tenement house above the bank.

Pellatro, who had been in this country only a few months, died at the hospital. Pati was forced to close his bank because of the panic among his depositors. He placed a note on the door saying why he took the action he did, but said "he had been molested and threatened, but would be back soon."[8] He wasn't. Pasquale Pati, who had built a business over 17 years, starting out as a cobbler, was a ruined man.

There were two cases involving scams that detective Petrosino investigated. The first began on December 22, 1898, when a Sicilian laborer was found wandering on the Bowery, looking and acting extremely ill. His name was Antonio Sperduto and he told police someone tried to poison him. He was able to explain his story, in his own language, to Joseph Petrosino. He had come to America six months before, leaving his wife and four children behind in Sicily. He worked at a job digging a subway tunnel for those six months. He had gone to the office of the steamship company to arrange to bring his family to the United States when he met a stranger who said he had known Sperduto in Sicily. He knew names of his wife and children and the two had a drink together. "I woke up in a dark alley," Sperduto said. "I was lying in a pool of vomit and my wallet was gone."[9]

It was the so-called "poison" gang that learned personal information of intended victims, pretended they had known them in the old country, shared a drink that was generously endowed with knockout drops, and then robbed the victim. It took a few days for Petrosino to make the arrest of the gang leader Giuseppe Giuliano and it was done in Hollywood fashion. They grappled at Giuliano's apartment building, rolling down four flights of stairs and into the street. Here the stronger policeman shoved Giuliano's head under a manhole cover while squeezing his throat until the subdued suspect was put under arrest.

In the next year, 1899, Petrosino put an end to the "insurance gang," all 112 members. The scam was that these men pretended to be insurance salesmen and persuaded their intended victims to take out life insurance policies on credit. The only condition they asked was that the policy holder show good faith by naming the salesman as beneficiary for a year, then it would be an easy matter to change the beneficiary—a reasonable enough request considering that the policy was free of premium payments. Needless to say, the insured seldom lived out the year.

An early arrival to Little Italy was the Morello gang. Their forte was counterfeiting but they were soon into other nefarious enterprises. On April 14, 1903, a woman named Frances Conners was on her way to work. At about 5:30 a.m. she came upon a barrel in the middle of the sidewalk in front of 743 East 11th Street near Avenue D. She saw that in the barrel was the body of a man. Her scream was heard by a police officer, Joseph McCall, who was patrolling the opposite side of East 11th, and he rushed across the street. Officer McCall summoned detectives and the mystery of the barrel murder case began to unfold. The corpse was doubled over, the knees up to the shoulders, and completely naked. His throat had been slit, nearly severing the head from the torso. There were 18 stab wounds on the body as well. The police found a small scrap of paper with the Italian words that said, "Come quickly." The head of the detective bureau George McClosky assigned Joe Petrosino to the case.

The Secret Service, who had been tracking the Morello gang for over a year concerning their counterfeiting activities, stepped in. The agent in charge was William Flynn, chief of the New York bureau of the U.S. Secret Service. Petrosino would work with him on a number of cases over the years. Flynn was the son of an Irish immigrant and a native of Manhattan. He was 36 years old and a former semiprofessional baseball player. Tall and powerfully built, he had left school at 15 to become a plumber. He worked for several years as a warden in a New York jail before joining the Secret Service. A member of the agency for six years, he had built a reputation through his service on cases in New Orleans, Washington and Pittsburgh. The Secret Service as a department of the treasury held jurisdiction over the crime of counterfeiting. When it was founded, just after the Civil War, nearly half of all currency in the country was counterfeit. Maintaining the value of the dollar was the principal function of the department and nine-tenths of the Secret Service's manpower was devoted to the war on counterfeiting. Flynn excelled in the qualities that it took for the effective consummation of his duties.

The Secret Service had been aware since the spring of 1899 of the Sicilian forgers in New York, but arrests had only been among the smaller fish in the gang. On New Year's Eve in 1902, a group in Yonkers had been caught passing counterfeit five-dollar bills. Four were convicted a month before the barrel murder, but none revealed any names or information. Through covert observation and information culled from informants, agents were drawn to a butcher shop at 16 Stanton Street. The store had recently changed hands and was now owned by a Sicilian named Vito Laduca. There were some avenues of concern for Flynn, however. Laduca had been arrested for counterfeiting a few weeks before and the previous owner of the shop had disappeared. When the police were unable to find any trace of him, they began to summarize that he had been killed. During the agents' surveillance of Morello gang members, an unknown man was seen with the group on April 13. He was recognized by Flynn's men as the barrel victim at the morgue.

Evidence, however, was missing. Especially since without the victim's identity, police were unable to establish a motive for the killing. They could hold them only for a limited period of 48 hours. Petrosino went to work on the details of the barrel the body had been contained in. The letters "W.T." were stenciled on the bottom and an address, 366 Third Avenue, was written on the side. The barrel's contents were carefully studied—burlap, sawdust, cigarette and cigar butts, and the peel of a red onion. The markings were traced to the Wallace & Thompson Company, one of the sugar refineries located on the Long Island side of the East River. When they checked in at Inzerillo's Café Pasticceria on Elizabeth Street, detectives found the same barrel contents and a barrel practically identical to the one that had held the body. It was filled with sugar. The purchase was verified at Wallace & Thompson but one of the barrels that Inzerillo had bought was missing.

At Flynn's suggestion, Petrosino took a photograph of the victim to Sing Sing Prison with the intention of showing it to several Morello gang members who were doing time there. One of them, Giuseppe DePrimo, identified the victim as his brother-in-law, Benedetto Madonia, married to his sister and a resident at 47 Trenton Avenue in Buffalo, New York. Apparently, according to DePrimo, he had sent his brother-in-law to Morello to get DePrimo's share of the counterfeiting money that was owed to him. When Morello refused, Madonia threatened to take his information to the police. They now had a motive.

The investigation further turned on Giuseppe Morello, the gang leader. From Corleone, Sicily, Morello had criminal records in two countries. He was arrested in Sicily for a double murder and was noted in New York for the counterfeiting ring. As a matter of fact, Morello had been tried in Messina and found guilty in his absence and sentenced. By the time the verdict was handed down, however, Morello had long fled to America. Dark-eyed with a deformed right hand, he was vicious and cunning. He arrived from Corleone in New York in 1892. Six months later the rest of his family and his Terranova stepbrothers arrived.

Morello worked for his father in New York as a plasterer, the businesses that followed were a coal basement, a saloon at 13th Street, and a second saloon on Stanton Street that was closed because of lack of business. He soon sold the first one. Then there was a date factory in which he employed around fifteen people but once again, running at a loss, the business was closed. On June 11, 1900, Morello and Colagero Meggiore were arrested for supplying counterfeit money that was being passed in Brooklyn. Morello was, once again, able to walk free from prosecution. Next came a real estate company, which eventually collapsed. In January 1903, Morello was charged with passing phony five-dollar bills that were printed in Italy and shipped to New York in empty olive oil cans. Other suspects refused to implicate him and so the "Clutch Hand," as he was known, walked again. In November 1909 officer Charles Carrao and Secret Service agents arrested Morello at 207 East 107th Street in connection with the counterfeiting ring operating in Highland, New York.

Black Hand letters were found on Morello, letters he himself had issued as part of a scam to convince the intended victim that he would take the letter and try to rectify the situation. By having the letter there would be no evidence should the victim go to the police.

Then came the barrel murder. Police believed the barrel murder had been committed at the little restaurant on Prince Street. Madonia sat eating a meal while the others in the room spoke in a Sicilian dialect. He was 43 years old, a powerful man of average height with a large moustache. He had only arrived in New York a week before and was now confronting this gang over money, his brother-in-law's share of the counterfeiting scheme. Among the men who had entered the room was Tomasso "the Ox" Petto and Giuseppe Morello.

Giuseppe Morello emigrated from Sicily and became one of the leaders of the notorious Morello-Lupo gang in east Harlem.

The deformed forearm Morello had was about half the length of a normal one. From birth his hand lacked a thumb and the first three fingers. He kept the clawlike hand hidden. It had earned him the nickname "Clutch Hand."

Madonia was dragged to his feet by two men to a sink where a third man stabbed him with a thin-bladed 14-inch dagger. Petto the Ox completed the job. An empty barrel covered inside with burlap and sawdust to absorb the blood was used as a container for the body, which was stuffed inside. The barrel was destined for a spot in the middle of the street where it was meant to be discovered.

On Thursday, April 16, more arrests were made in connection with the murder. Ignazio Lupo, a wine importer who had a shop at 9 Prince Street, was arrested in his apartment. The police found a dagger and three revolvers. He was born in Palermo, Sicily, in March 1877. He had worked in a dry goods store at 35 "Matatazzia" in Palermo, until he shot a business rival named Salvatore Morello during an argument in the store. By the time he was convicted of "deliberate and willful murder" in March 1899, Lupo had fled the country, arriving in New York in 1898.

He opened a store on East 72nd Street in Manhattan, but after a disagreement with a partner, Lupo moved his business to Brooklyn. He was back in Manhattan in 1901 at 9 Prince Street, and also ran a saloon across the street. Giuseppe Morello owned a restaurant in the rear of the premises. The saloon soon became a base for the Morello gang. Lupo's father, Rocco, upon his arrival in New York in 1902, joined with Ignazio and another son, Giovanni, and opened a retail grocery store on 39th Street between 9th and 10th avenues. Lupo and Morello ran a counterfeiting ring and indulged in drug dealing. They preyed on successful businessmen. One such was Salvatore Manzella, who owned a shop on Elizabeth Street, importing wines and Italian foods. His life was threatened by the fiendish pair and he paid out $10,000 to them.

The next day arrests were made. The police had been watching the usual hangouts of gang members and they moved in quickly, arresting eight on April 15. Those apprehended were Giuseppe Morello, Thomas Petto, Joseph Fanaro, Antonio Geneva, Lorenzo and Vito LoBido, Dominico Pecoraro and Pietro Inzerillo. It wasn't the whole gang, as several remained on the loose. The arrests of Morello and Petto were made by Flynn and his agents on Delancy Street one evening about 8 p.m. on April 15. Having followed Morello on his walk home and after he was joined by Petto, four detectives jumped the counterfeiters, knocking them to the ground. Both suspects reached to their pockets, but the detectives prevented them

Detective Joseph Petrosino (left) and Inspectors Carey and McCafferty escort prisoner Tomasso "Ox" Petto (second from left) (Library of Congress).

from drawing the weapons they were carrying. They were handcuffed and searched. "Ox" Petto carried a pistol and a stiletto, and Morello had a .45-caliber revolver and knife strapped to his leg.

On the date that Lupo was apprehended—Thursday, April 16—the police nabbed Vito Laduca and Nicola Testa. Petrosino also arrested Giuseppe Lalamia, whom he recognized as one of the gang. Lupo was a suspect in the killing of Giuseppe Catania, a Brooklyn grocer who was found murdered on July 23, 1902. Lupo was one of the last men to see him alive. The police and the Secret Service were unable to get enough evidence on Lupo in the case. He was also cleared in the barrel murder for the same reason. The police found a pawn ticket in the possession of Tomasso

Petto that when redeemed was a watch that appeared to belong to Madonia. Petrosino traveled to Buffalo to question the murder victim's wife and stepson. They identified the watch as belonging to Madonia. Petrosino was sure that the murderer was Petto and now he believed he had enough for a conviction in court.

It was here that a ploy used by the gang turned the proceedings upside down. The investigation conducted by the Secret Service and the police led to the arrest of Tomasso Petto on Saturday, April 25, for the murder of Benedetto Madonia. The gangsters, possibly on the advice of Vito Cascio Ferro, replaced Petto with a look-alike who was arrested in Petto's place. The man who recently arrived from Italy was Giovanni Carlo Costantino, but upon arrival in America had changed his name to Giovanni Pecoraro and told the arresting officers he was not Tomasso Petto. He bore a physical resemblance to the suspected killer and he was not believed. At the arraignment two days later, on April 29, 1903, as Petto was charged with the murder, his double reiterated that he was not Petto. He had papers to prove his identity and he was released from custody.

"They were smarter than we were," was all Petrosino could say.[10] There were two positive factors that Petrosino took from the barrel murder investigation. There was a great deal of publicity surrounding the case and the knowledge the detective gained of the interrelationships between the various Sicilian bands. The uncertainty of cooperation between Black Handers and the Mafia was no longer such for Petrosino.

Two years later Giuseppe DePrimo, Benedetto Madon-

Ignazio Saietta, known as "Lupo the Wolf," was the other leader of the Morello-Lupo gang.

30

nia's brother-in-law, was released from Sing Sing. He soon dropped out of sight, but a month later the police department of Wilkes-Barre, Pennsylvania, notified the NYPD that Tomasso Petto had been killed by an unknown assailant.

Ignazio Lupo was a key suspect in the entire case since he was suspected in three murders but managed to elude prosecution. Lupo was arrested again on April 30, 1903, and held on $5,000 bail and Pietro Inzerillo was indicted with him on a 1902 counterfeiting charge. Lupo had mailed a letter to Salvatore Matise aka Andrea Polora in Canada; the letter contained a five-dollar counterfeit note. The charges against the two, however, were eventually dropped. Arrested in 1904 on a concealed weapons charge, Lupo then married Salvatrice Terranova, a sister to the Terranova brothers. In 1906 he was arrested again after being identified by a kidnap victim. The kidnapped boy, Antonio Bozzuffi, was the son of a wealthy banker named John Bozzuffi. However, once brought face-to-face in court, the youth failed to identify Lupo. Lupo continued to break the law and continued to evade prosecution. In 1908 he claimed bankruptcy of his import business. A store of his product was found in a warehouse on Washington Street and it was known that there were real-estate transactions Lupo made before he disappeared after the bankruptcy declaration and didn't turn up for another year.

A merchant at 196 Elizabeth Street, Salvatore Manzella, filed for bankruptcy in December 1908, claiming that he had been a victim of extortion from Lupo for over three years. Lupo was finally arrested in November 1909 in connection with the extortion charges. He was released when Manzella failed to appear in court. But Lupo was again arrested on charges related to counterfeiting. He and seven others including Giuseppe Morello stood trial on the counterfeiting charges beginning on January 28, 1910. Judge George W. Ray received death threats in the style of the Black Hand during the course of the 17-day trial. It drew to a close on February 19 when the jury brought in a verdict of guilty for each defendant.

Giuseppe Morello was sentenced on one count to 15 years of hard labor and a $500 fine. On the second count, ten years of hard labor and a $500 fine. Ignazio Lupo was sentenced to 15 years of hard labor on the first count and a $500 fine. On the second count, 15 years of hard labor and a $500 fine. Morello's sentence was ultimately commuted to 15 years and he was released in 1920. Lupo received a conditional commutation and was also released in 1920.

In 1906 Petrosino headed an investigation into the murder of a man named Salvatore Svelazo, who was killed in his saloon on Forsyth Street.

Petrosino determined that the man had Black Hand connections and was related to Benedetto Madonia. Other gang members were killed over the next few years seemingly because of their connection to the barrel murder of 1903. The Secret Service believed that the one murder that was certainly linked to the barrel case came in 1912 and it was the shooting of Calogero Morello, Giuseppe Morello's only son. The reign of the Morello-Lupo gang had come to an end when they were imprisoned.

As previously mentioned, there is often some confusion over the terms "Black Hand" and "Mafia." But there is a distinction. The Mafia being a criminal organization, while the Black Hand was more a method of operation rather than an organization. There was no one person guiding its actions. As a result the intended victims came out of all walks of life. In 1907 at the Polo Grounds in New York, the manager of the Chicago Cubs was greeted with a letter threatening him with "If you do not let the Giants win the first place this year, gang of Black Hands will see you after ... we will use bombs on your players on train wreck." It was signed "Black Hand" with a bony hand and clawlike fingers drawn at the bottom.[11] The police, however, considered the letter to be a phony since no one was harmed and the Giants finished in fourth place. But a Chicago group had the temerity to go after a big-time mobster, Big Jim Colosimo. Big Jim actually paid out $5,000 to the Black Hand Society, like so many others, before realizing that the society would not be satisfied.

Big Jim reached out for help from a Brooklyn mobster named John "The Immune" Torrio, who had been targeted by the Black Hand himself. However, his retaliation had been swift and final: he merely killed everyone connected with his extortion demands. Torrio reported to Colosimo and put into effect his proven method. The bodies he left as messages to others did the trick. Colosimo made Torrio his right-hand man and as he became entrenched in the Chicago underworld, he brought a rising gangster from Brooklyn to act as his bodyguard. The man's name was Al Capone.

The word "Mafia" first appeared the newspapers in the United States in 1891. It was in conjunction with one of the most disgraceful and tragic events in U.S. history, the New Orleans lynching that took the lives of 11 Italians. The event nearly caused a threat of war by Italy. There were two gangs extorting the immigrant farmers in a large Sicilian community in Louisiana when the gangs came into conflict. New Orleans authorities didn't care much as long as the trouble was between the Italians. But when the Chief of Police David Hennessy was killed on October 16, 1890, and in his last words he blamed the Italians ("It was the dagoes, the Italians") it was enough to set off an explosive situation. There were more Italian immigrants in New Orleans than any other southern state. Between 1884 and 1924, nearly 300,000 Italian immigrants, mostly Sicilian, came to New Orleans, earning the nickname "Little Palermo" for the French Quarter.

Hennessy was no saint and New Orleans was no Eden at the turn of the 20th century, though he gained a reputation as the "first American victim of the Italian Mafia." In his checkered career, Hennessey had been tried and acquitted for murder on two occasions. He had lived throughout the west for some years before settling in New Orleans where he got himself elected to the position of chief of police. While being a tough, no-nonsense cop, Hennessy was also known to have done favors for the noted Provenzano gang, some members of which were on trial for murder when Hennessy intervened with favorable testimony. Joseph Petrosino came to the attention of many Americans when he was described by the newspapers as being an expert in Italian matters. He was asked his opinion of the crime when Hennessy was murdered and he suggested some tie-in between Hennessy and the Mafia. It was found by New Orleans investigators that he'd had run-ins with the other gang, the Matrangas, who accused him of taking the side of the Provenzano gang.

Hennessy had spent the evening of October 15 at a meeting of the police board at the old city hall. Afterward a friend of Hennessy's, Bill O'Connor, stopped by and the two walked home. On the way, Hennessy suggested they stop at Dominic Virget's Oyster Saloon for a late snack. They continued their walk along Rampart Street and the two men parted at the corner of Girod Street. The men walked in opposite directions as Hennessy headed for his home at 275 Girod Street. Then five men appeared directly across the street and opened fire with shotguns and probably rifles and pistols as well. Although hit many times, Hennessy drew his pistol and began to chase the fleeing assailants. He fired two shots near the corner of Basin Street, striking no one, and then collapsed in front of a frame house at 189 Basin Street.

O'Connor, hearing the shots, ran toward the sounds accompanied by a couple of police officers. It was when O'Connor bent over the wounded police chief and asked him who shot him that O'Connor said, "As I bent down, he whispered the word, Dagoes." No one but O'Connor heard Hennessy's reply.[12]

During the night at old Charity Hospital, Hennessy was conscious, and accounts of his conversations indicated his mind was clear and calm. He was asked three times during the night about the shooting and each time his answer was evasive, assuring his questioners that he was going to be all right. He was pronounced dead at 9:06 a.m., nine hours after the shooting. According to writer Richard Gambino, what followed was "a persecution of Italians rather than a true investigation of the murder."[13]

At the moment of Hennessy's death, some fifty Italians had already been arrested. All 17 members of the Matrangas' gang plus Charles Man-tranga and a boy, all Sicilians, were arrested. They all denied any part in the crime but the public outcry was heavily against the Italians. Pietro Monasterio was arrested because he lived across the street from the place where Hennessy was shot. Antonio Marchesi, a fruit peddler, was arrested because he was a friend of Monasterio's. Emmanuele Polizzi, who was mentally handicapped, was arrested when a policeman identified him as one of the men he had seen running from the scene of the crime.

A council of 50, made up of influential citizens and a vigilance committee, took it upon themselves to see that "justice" was done. The Ku Klux Klan aimed at the Italians as they had the blacks, for the purpose of "safeguarding racial purity."[14] The hatred prevailed. Two thousand Sicilians arriving in New Orleans at this time with no knowledge of the events were welcomed by a screaming mob hurling rocks at them. A certain Thomas Duffy, a 29-year-old newspaper salesman, went to the prison and asked to speak to Antonio Scaffidi, one of the suspects, whom he had never seen before. Duffy put a bullet into his neck. For this, he was sentenced to six months imprisonment.

Nineteen Italians would go on trial for the murder of David Hennessy in two installments, nine in the first trial and the other 10 in a later trial. The first began on February 28, 1891, before Judge Joshua G. Baker, who had presided over the Provenzano trial in a suspicious manner. The district attorney and two members of his team had acted as defense lawyers in the Provenzano trial. The state called 67 witnesses; the defense called eighty-four. There was no credible evidence presented and on March 13, 1891, six defendants were acquitted. The jury asked the judge that a mistrial be declared for the other three. Jurors were accused of being bought off and defense lawyers were attacked. After the trial Federal District Attorney William Grant looked into the case and reported that the evidence against the men was "exceedingly unsatisfactory" and inconclusive.[15]

The public, however, at the decision, turned to mobs at the prison. They were incited by city officials including the mayor. A few days after Hennessy's death, Mayor Joseph A. Shakspeare gave an inflammatory speech condemning Sicilians and called upon the citizenry to "teach these people a lesson they will not forget."[16]

The Italians had not yet been released. The mob broke into the jail.

However, John Davis, the prison warden, released the prisoners from their cells and told them to hide wherever they could. They were found one by one: from under a heap of dirty clothes, dragged out of a dog kennel, from behind a pile of garbage. The mentally handicapped Emmanuele Polizzi was taken outside, hung from a lamppost and shot. Another was shot to death. The prisoners, eleven of them, were finally taken out and hanged from the trees on Treme Street. Five of the murdered men had not even been on trial. Although the mob was huge, the killings were committed by a smaller, disciplined group that included city leaders like lawyer William S. Parkerson, local politician James D. Houston, and John Wickliffe, editor of the New Delta newspaper. Other members of the lynch mob included John M. Parker, who was elected as Louisiana's 37th governor, and Walter C. Flower, who was elected as the 44th mayor of New Orleans.

The mob actions, however, horrified the world, and there were even demands for declarations of war by the Italian government. Though the dispute with Italy was settled in time, there were lynchings of Italians in parts of the country throughout the rest of the decade. In spite of the general outrage, many Americans applauded the killings. The *New York Times* called the victims "desperate ruffians and murderers."[17]

The tragedy loomed even larger due to the fact that New Orleans' government leaders were complicit in the mob's actions. A grand jury issued its report on May 6, 1891, and "in one of the most glaring examples of official mendacity in American history"[18] failed to present indictments against any of the mob leaders.

In the ensuing 128 years there was no attempt at an apology by any members of the New Orleans city government. Then in 2019 the efforts of Robert M. Ferrito, state president of the Order Sons and Daughters of Italy, John Fratta, chairman of the New York State Commission for Social Justice, and Michael A. Santo, prompted the long-overdue apology. On April 12, 2019, an Official Proclamation of Apology was made by the mayor of New Orleans, Latoya Cantrell, at the American Italian Cultural Center in New Orleans.

There were no lynchings in New York, but the Black Hand extortions and the primitive Mafia organizations took such a strong hold that the new century began with a precarious balance between those good and bad, criminal and honest citizens—with Detective Joseph Petrosino, virtually the only police officer strong enough to make the challenge plausible. By 1904 his persistent pleas for a specialized "Italian Squad" of police officers created specifically to combat those crimes prevalent in the Italian immigrant community were finally granted.

Chapter Three

The Italian Squad—NYPD

There were two steps that Joe Petrosino wanted to see taken that in his opinion would strengthen the NYPD in its dealings with Italian crime. One was to petition the Italian government to toughen their policy in granting passports to so many of their nation's criminals. He wanted the federal government to round up the undesirable aliens and send them back to Italy. The NYPD could not handle the multitude of crimes that had broken out in the Italian communities, particularly in Manhattan's Little Italy. The department had no way of dealing inside the Italian community, and little understanding of the language and culture, thus Detective Petrosino's persistence in asking for an Italian unit to deal exclusively with crime in that community. It finally paid off paid off when, on September 14, 1904, Police Commissioner William McAdoo granted his request to establish a Secret Service in the NYPD made up of Italian officers to be known as "The Italian Squad." Their activities were to be clandestine as they would operate within the borders of the Italian immigrant community. To this day, the records of the NYPD are void of details regarding the work of the Italian Squad. They would be paid by the city of New York, but additional funds needed for the maintenance of the unit were to come from unknown sources which the police commissioner assured was not public money. It is believed that contributions from Italian merchants and bankers provided these funds.

In a report issued by Police Commissioner William McAdoo regarding the city and its police protection, he made two important points: one, that from 1898 to 1905 the increase in population had been 20½ percent while in the same period the number of police officers had only increased by 4⅓ percent. Police protection needed to be increased in order to keep up with the rapidly growing population. One step had been taken, he pointed out, by the formation of an Italian Secret Service. He pointed out that "in a general way this Bureau will be able to more successfully cope with any crimes that are perpetrated by the so-called 'Mafia' or Italian bands of a similar nature."

Petrosino was to head the newly formed unit. He gave his views on the Black Hand criminals: "The gangsters who are holding Little Italy in the grip of terror come chiefly from Sicily and Southern Italy, and they are primitive country robbers transplanted into cities." He went on to point out that the crimes that occur among the Italians are the same as those

Det. Rocco Cavone

Det. Ralph Micelli

Det. Joseph Di

Lieut. Joseph Petrosino

Office of Italian Squad 316 Lafayette St.

Lieut. Maurice Bonnoi

Det. Peter Dondero.

Det. Michael Meali.

Det. Paul Simonelli.

Det. John F. Archiopoli.

Original Italian Squad
· 1904 ·

The original Italian Squad was formed in 1904 with these nine members and Detective Petrosino was put in charge (author's collection).

committed at one time by rural outlaws in Italy. The victims, he said, "like the killers, come from the same ignorant class of people. In short, we are dealing with banditry transplanted to the most modern city in the world."[1]

Several authors have varied in stating the number of original members that were selected for the Italian Squad. Talty in his book *The Black Hand* puts the number at six including Petrosino. Thomas Reppetto and James Lardner in *NYPD: A City and Its Police* mentions four names in addition to Petrosino. Mike Dash in *The First Family* expresses the fact that with Petrosino as the leader, Commissioner William McAdoo would "eventually unearth eight more men."[2]

I have in my possession a family-owned photograph labeled "The Original Italian Squad—1904" that displays the images of nine men including Petrosino. Petrosino and Maurice Bonnoil are the only names that appear on all lists (Dash mentions no names, only a number). Petacco gives the names Bonnoil, Dondero, Cassidi, Silva and Lagomarsini. The NYPD has no records today of the names of Italian Squad members. The photo being the only documentation, I will identify all nine as original members of the Italian Squad.

With one exception, all members of the newly formed squad were Italian. The exception was Maurice Bonnoil of French-Irish heritage, who had grown up in Manhattan's Little Italy. Bonnoil spoke the Sicilian dialect fluently. Peter Dondero was a 27-year-old who had been on the force for three years. Dondero was tough and carried a scar across his face from a fight he'd had with a collar named Harry "Pussy" Meyers. Another time a criminal pressed a gun to Dondero's mouth and cocked the weapon. Just before it went off, Dondero managed to grab the gun away, literally dodging a bullet. Then there was Rocco Cavone, Ralph Micelli, and John Archiopoli. Joe DeGilio was five-foot-six with gray hair. Paul Simonetti was often in on arrests with Michael Mealli, as the two teamed up on numerous cases over the years. The ninth member and the leader was, of course, Joseph Petrosino. Additional names have been mentioned, like Hugo Cassidy (Ugo Cassidi), George Silva, and John Lagomarsini.

In January of 1906, the new police commissioner was General Theodore Bingham and his support for Petrosino was evident in his enlarging the Italian Squad. It is therefore feasible that all of the names mentioned above were members of the squad by 1906.

Petrosino numbered among his many friends in Little Italy the Cavone family. This family had come from Italy a few years before and with them came their son Rocco. An enterprising and intelligent young man, Rocco had, at the age of 10, worked as an errand boy for a wholesale fruit firm. Like so many immigrant children, he had quit school to go to work and help his family. At age sixteen, he became a managing clerk of the store. Not long after that he rose to the position of production manager of a Manhattan factory, apparently well on his way to a successful and prosperous future. It was about this time that Petrosino, who'd been given authority to recruit new officers, paid Rocco a visit. He wanted him for his Italian squad. It would seem to have been a difficult decision for the young man, but respect for the detective probably oversaw any objections he might have and Rocco Cavone joined the police force.

Just a short while later (a matter of weeks), Cavone disappeared from his regular assignment in the department. As mentioned above, members of the Italian Squad officers assigned to the squad were virtual non-entities to the rest of the department. It turned out that Rocco, under an alias, began hanging around the bars and assorted dives of Little Italy. He slept in Mulberry flophouses and cavorted with laborers as well as Black Hand murderers. He soon began passing the information he had accumulated to Petrosino. Ultimately many arrests took place as a result of Cavone's undercover activities. In Brooklyn the NYPD established an offshoot of the Italian Squad, a similar unit of ten men under the direction of Detective Sergeant Antonio Vachris, a Genoese with 11 years on the force. Vachris had supported Petrosino's idea of an all Italian Squad to specialize and combat Italian crime, noting that non–Italian officers in Brooklyn faced the same obstacles that Petrosino's men did in Little Italy—the inability to communicate with the populace—and to comprehend the traditions that the people lived with.

One of the problems that confronted Petrosino and his new Italian Squad was the lack of respect and cooperation they received from the NYPD. It seemed the department went out of its way to stymie their operations. They set up a headquarters at 175 Waverly Place and Italian men were soon observed going in and out at all hours of the day and night. Suspicions aroused and an ambitious cop took special notice of the activity, believing the men to be members of the Black Hand, and he reported it. Captain John O'Brien was in charge of the squad assigned to raid the building. When they found the door locked they broke it down and entered the premises. During the search, Petrosino returned dressed as an Italian laborer, and stumbled into the scene. A cop identified him as the leader of the gang and O'Brien tried to wrestle Petrosino to the ground but the detective overpowered him, knocking the captain to the floor. O'Brien then pulled out his revolver and pointed it at Petrosino's face. The detective slowly moved his jacket aside revealing his detective's shield. It seems that soon after Captain O'Brien was demoted to foot patrol in Greenpoint, Brooklyn.

Three months later the Italian Squad had its first notable success in what became known as the case of the mushroom picker. The body of a young man with 36 stab wounds was found on Sunday, August 13, 1905, in Van Cortlandt Park in the Bronx. The body was discovered by Frank Lo Cascio, a 40-year-old textile worker who was in the park foraging for mushrooms. He told police that he had met two men, both Italian, who asked for directions. One of them, the younger of the two, was the murder victim whose body he had found. Police doubted his story but because the victim was Italian, the case was turned over to Petrosino and his newly formed Italian squad.

Petrosino absolved Lo Cascio as a suspect because he had no marks or wounds on his body. The detective reasoned that such a violent crime would have meant that the victim fought and would have inflicted some injury on his attacker. In the meantime a note was found on the victim with a name and an address in Lambertville, New Jersey. Peter Dondero of the squad had found a subway conductor who identified the two men getting off the train at Van Cortlandt Park. In Lambertville they found a number of Italians employed in the construction of a railway, one of which was the name on the note, Sabato Gizzi. Gizzi identified the body as that of a fellow worker, Antonio Torsiello. Through further investigation and continued questioning of Gizzi, Petrosino learned the identity of the second man at Van Cortlandt Park, Antonio Strollo.

The young victim, Torsiello, had come to America to search for his brother Vito, and in time received a letter from him saying that he had become a rich merchant living in Yonkers and invited his brother to join him. Antonio took all the money he had and sold anything he possessed, gathering up about $500. Strollo had, of course, written the letter and was accompanying young Torsiello to Yonkers as they passed through Van Cortlandt Park. Strollo had a knife wound on his leg and he was identified by postal workers in Lambertville where he had mailed the letter. Not satisfied with the mostly circumstantial evidence that the squad had gathered, Petrosino planted an informer in Strollo's cell. After gaining the suspect's confidence, the informer, whose name was Reppetto, and who would later become a policeman and work with the Italian branch, agreed to testify in Strollo's favor at the trial. He did testify, but rather than tell the story Strollo had concocted as an alibi, he told the facts as Strollo had relayed them. Antonio Strollo was found guilty of murder and sentenced to the electric chair. He was executed on March 11, 1908.

When Police Commissioner McAdoo passed along the decision of the aldermen to establish an Italian Squad, it was done with some reluctance. McAdoo had never been a real supporter of the idea, believing it to be detrimental to the NYPD's dealings with other ethnic communities. The next commissioner, however, had a decidedly different point of view, one favorable to Petrosino and his pet project. Theodore A. Bingham, nicknamed "The General," was a personal friend of Teddy Roosevelt and described as able, ambitious and authoritarian. The *Los Angeles Times* referred to him as "an animate picture of vigor, rough grace, and daring."[3] He was valedictorian at Yale, then attended West Point where he received a commission as second lieutenant. Bingham was following the family military tradition that included Revolutionary War soldiers. However, he never saw combat action in any war. In 1897 he went to Washington as a full colonel to oversee the city's public building in his capacity as an engineer.

His next mission was the White House where he served President McKinley as an all-around organizer, secretary, and advisor. When Roosevelt became president a riff, the details of which were never revealed, developed between the two men, and Bingham took a promotion to brigadier general as his send-off to upstate New York on another engineering project. His military career came to an abrupt end when a leg amputation resulted after a 700-pound derrick collapsed on his leg. It was at this point in his life and career, on January 1, 1906, that Bingham received the appointment as commissioner of the NYPD.

He immediately established a reputation of being a "straight-talker," of not pulling punches and he verbally expressed support and appreciation for the job Petrosino was doing. "From this moment on," he stated at his appointment, "the goal of my life shall be to crush the Black Hand and to destroy these vile foreign criminals who have come to disrupt the serenity of our peaceful land."[4] Within four months he had expanded the Italian Squad to 25 men with another ten as part of a unit in Brooklyn under Sergeant Antonio Vachris. He kept a close tab on all his officers and gave every indication of running a tight ship from the beginning.

The new commissioner ordered all known leaders of Black Hand gangs be kept under constant surveillance. He hired an effective Arthur Woods as deputy police commissioner, one of whose duties would be to oversee the Italian Squad. In July 1907 a new immigration law went into effect. It was, however, so full of loopholes that neither Petrosino nor Bingham could see any advantage in their struggle to keep criminals out of America. One of the most difficult of the law's amendments stated that a criminal could not be deported if he had been in the country over three years. The new law could work on criminals new to the country.

Enrico Alfano was the leader of the Neapolitan Camorra (Mafia) and was accused of murdering Gennaro and Maria Cuocolo, rivals to him in the Camorra criminal society in Naples.

After he was charged with the crimes, he fled to Rome, obtained a false passport and sailed for America. He came to the United States and was hiding out on the Lower East Side. Petrosino went after him himself. After learning where Alfano was hiding, he entered a room on April 17, 1907, where six men, including Alfano, were sitting around a table. Petrosino identified himself and then placed Enrico Alfano under arrest. He offered no resistance, believing that there must have been many more police in the vicinity. There weren't. Now came the more difficult job of deporting the criminal. There was a difficult court case and, in the end, Alfano was deported on May 9. It was settled by the fact that Alfano had come to America from Le Havre, France, and he was ordered to be deported back to France.

Usually failing to cooperate with the American police, the Italian police, however, this time did their job. They worked with the French police and had Alfano taken immediately from France to Italy. Alfano was tried in the Court of Assizes at Viterbo, Italy, and was convicted on July 8, 1912, of the Cuocolo murders and sentenced to 30 years in prison. By the conclusion of the Alfano affair, Joe Petrosino was noted as one of the two or three most famous policemen in the city, if not the entire country.

The job for the members of the Italian Squad was a dangerous one and on December 28, 1907, it almost cost the life of Rocco Cavone, recently promoted to lieutenant. He had entered an apartment building in Kingsland, New Jersey, where he had reason to believe a murder suspect named Nicolo Bonanno was in hiding. On Christmas Day a Manhattan barber had opened his door and was shot twice in the chest with a pistol. Cavone had a suspect under surveillance for two days and prepared to close in. Cavone was married with a baby and lived in an apartment in Lower Manhattan.

As the young detective climbed the stairs, he was unaware of the crouching figure at the top of the stairwell. Bonanno waited for Cavone to get close and then two shots rang out. Cavone was hit in the face and as he cried out, other members of the squad raced up the stairs. The gunman reached the roof, got to a fire escape and climbed down to the street below. The officers gave chase and Bonanno found himself cornered in a wooded area, so he put the gun to his cheek and pulled the trigger. However, his attempt to kill himself failed and he was taken into custody. Though bleeding from the face when his partners found him, Cavone was lucky. One of the bullets had hit him in the forehead but at such an angle that it only grazed him, and though bleeding profusely, the wound was superficial. Hit also in the left hand, he was taken to St. Vincent's Hospital where it was determined that some of the nerves in the hand had been damaged.

Members of the squad did all that it took to accomplish their ends in the battle against crime in the city. In one case in late 1907, Detective John Archiopoli hid in a coal box in a saloon in order to apprehend two Black Hand criminals. The squad got word from a complaint by a musician named Pittoro Menucci, charging Carlo D'Angelo and Michele Quatrono with trying to extort him of $30 or he would be "cut up into small pieces."[5] Archiopoli went to the place specified, a saloon at 121 Mulberry Street in Manhattan, in the morning and hid in the coal bin. Two other detectives from the Italian Squad, detectives Trabucci and Devoti, were stationed outside the saloon. The bills that the musician was to turn over to the Black Handers were marked for later identification. When the extortionists arrived to meet with Menucci, the detectives revealed themselves. A melee ensured in the crowded saloon, but soon both D'Angelo and Quatrono were subdued. The two were arraigned on charges of extortion and attempted blackmail.

The more the Italian Squad seemed to find success, the more crime they had to face. It was said that they reduced crime by 50 percent and put away hundreds of criminals, but that figure was just an estimate, and Petrosino felt the almost endless frustration that accompanied their work. The gangsters of the Black Hand were relentless in the vicious means that they sunk to in trying to achieve their goals of terrorizing and extorting victims. They even went to kidnapping young children. On September 21, 1906, Willie Labarbera was playing on the street in front of his family's fruit stand on the East Side of Manhattan when he simply disappeared into the crowded walkway. His friends didn't realize he was gone until the kids regrouped a while later. His parents, William and Caterina, frantically searched the neighborhood, but could not find little Willie and the cryptic fear that went through the minds of all the people in Little Italy struck them—*La Mano Nera*, the Black Hand, had the child. The Labarberas reported the kidnapping to the police and Joseph Petrosino responded. He was shown the three letters that had been received but that was all the information the parents possessed.

The detective went right to work. He began by cornering all of his informers and contacts of which he had many in the area. The boy's description was put in all the newspapers. Another letter arrived telling the family to sell their home in order to raise the $5,000 ransom money. Included in this letter was a lock of Willie's hair. Days passed, then the squad received a tip from one of the network of informants—called *nfame*. The story was that a woman in Kenilworth, New Jersey, had passed a man on the street who was carrying a large bundle. As he passed her she heard a cry from inside the bundle. The man hurried into a nearby house and while the woman watched he emerged a few minutes later, still carting the bundle which was now silent. He got into a wagon and drove away.

As soon as word got to Petrosino he boarded a ferry at West 23rd Street and crossed the Hudson to New Jersey. On the Jersey side he hired a carriage for the journey to Kenilworth, about twenty miles, and returned to the dock a few hours later without the boy. But a few weeks after while reading police bulletins, when he saw one from Brooklyn saying a boy crying had been found wandering the streets. Petrosino hurried to Brooklyn and to the local branch of the Society for the Prevention of Cruelty to Children. It was 3 a.m. and from the description, the detective recognized the sleeping boy as Willie Labarbera. He went to the Labarbera's house and when the door opened a revolver was put in his face. Fear had taken hold of so many, and not just the victims. William and Caterino accompanied Petrosino to police headquarters at 300 Mulberry Street where he had taken the boy. Caterino grabbed her son and embraced him. "I thought she would eat little Willie," Petrosino said later.[6]

Petrosino confronted the Sicilian Mafia's Raffaele Palizzolo in 1908. A dominant figure in the Sicilian Mafia underworld, and a member of the Chamber of Deputies in Palermo, Palizzolo was charged in an Italian court in 1899 with ordering the murder of a political opponent. Emanuele Notarbartolo, a former bank director, was found dead of 23 stab wounds in the rear of a railway carriage in February 1893. Convicted in 1902 and sentenced to 30 years, the Mafia chief won a new trial and was acquitted in 1904. On June 8, 1908, the 63-year-old Palizzolo arrived in New York City aboard the steamship *Martha Washington*, and stayed with a friend at 105th Street. He was a hero to some since his Mafia activities were kept quiet from the general public. In spite of his denials, Petrosino decided to keep a quiet eye on the Italian celebrity. But when Palizzolo made contact with the local Mafiosi, the detective paid him a visit. The meeting was kept discreet with no reporters in evidence, but the outcome was that Palizzolo sailed back to Italy on August 2.

In spite of their successes, Sgt. Petrosino and his Italian Squad had a most difficult time, having to face opposition from their fellow officers of the NYPD. The heavily Irish force was hostile toward the Italians and did nothing to aid or support them. In the earliest days they actually used Petrosino's apartment as a headquarters and then a tiny office at 300 Mulberry Street until they established themselves at a rental at 175 Waverly Street. They placed a few desks and hung a sign on the window that said "Real Estate." In an interview with a reporter from the *New York Times*, Petrosino repeated his oft-stated opinion that the ignorance of the new citizens was their greatest enemy. Ignorance of their rights as citizens of their new country. He persisted in his stress on the Italian's need to feel a part of the United States.

During this same difficult period the Italian immigration continued to increase. In 1904, the year the unit was founded, 193,296 Italian immigrants entered the United States. The number increased to 285,731 by 1907. The population of Italians in the new land equaled, then exceeded, that of Rome. Criminals entered the country along with the honest people and Petrosino was to put the estimate of Italian criminals in Manhattan at between 35,000 and 40,000 in 1905. It's no wonder the Italian Squad had their work cut out for them.

Each case required many man hours of work and tied up men in surveillance as well as paperwork, so at times when a false alarm or a joke were played it was costly for the squad. At times the truth could not be determined. A contractor and a builder living at 54 Norwood Avenue in Brooklyn named Henry Meyer received what was presumed to be a Black Hand letter threatening harm to him and to the property he owned if a payment of $50 was not forthcoming. The handwriting was scrawled and appeared to be that of a schoolboy. It was ordered that the money be placed in a fire hydrant near the Carnegie Library at Warwick Street and Arlington Avenue that evening. Unless the money was paid, the note said, his row of houses in Cypress Hills and his shop on Norwood Avenue would be blown up. Meyer believed it to be a practical joke and turned it over to the police.

Although they were inclined to agree with the contractor, they still investigated the matter. It meant posting plain-clothed men near the fire hydrant and the area, to no avail. Meyer was in the process of taking a trip to Germany and he and his wife went ahead with their plans, with the police calling the letter a hoax.

The workday for members of the squad began almost the same every morning. They reported for work at 175 Waverly Place in the guise of workmen, received their assignments from Petrosino for the day and left the office in ones and twos so as to draw as little attention as possible to themselves. Violence continued to accelerate all around them and the frightening letters perpetuated. A baker named Serrino Nizzarri resisted the Black Hand and an attempt was made on his life. Anthony Fazio attacked him with a knife in a barbershop when Nizzarri managed to elude the attempt on his life. He received another letter warning him not to make its contents known and that he should place a red handkerchief in his window when he was ready to pay. The handkerchief never appeared. While working in his shop one evening in the presence of his daughter and her baby, the baker was confronted by the same Black Hander, Anthony Fazio, who fired two shots. They missed Nizzarri but his daughter knocked over a pot of boiling water that spilled onto the child, scalding it to death.

Fazio was pursued by the squad and arrested. In spite of his tragedy, Nizzarri testified amid Fazio's threats even in the courtroom. The defendant was found guilty and went to Sing Sing. Petrosino's hope was that the Italians would like Nizzarri and stand up to the Black Hand. He believed that such strength and courage on the part of the people would ultimately cripple the Black Hand. But it would be a difficult turning point to achieve, as many were too afraid to consult the police. In Brooklyn, the young son of a contractor, Tony Marendino, was kidnapped one afternoon. His father refused to talk to the Italian Squad. The squad did, however, track down the kidnappers, Salvatore Peconi and Vito Laduca. Peconi had been arrested before for kidnapping as a Black Hand associate. The father was so fearful of consequences that, upon hearing of the arrests, he tried to pay the kidnapper's bail. He refused to testify and the case was dropped.

Violence continued to spread, even to other communities. In Westfield, New Jersey, John Clearwater, the owner of a restaurant and a non–Italian, was confronted by a Black Hand member who had threatened his life. At 1 a.m., Clearwater found a revolver pointed at him. He pulled out his own gun and began firing. The restaurant owner was hit by two bullets and the Black Handers jumped on him with daggers, stabbing him to death. There were incidents of witnesses on the stand in courtrooms being intimidated by a spectator in the room giving them the death sign. In one case in Baltimore, the judge ordered the jury box and the witness stand to be turned to face the wall so that no eye contact could be made by anyone sitting in the room and the witnesses. It was Petrosino's guess that for every witness who came forward there were 250 who did not.

Detective Petrosino constantly advised and expressed his wish that victims would not relinquish to the demands of the Black Hand, but fear was the criminals' most powerful weapon. They were vicious and violent and the detectives of the Italian Squad were putting their lives on the line every day for the benefit of the good and honest people who were victimized. John Bozzuffi was a banker in the Manhattan colony on the Upper East Side. He was visited one day by three Italian merchants; Mr. Christina was a cobbler, Mr. Campisi owned a grocery shop and Mr. Fascietta had a barbershop on First Avenue. They were friends of Bozzuffi and all three had been recipients of Black Hand letters. Christina's letter said they would drink his blood if he did not meet their cash demand. Campisi was warned that he would be cut up and stuffed in a barrel and Fascietta had been bombed once before.

Mr. Campisi wanted to leave the city before they would kill him or kidnap his children. Bozzuffi understood the fear in his friends. He had a family too—seven children, the oldest, Antonio, was named for his grandfather, who brought his family to America in 1872 and had worked as a laborer on the streets of New York. John had worked his way up from a ticket taker on the elevated subway to buying a little grocery store, and then he went into insurance and banking. He was respected, he was honest and he had earned his reputation. Bozzuffi had also heard from the Black Hand; he had his own letters, but as Petrosino urged, he had refused to give in to the extortionists. He advised his friends to resist, for to give in, in his mind, meant other Italians would do so also.

Over the next two or three weeks more letters arrived. The three merchants sought their friend's counsel once again. His advice was the same and he was more adamant than before. The men bravely held on knowing that anyone entering their shops could be the instrument of their death. One of the men, Mr. Christina, had his own system of defense. Every time he heard the Black Hand mentioned, he whispered a word, *Petrosino,* his way of giving himself the strength to carry on.

The letters continued to come over a period of months, but there were no attempts at violence until one day Bozzuffi's 14-year-old son, Antonio, was confronted as he exited from a drugstore near his home. A stranger asked him if he would accompany him home to translate some letters from Italy. The boy agreed. They entered an apartment and there were three men instead wearing black masks. The door was locked behind him and Antonio was told to write a letter. He dictated the words. Bozzuffi would pay $20,000 or Antonio would be killed. The teenager was frightened and very upset. He knew the amount of money was beyond what his father could afford. The men also told him to include in the letter that if Petrosino or the police were contacted, he would surely die. He was bound and gagged and a ransom letter was sent to Bozzuffi, who upon reading it believed his son was already dead. He contacted Petrosino. The detective began by contacting the area hospitals, then inquired throughout the neighborhood.

As word of the situation got out, depositors at Bozzuffi's bank, thinking the banker would use the bank's cash for the ransom, began making withdrawals. The run on the bank began almost immediately and by the next day $7,000 had been withdrawn. Another letter came for Bozzuffi. This one contained specific instructions. If he was willing to settle the payment on March 7, he was to put a sign in the window of the bank that read "Seven men wanted." If he decided to pay on March 8—the sign would read "Eight men wanted." On that day the kidnappers would appear to collect the ransom. Bozzuffi then wrote a message on a sign, in Italian, and hung it on the window facing First Avenue. Bravely or foolishly, he had written, "The money in this bank belongs to the depositors and it will be paid to them if I never see my son again."[7]

Friends and family begged him to reconsider, but the banker held fast. He refused to be part of a crime and insisted that he would never give in no matter the cost. Three days later, with only one guard watching him, Antonio was able to get out of his bonds and escaped through the door and out on First Avenue. Some believed that the kidnappers may have come to believe that Bozzuffi would not budge and they let the boy escape as the best way to unburden themselves from a difficult situation. In any case, the boy was reunited with his family. As difficult as his decision was, Bozzuffi was a hero to Italians who read the story all over the country. He was admired and applauded as the Italian who'd risked his child's life to defy the evildoers.

He went so far as to have all seven of his children photographed in case they were kidnapped and photos of them had to be circulated. This was one story of Black Hand extortion attempts that had a happy ending. His son came home, the run on the bank ended and his actions even won him new customers. Petrosino was happy for Bozzuffi, but delighted that the man had stood tall under dire circumstances. This was exactly what the detective was fighting for.

For every happy ending there was at least one that ended on a different note. Francesco Abate had gone to live in the east New York section of Brooklyn. At 24 years old, neither he nor anyone else in east New York had received Black Hand threats before. In his apartment at 136 Sackman Street, he began to learn how to make a bomb, in books he read how extortion gangs had worked and built a library of literature on everything pertaining to Black Hand activities. He sent Black Hand letters to local merchants and businessmen, and they paid. His lifestyle became notable in the area. He dressed well and spent money lavishly, appealing to the young ladies, even courting some whose fathers he had extorted. Spending as freely as he did, he felt the need to raise the demands he made. A meeting was arranged between Abate and the local merchants to establish the new rates. At the gate to Acacia Cemetery in Ozone Park as Abate awaited his prey, the merchants showed up armed with knives, axes, and pickaxes. They attacked Abate, literally cutting him to pieces. A sad ending for the young man, but also an end to Black Hand activity in East New York.

Once Petrosino got his Italian Squad he began to organize it in such a way as to be most effective in searching out suspects and solving crimes. They built a network of informants, an essential ingredient in law enforcement, especially in a large city. Next he created a list of known or suspected criminals to keep tabs on and to have someone to go to as chief suspects when a crime was committed. They received publicity especially since Petrosino made it a habit of notifying the press when a certain bust was about to go down. The war between the Black Hand and the new Italian Squad was a point of interest throughout the city. It became a craze and articles related to the Black Hand were sold by street vendors and in stores. There were metal black hands as charms, stationery with the Black Hand insignia and envelopes to match. Symbols of death became a fad. But it did nothing to alleviate the criminal activity.

The squad learned how to distinguish between a genuine Black Hand letter and a phony one by the phrases and dialect. In some cases a writer who was not Italian tried to mimic the broken English wording. A Mr. Nussbaum of Manhattan received a letter in 1905 demanding $50 on September 30 before 11 a.m. or the letter writer was going to "kill you and your girl." It was signed "The Black Hand." The police recognized it as a bogus note. It was written by Nussbaum's 15-year-old daughter "just for fun," as she said.

But the squad and its methods were bearing fruit. They uncovered a scheme involving laborers working on subway tunnels, and buildings. Petrosino's men spent much time and effort to determine the racket and how it was being perpetrated. When a new construction project was announced, the Black Hand sent in a man to apply for a job. He would let it be known to other workers that he received a Black Hand letter and fear would be created among the work crew. They wondered who among them was involved and when additional letters would be received. After time it was easy pickings for a society member to capitalize on the men's fears and they would readily pay up.

Though the Italian Squad and Joe Petrosino had their work cut out for them, they proved to be up to the task. From the onset in 1904 to the expansion beginning in 1906 under the new commissioner Bingham, the squad grew in manpower and in style and method. They were a force to be reckoned with.

Chapter Four

The Italian Sherlock Holmes

Detective Sergeant Joseph Petrosino's reputation grew immeasurably during his first few years on the police force. His prestige aided in getting his Italian Squad as he was known to be knowledgeable about the ways of his countrymen and tough when dealing with the criminal element among them. A newspaper called him "the greatest Italian detective in the world, the Italian Sherlock Holmes."[1] After his promotion to detective he wore civilian clothes, usually black, and the Prince Albert overcoat, dark suit and black derby hat became a trademark of his dress. It was written, however, that "even dressing like a gentleman could not make Petrosino look attractive. He was a squat, heavy man with a peasant's round face that still showed traces of the smallpox from which he had suffered as a child in Padula."[2]

Author Luigi Barzini described him as a "stout, strong man. His clean-shaven face was coarse-featured, and marred by light pocking. But in that butcher's face there was the impress of a stubborn will and of courage. There was more of the wrestler than of the policeman in Petrosino. One sensed that he was better at thrashing the evildoer than at finding him."[3] He was tough and as time was to tell, a good cop. Even in a time that police had more freedom in dealing physically with criminals, Petrosino maintained a strong reputation. It was said that he "knocked out more teeth than a professional dentist."[4] The image, however, of a tough, hard-nosed bully of a police officer was tempered somewhat by his aesthetics. He played his violin and loved opera. His favorite composer was Verdi, an aria from *La Traviata* a favorite violin piece.

One reporter after interviewing Petrosino said he had a "determined jaw.... The eyes are not the searching eyes of the inquisitive plodder, but the intelligent eyes of a student. There is generally a kindly light in them, a light that makes one feel easy in mind. You can readily imagine that you are talking to some gentle and thoughtful person who has your interests at heart."[5]

As an ambitious youngster to one of the first Italian policemen hired by the NYPD, Petrosino showed grit and determination. His early days on the force were not easy since even Italians distrusted authority and he was often insulted and received death threats in the mail. In Sicilian, *petrosino* means "parsley" and the call "Fresh parsley for sale" from street peddlers was often a warning to local thugs that he was approaching. His existence was Spartan, as he had no wife or family and lived alone. "The police department is the only wife I have a right to have," he once said. "There's so much sudden death in this business. A man hasn't the right to bring a woman into it."[6] His life was his work. As he patrolled the Tenderloin district of Manhattan, he made his first arrest, an actor who'd broken the ban on Sunday theatrical performances.

When Petrosino joined the police force, it was in the days of the Democratic political machine Tammany Hall, and corruption among both the politicians and the police was widespread. Petrosino was to make many friends and acquaintances during his years on the force and one who appeared at this juncture in his life was Theodore Roosevelt. Roosevelt had been born in New York on October 27, 1858, attended Harvard and became a member of the New York State Assembly when he was 23 years old. In 1886 he lost his bid to be mayor of New York City. He then went to Washington, D.C., to serve on the U.S. Civil Service Commission for the next six years, before returning to his home. At the time, the police commission consisted of four members, as the New York Board of Police Commissioners (it was not until 1901 that a single commissioner was chosen to run the NYPD). An effort was made to eliminate the vast corruption in the department and it was decided that by making Roosevelt the head of the commission it would go a

Lieutenant Detective Joseph Petrosino was the first detective of Italian heritage in the country and the first commander of the Italian Squad of the NYPD (Library of Congress).

long way toward achieving that end. On January 1, 1895, the future president of the United States was sworn in as the head of the police commission of New York City.

The task that the new commissioner faced was enormous. His opinions closely resembled Petrosino's. He hired cops on the basis of their abilities, not their political affiliations. He had telephones installed in the precinct houses, ordered regular physical and firearms inspections and conducted walking tours to inspect his officers on patrol. He was strongly of the opinion, like Petrosino, that special requirements for officers were necessary in order to properly police the immigrant neighborhoods. Inevitably he discovered Joseph Petrosino.

The police were commonly involved in shakedowns of brothels and beat cops regularly took bribes from fruit vendors and bootblacks, of which Petrosino was familiar because of his days shining shoes. One of the earliest and most renowned actions by the new commissioner was the night he and a friend, journalist Jacob Riis, wandered about the city streets after midnight. They observed police officers asleep while on duty or socializing in cafés and saloons instead of tending to their duties. A number of them were formally reprimanded by Roosevelt.

Not all actions on the part of the commissioner were successful. One mistake was trying to shut down the saloons on Sundays. The motivation for the backlash that followed came from the many workingmen who labored six days a week and had only Sundays for relaxation at their favorite stops. Roosevelt served just two years, as one of his motives in taking the job was to further his political career. He and his board created a pistol shooting range, which as a result he is credited with the founding of police academies. On July 20, 1895, he named Joseph Petrosino the first Italian detective sergeant in the nation. In one year the new sergeant won 17 murder convictions and by the end of his career he would send one hundred killers to the electric chair or to long prison terms in Sing Sing Prison.

Raymond and Carmelo Farach were early immigrants from Palermo, having arrived in America in 1853. In April 1884 Carmelo's body was found stabbed to death on Staten Island. A man seen with him just minutes before his death was identified as Farach's business partner, Antonio Flaccomio, and immediately became a prime suspect. He disappeared, however, soon after the killing and did not reappear for two years. He had been traveling throughout the United States and upon his return went to live in Little Italy. It was not until two more years had passed that Flaccomio met his own death. On October 14, 1888, after playing cards with friends, he was attacked while walking home. Stabbed in the chest with a bread knife, his murderers escaped but were recognized as being Italians. At the time, Joe Petrosino was one of only two detectives who spoke Italian. Responsible for the investigation was Inspector Thomas Byrne and it was swift and complete but the arrested suspect, Vencinzo Quartararo, was acquitted because of testimony as to an alibi that came from Sicilians of low repute. As a result the police chose to shy away from Italian crimes, leaving the door ajar for the eventual approval of Italians as detectives to act on and specialize in crimes committed in the Italian community. The first of note, of course, was Joe Petrosino.

One of the most notable cases for Joe Petrosino had been the infamous barrel murder in 1903. The case brought Petrosino in touch with Don Vito Cascio Ferro and he couldn't know then that this gangster would one day in the future claim responsibility for the death of the detective. Cascio Ferro was associated with the Morello-Lupo gang, whose members were arrested in the case. But Don Vito had left town before the police made the arrests. He fled to New Orleans and then back to Sicily. It was said that he vowed vengeance on the detective and Petrosino's biographer tells us that Ferro kept a photograph of the policeman in his wallet so he would be absolutely sure of his identity should their paths cross in the future. This was a practice of American killers who wanted to be sure they had the right target.

Vito Cascio Ferro was born in Palermo, Sicily, on January 22, 1862. His father worked for the Inglese family, managing their farm in Bisacquino, near Palermo. He never went to school. While still a young man he married the village school teacher, Brigida Giaccone, who bought the house the couple would live in as a dowry, and taught him to read and write. He was considered a handsome man with the dress and the habits of a gentleman. He smoked a long-stemmed pipe and his manner drew respect from the peasants so that they began to refer to him as *Don,* a title of respect. He didn't care for work and spent much of his time in local bars and taverns and in time joined an anarchist movement as it became popular in Sicily. He made speeches preaching the socialism of the anarchist. Once when he was brought into court for not paying his bills, his claim was that as an anarchist, he didn't believe in property rights.

Even with his political ideology, he found the time to indulge in crime, a career choice that began before he immigrated to America. In the 1880s he was inducted into the Mafia. He worked as a revenue collector, which was a cover for his protection racket. His criminal record began with an 1884 assault charge and was to include extortion, arson, and kidnapping. Recruited into the Fasci Siciliani, a popular socialist movement, he eventually became president of the Fascio of Bisacquino. When in January 1894, the Fasci were outlawed on the orders of the prime minister, Cascio Ferro fled to Tunis to avoid jail. He returned a year later and got himself a position in charge of granting emigration permits in the district of Corleone.

In 1898 he was involved in the kidnapping of Baroness Clorinda Peritelli di Valpetroso. She was released unharmed a day later, presumably after the kidnappers received a ransom. However, Vito and two others were arrested and incredibly talked themselves out of trouble when Ferro offered a far-fetched story that the motive for the act was love. He explained how one of his fellow kidnappers, in his infatuation with the 19-year-old baroness only wanted her attention to present his case for marriage. He was turned down,

Vito Casio Ferro became a noted mafia leader in Sicily and was linked to the murder of Petrosino.

but the Italian police accepted Ferro's explanation, and he was freed after receiving a suspended sentence. Apparently determining that crime was more profitable than politics, he organized his first criminal gang.

Much of the accusations against him were not based in fact. He became a master of disguise so that his victims could only offer speculation. There was a robbery of three merchants when their carriage was halted on a road and a priest held a rifle on them. The priest was believed to be Don Vito Cascio Ferro. At this point Cascio Ferro traveled to Marseilles and from there sailed to the United States arriving in New York in September 1901. He lived for a time with his sister Francesca on 23rd Street, before getting his own place at 117 Morgan Street. His earliest activities labeled him as one of the first Mafioso leaders in this country. His extortionist activities were "gentlemanly"; that is, instead of threats, he used soft talk and reason to convince merchants that he only wanted to protect these good men from bad men. Cascio Ferro was "dressing the Mafia in new clothes."[7]

He became involved with a counterfeiting operation in Hackensack, New Jersey, and was arrested at a barbershop on First Avenue, from which the counterfeit money had been distributed. Somehow he escaped prosecution with an alibi that he worked at a paper mill, while the other gang members were tried and convicted. It was only a matter of time before he would become associated with the Morello gang in Harlem. When he was sought for arrest in the barrel murder case he returned to Sicily by way of New Orleans where he was traced by Detective Petrosino, but he had already left the city. He was credited with being the first to introduce the practice of protection payments into the United States, the practice being a familiar one in Sicily.

Once back in Sicily, Cascio Ferro became a local notable. He worked closely with the mayor of Burgio as a ward healer and developed good terms with a number of other local influential men. He came to be a significant figure with the local Mafia clans, including some in districts of Palermo. Journalist Luigi Barzini explained Cascio Ferro's approach to his vocation and why he became so successful at it. "Don Vito brought the organization to its highest perfection without undue recourse to violence. The Mafia leader who scatters corpses all over the island in order to achieve his goal is considered as inept as the statesman who has to wage aggressive wars. Don Vito ruled and inspired fear mainly by the use of his great qualities and natural ascendency. His awe-aspiring appearance helped him. ...His manners were princely, his demeanor humble but majestic."[8] He was described as associated with the "high" Mafia, led a life of luxury, going to theaters, cafés, and gambling huge sums of money at a place called Circolo dei Civili, a gentlemen's club for the pretentious and elite.

With all the polite conversation and high-class company, Cascio Ferro was a murderer as well. Authorities believed him to be linked to a hundred or more killings over the years. He was an organizer as well, organizing a gang of thieves to work specific crimes and thought to have brought the Mafia into the modern, big-city world. Although he evaded prosecution in Sicily, a wide range of crimes such as arson, murder, extortion, kidnapping and racketeering were attributed to him by the Palermo police. They considered him to be the head of the Mafia of Bisacquino, Palermo, Burgio, Corleone, Campofiorito, Contessa, Estellina, Chiusa, Sclafani, Sciacca, Sambuca, Zabut, and Villafranca Sicula. His reputation among his kind was solid. He was the mind behind the impersonation ploy in the barrel murder and his organizational skills made the Black Hand more efficient and more deadly. After his trip back to Sicily in 1904 he was somewhat of a link between the Black Hand and the Mafia, and his star in the underworld continued to rise.

Known as he was as the controlling faction of a number of Mafia organizations in Sicily, his sophisticated approach led to a unique interpretation of protection whereby some victims actually complimented him on it.

The living conditions in Little Italy in Lower Manhattan at the turn of the century were deplorable. They have been described as an anthill in constant movement, squalor and degradation and neighborhood disorder. More than 5,000 pushcarts clogged the streets, where every dialect of Italy was spoken. On the Lower East Side of Manhattan beneath the Brooklyn Bridge, a half-million Italian immigrants clustered. As they tried to survive in this new and unfortunate environment, the criminal elements who emigrated from the homeland with them held them at their mercy. Hundreds of criminals were successful in leaving the country through the system of issuing passports that the Italian government set up with the purpose of ridding themselves of this element. The conditions made the job of the police almost impossible. Commissioner William McAdoo in a report wrote, "It is simply impossible to pack human beings into these honeycombs towering over the narrow canyons of streets and then propose to turn them into citizens who respect and obey the laws."[9]

The McKinley incident previously mentioned began with the July 30, 1900, assassination of Italy's King Umberto I at Monza by an anarchist from America, 31-year-old Gaetano Bresci, who was born in Prato, Tuscany. The Italian consul general in New York, Carlo Branchi, and the Italian ambassador in Washington, Mayor des Planches, both asked on behalf of the Italian government for the assistance of the American police in solving the conspiracy that led to the murder of the king of Italy. Bresci had gone back to his country from Paterson, New Jersey, where he had been a part of a large Italian community, whose members were almost all from the north-central region of Italy and were connected with an anarchist movement.

The United States, however, did not have much interest in the anarchist attacks that had been carried out in Europe over the past few years—they were "Old World" problems and better left for the Europeans to solve themselves. As a result, the investigation that had gotten underway in Paterson was superficial. The Italian government was not pleased with this attitude. Their concern was that rather than a lone malcontent, Bresci and

Hester Street in Little Italy in NYC was indicative of the appalling conditions that Italian immigrants lived under at the turn of the 20th century (Library of Congress).

his actions had been a part of a broader plot. The Italian ambassador was instructed to address the president of the United States directly so that he may authorize a new investigation. William McKinley entrusted the matter to the Secret Service. The agent selected, named Redfern, pointed out that he would be incapable of carrying out the assignment due to his ignorance of the Italian language.

McKinley's vice president was the former police commissioner of New York, Theodore Roosevelt, and when he became aware of the situation, he immediately recommended that Joe Petrosino be called in. A few days later, an Italian immigrant named Pietro Moretti checked into the Bertoldi's, a small, cheap hotel in Paterson. The immigrant was, of course, Joe Petrosino. He was aware that Bresci had lived there for some time. The detective got a job as an unskilled laborer and lived at the hotel for three months. He showed an interest in anarchist ideas without being overly enthusiastic, gaining the confidence and friendship of several of the residents who were among the anarchists. He observed and noted everything he saw or heard and when he returned to New York, he carried a notebook filled with his information. He then went to Washington to report in person to President McKinley and Vice President Roosevelt.

According to Petrosino, the assassination of Umberto I was the result of a conspiracy arranged by the group in Paterson that was affiliated with the European Black Hand, an anarchist subversive organization. He said that Bresci was chosen by lot to be executioner. But the most sensational discovery that Petrosino made was that the group planned to assassinate the president of the United States. He was not taken seriously by the president.

"McKinley received it [the news of an assassination attempt] with a patronizing smile, convinced as he was that he was the best-loved man in America. Teddy Roosevelt, with his usual snobbish cynicism, offered no more than a witticism: 'I certainly hope it will not be the anarchists who will make me President.' And that was the end of it."[10]

McKinley was not affected by Petrosino's warning and he naively refused effort to assure his personal safety. On the morning of September 6, 1901, McKinley had gone to Buffalo, New York, for the Pan-American Exposition. He was scheduled to meet the people in a vast pavilion that was called the Temple of Music. His private secretary, George Cortelyou, tried to impress upon him the possible danger by reminding the president that in Petrosino's report, McKinley was on the anarchists' assassination list, as were the Tsar, Emperor Wilhelm II of Germany and Emperor Franz

Josef of Austria-Hungary. Sadly, it did not deter McKinley nor seem to cause him any concern.

At four o'clock in the afternoon, William McKinley took his place in the Temple of Music and prepared to greet the electorate. A long line of people waited to shake the president's hand. One of them, a 28-year-old Polish native, Leon Czolgosz, approached the president with a small .32 caliber revolver wrapped in a handkerchief in his hand. Twelve minutes after the line had begun to move, the young man stepped up to President McKinley and shot him twice in the abdomen. Czolgosz was an anarchist and they found in his wallet a newspaper clipping of Bresci's crime. McKinley died eight days later.

In New York, as soon as they received word, reporters hurried to police headquarters at 300 Mulberry Street to give them the news and to get reactions. When they saw Petrosino and told him, they reported that the detective began to sob. When he gained control of himself, he said to the journalists, "I warned him!" The next day the headlines read, "PETROSINO WARNED HIM!" and "ITALIAN DETECTIVE TRIED TO SAVE MCKINLEY."[11] In the ensuing years Petrosino often worked closely with the Secret Service, and certainly his value to law enforcement was enhanced by the McKinley case.

By 1905 relations between Petrosino and the police force should have been one of cooperation but that kind of joint existence had not yet been achieved, and Little Italy and the Italian immigrant population remained underpoliced and underprotected. A small Italian grocery store at 13 Stanton Street and the owners, the Gimavalvo brothers, became a target for the Black Hand. The brothers had come from Sicily in shifts and brought their family over bit by bit, funds all coming from the little store on Stanton Street. When the Black Hand letters began to arrive, they called Joe Petrosino. On the afternoon of October 16, 1905, Petrosino stood outside the Gimavalvo store on guard but had to leave to keep an appointment with a fruit peddler on the Brooklyn Bridge, who was also a recipient of a Black Hand letter. He called over Sergeant Funston of the local precinct and explained to him that the store must be guarded constantly and that he would return a bit later. Funston said he would guard the store and get a note to his superior, Captain Murtha, who would be sure that a guard would be at the store around the clock.

Petrosino kept his appointment with the fruit peddler on the bridge and the two set up boxes of fruit as the detective pretended to be the man's assistant. A policeman came by and ordered the two men to remove their wares and get off the bridge. Petrosino explained who he was—but the cop wouldn't accept that. The clamor that he made ruined any chance of Petrosino having a rendezvous with the extortionists. Furious, Petrosino and the fruit peddler left the scene. That night, at 3 a.m., a terrific explosion ripped through the Gimavalvo's store and apartment above it. There were injuries due to flying glass, but miraculously no one was killed. What Petrosino learned of the disaster infuriated him all the more. When the bomb throwers had arrived there were no cops anywhere. Captain Murtha and Sergeant Funston had lied about keeping an officer on guard. The Italian Squad was protecting the family but as soon as the job had been turned over to an Irish cop, an attack was made.

There seemed to be no limit to the audacity of the Black Hand and New York's criminal element. A letter appeared at the office of Joel M. Marx, the assistant district attorney of New York City, on an August day in 1904. Marx had been going after Italians who were selling false citizenship papers, and had been successful in putting away dozens of them. The letter threatened to kill Marx and the Italian detectives if he did not stop his pursuit of these criminals. "If you don't stop we will kill you and your children. Revenge." It was signed by a recognizable Black Hand symbol; two crosses flanking a heart pierced by an arrow.

The Secret Service was called in though their jurisdiction in this case was debatable. Petrosino was surprised by the federal attention. He and his squad had received hundreds of death threats and never had the government agency been brought into it. Petrosino publicly questioned the lack of attention his squad got from the Secret Service in combating the Mafia or the Black Hand. The response was simply that the Service would only get involved when a federal law was broken. At this point in time the federal government was staying clear of rendering any assistance to the Italian communities.

One of the most notorious underworld figures of the early 20th century was Giuseppe Morello, a counterfeiter who, with his partner, Ignazio Lupo (aka Lupo the Wolf), would be implicated in the infamous barrel murder case in 1903. Morello was born May 2, 1867, and grew up in Corleone, Sicily. His father died when he was five years old and at the age of six had a stepfather, Bernardo Terranova. Morello and the Terranova family would be allied in criminal activities in the future. Terranova and then Morello would become members of the Sicilian Mafia. Generally considered his first murder, Morello shot and killed a Mafia head in Corleone. A witness to the crime was later murdered as well, who was shot in the back. Although arrested and questioned, Morello was released for lack of evidence—there were no witnesses to the murder. The counterfeiting operation that Morello conducted in Sicily resulted in warrants being issued for his arrest. By this time Morello had long since fled to America.

In an attempt to keep a low profile and avoid deportation, Morello apparently lived within the law, at least until about 1899, when he returned to counterfeiting. It was a few years hence that his involvement in the barrel case brought him in contact with Joe Petrosino.

As the gang activities proliferated in the early 1900s, the undisputed leader was Giuseppe Morello. Although it was nearly impossible to connect them to the crimes without direct evidence, the police were usually certain when the Morello gang was responsible for a crime. They were connected to as many as one hundred murders during the first decade and a half of the 20th century. Salvatore Marchiani had come to the United States from Sicily, having been associated with the Sicilian Mafia. He became associated with the Morello gang and in February 1908 his mutilated body was discovered in Brooklyn. The last person he was seen with was Joseph Fanaro, a Morello operative. The Brooklyn police could not turn up any evidence linking the gang with the killing nor the reason for it. Marchiani had obviously done something to make his life expendable. Detectives could charge no one with the crime but never had any doubt that Morello was behind it.

Already suspicious of the police because of their past lives in Sicily and southern Italy, the inability of the local cops, for the most part Irish and Jewish, to communicate with these immigrants not only made it difficult for these new citizens to be comfortable with authorities, but also aided in the growth of the Mafia. Criminal activities also caused non–Italians to see all of them as criminals or potential ones and to view them with suspicion. Into this climate of confusion, doubt, and crime stepped Joseph Petrosino. Quick to assess the problems, he offered his idea of solutions: one being the formation of a special Italian Squad, men who spoke the various dialects and were cognizant of the customs and traditions that guided their existence. He got his squad in 1904 after two years of cajoling and pleading and arguing for it.

Another idea that he persisted on expounding was the support of the community. He wanted them to rise up against their tormentors. "The problem with my people," he said, "is that … they are timid, and will not give information about their fellow-countrymen. If they would form a Vigilance League, they would be as safe as anyone else."[12] He called his countrymen sheep and failed to understand why they didn't unite against the barbaric invaders. Petrosino had gained the voice of the newspapers where he was popular. He often informed reporters of his projected arrests so they were able to be on top of the story. His statements, for example, about forming a vigilance league was printed in the *New York Times* on September 22, 1905. By 1907 the squad consisted of 40 men, but their work was increasingly difficult.

In February 1908, 500 Italians held a meeting in the offices of *Bollettino della Sera*, an Italian newspaper edited by Frank L. Frugone, who was elected president of the new organization called "The Italian Vigilance Protective Association." The highest number of Black Hand cases recorded was in 1908. Commissioner Bingham issued a report that stated there were 424 cases reported, with 215 arrests and 36 convictions. Sicilian gangsters had made their way to Tunis as a refuge and when the French decided to clean out about 10,000 criminals from that country, most made their way to America. This led to another step for Petrosino, which was to revamp immigration laws in order to more vigorously control the elements who entered the country. This work would ultimately lead to Petrosino's fatal trip to Italy in 1909. He gave an interview to the *Bollettino della Sera* in 1908 in which he said, "The United States has become the refuge of all the delinquents and the bandits of Italy, Sicily, Sardinia, and Calabria... When the French government proceeded in the expulsion of 10,000 Italians from Tunis ...they were welcomed with open arms by Uncle Sam.... Our Penal Code should be made more severe."[13]

For the years that Petrosino had been urging the Italian Americans to ban together, it finally seemed to be happening. In Chicago prominent Italian Americans in the city held a meeting on November 17, 1908, with more than a thousand people showing up. On this night they founded the Society of the White Hand. They planned a war chest of $50,000 and they would recruit one thousand detectives to hunt down Black Hand members operating in the city of Chicago. The chief of the Chicago Police Department enthusiastically endorsed the project, while the newspapers published positive editorials. Other cities around the country joined in. Carbondale and Reading, Pennsylvania; Clarksville, West Virginia; Brockton, Massachusetts; New Orleans and Baltimore among them. In Pittsburgh a White Hand group armed themselves and took after the local Black Handers. There was a gun fight in a railroad yard. One White Hand member was hit by a bullet. The shooter was chased by two others and caught and shot dead.

The federal government inserted a clause in the Immigration Act of 1907 that allowed the arrest and deportation of any immigrant convicted of a crime in his home country, up to three years after his arrival in the United States. It was a step but not strong enough to suit Joe Petrosino.

He cried that most of the imported criminals were in the country more than three years before they even knew they were here. He pointed out to Commissioner Bingham that of 5,000 criminals his squad tracked down, only 20 were eligible for deportation. The commissioner agreed and informed Petrosino that he was working out a plan, but in the meantime he explained, "we'll have to go it alone."[14]

Michael Mealli was promoted to detective in April 1905 and would have taken part in investigations conducted by the Italian Squad at that time. The squad and the Black Hand clashed constantly. Once a butcher at 211 Bleecker Street received an extortionist letter and reported it. Several members of the squad arrived early one morning and hid in the butcher's freezer and waited for several hours. They drank hot cocoa to stay warm while sitting on cakes of ice and moving around to keep their limbs loose until late in the afternoon. Finally a man identified as Gioacchino Napoli came into the shop and collected $50 in marked bills. The detectives came out shivering from their hiding place and cuffed the extortionist.

In another case detectives worked the counter in a drugstore. The cousin of a Black Hand victim stood outside the shop awaiting the arrival of someone to collect the ransom he held. Soon three men appeared. The cousin handed them a package then wiped his brow with a handkerchief, which was the signal. At that, the detectives rushed out of the store as the three criminals took off down the street. The squad members gave chase as the three leaped aboard a streetcar. One of the detectives reached the vehicle and pulled himself aboard. A Black Hander, Paolo Castellano, jumped through the car's open window and took off down the street. Gunfire erupted as the detective and a patrolman fired at Castellano, and a bullet struck him in the hip. He and the other two were nailed by the detectives and dragged to the nearest precinct.

Petrosino schooled his detectives in the ways of the Black Hand, and one of their lessons was to learn how to read the threats and determine which were real and which were not. They certainly could not investigate every threat, possessing neither the time nor the manpower. But he taught them well. The squad became an efficient, tightly run unit and their successes, in spite of the tens of thousands of New Yorkers being victimized by the Black Hand, were numerous. In November 1906, Commissioner Bingham promoted Joe Petrosino to the rank of lieutenant. He celebrated with a few friends at Vincent Saulino's restaurant at the corner of Lafayette and Spring Streets.

Vincenzo Saulino came from the Italian town of Agnone, a hundred miles east of Rome in the province of Campobasso. Saulino was a veteran of the Italian Legion and had fought during the Crimean War at the Battle of Sevastopol against the Russians. Then in his return to Italy he fought in the War of Italian Unification through 1871. He decided at that point to seek a new life in America where he took his French-born wife, Maria. He opened a comfortable little restaurant where his wife did the cooking and Vincenzo sat and chatted with customers while sipping wine. Petrosino found the restaurant a refuge, a place where he could enjoy the cuisine of southern Italy and get the attention he needed so as not to waste valuable time waiting to be served. He often accomplished this by calling ahead so that his meal would be prepared when Petrosino arrived. As a precaution he usually sat with his back to a wall so that an attacker could not surprise him from behind.

There were times when Petrosino could be more leisurely and he would engage in card games with Saulino. There was, however, another reason for Petrosino to spend time in the restaurant: Adelina, the owner's daughter, who was 11 years younger than the detective. She had been married and was living in Boston when her husband, Edward Vinti, died. The couple had no children and for a time, Adelina lived alone in Boston. Her father prevailed upon her to come to New York, as the mores of the time made it difficult to accept a woman living alone, and so she came to her parents' house and worked in the restaurant. Petrosino was taken with the younger woman and the two often engaged in conversation when he was in the restaurant. Her English was elementary so they conversed in Italian.

The relationship apparently developed over a period of time, perhaps two years, but there was no doubt that Petrosino had fallen deeply in love. Saulino, however, at first refused to agree to the wedding. There was the fear of assassination, as Vincenzo knew the dangers Petrosino faced nearly every day. It probably helped that Maria was in favor of the union, so on the occasion of his promotion to lieutenant, Joseph made his proposal of marriage to Adelina Saulino and she said yes. The couple were married on the first Sunday of April 1907 at St. Patrick's Church on Mott Street. Monsignor Patrick J. La Valle, an old friend of Petrosino's, performed the ceremony. In attendance was the Italian Squad and Theodore Bingham. A wedding luncheon was held at Saulino's Restaurant and the newlyweds moved into a four-room apartment at 233 Lafayette Street. Adelina apparently was a sensible enough woman to grasp the life she would be forced to live as wife of the most famous and yet often despised detective in New York. They did not go on a honeymoon and she spent most of her time at home. She was aware of the threats her husband received and in time became accustomed to them. This then was their life together, and they were happy.

Petrosino, however, lived in perpetual anxiety knowing that there were many threats to his life, and he didn't have any reservations about the reality. One night as he returned to his home, a reporter was awaiting him while standing in a dark hallway. When the reporter called Petrosino by name, the detective, startled, leaped toward him and pinned him against the wall. When he realized his mistake, he immediately let him go. The reporter recalled that "Petrosino did not laugh." He simply nodded and told the man, "I thought it was my time, at last. Someday they will get me."[15]

Chapter Five

The Mission

There were Italians among the immigrants who wanted to raise their people from the degradation many of them were bogged in. One who used his success to uplift his fellow Italians was Dr. Vincenzo Sellaro. His apartment and offices at 203 Grand Street had been bombed. The warning was for him as was the demand for $5,000. He was warned not to contact Petrosino. The doctor was a Sicilian, born in Palermo, and had received a medical degree from the University of Naples. In 1897 he came to America and enrolled at Cornell Medical School and by 1904 had developed a successful medical practice. In the summer of 1905, the doctor invited a number of influential Italians to a meeting with the idea of forming an organization whose aim would be "to emancipate Italians from every prejudice."[1] The society they founded was *Figli d'Italia*, the Order Sons of Italy in America.

Other help for the Italian Squad came, at times, in the form of retaliation by intended victims. Sometimes the Italians knew their tormentors and fought back. One immigrant bought a gun upon receiving a letter. He went to see some men he knew who had Black Hand connections. He told them that if any harm came to him or his family, he would kill them. It ended there. Another story was of a powerful individual whose brother and his business was the target of the Black Hand. He stood guard at his brother's establishment for three days. Finally he recognized someone who he knew to be a member of the society. He grabbed the man, held him in the air and began shaking him violently. He put the man down with a threat: if anything happened to his brother or his business, he would hunt down and eliminate each member of the gang. Again, there were no more letters.

Though it happened infrequently, there were instances of resistance. In Westchester, Giovanni Barberri had a bakery shop, the letters he got demanded $500. He did not respond. Antonio Fotti came up by train from the city and walked into Barberri's shop and pointed two pistols at the baker. Barberri ran into the street followed by the gunman. Two women passing by grabbed Fotti's arms as the baker ran back into the shop and grabbed a shotgun loaded with birdshot. He yelled to the women to let Fotti go. They did and he fired both barrels. The police followed a trail of blood to a Yonkers hospital and arrested Fotti.

Just two days later in Mamaroneck, another Westchester community, three men walked into a hotel bar. The leader of these men was known as Big Pietro. When the hotelkeeper, Pietro Caputo, poured the drinks, Big Pietro reached over with a knife and slashed Caputo in the throat and head. Caputo, though fatally wounded, reached for a shotgun he kept behind the bar and fired at Big Pietro, blowing away the top half of his head. The other two ran into the surrounding woods local Italians formed a posse and hunted down the two accomplices.

This kind of resistance is what Petrosino tried to instill in the local Italian populations. Further along this line he encouraged organized resistance. He wished that Italians would band together and form vigilance leagues. Petrosino's battle plans, which included the Italian Squad, vigilance resistance and strengthening the immigration laws so that criminals could be deported, were all solid procedures that if put into effect could end the threat of the Black Hand. He had his squad, so the next thing that he could do was go to Italy and begin preparation for methods of keeping criminals out of the country and deporting those that were already in the U.S.

The Immigration Act of 1907 simply was not working and the influx of criminal elements continued to infiltrate the United States. Prosecution of these criminals was difficult as best, but at this time, an enterprising young prosecutor in Brooklyn named Francis Carrao was working his way up. He publicly pushed for an Italian prosecutor, one who could speak the language and knew the ways of the immigrants. Carrao was eminently aware of the need to crush the Black Hand, since his brother Charly was a member of the Italian Squad. Then, on April 2, 1907, Francis was given the position of prosecutor, the first of his heritage to hold it. His brother and Lt. Petrosino could arrest the Black Hand and he, Francis Carrao, would prosecute them. Arrest, prosecution and deportation would be the line of fire to combat the criminals.

When General Bingham told Petrosino that they would have to "go it alone," he meant until his plan could be put into effect. Bingham was just as frustrated as both Petrosino and Carrao were by the ineptitude of the laws to support their actions. There were cases where a man had been in the country three years and five days and the statute disallowed deportation after three years, and another failed because authorities couldn't decide where to deport him. Out of 5,000 Italian criminals tracked down by the squad, only 20 had been deportable. Because of the ineffectiveness of the immigration laws, committees from the senate and the congress had made the trip to Europe, and in particular to Italy, to study the problem firsthand, with the hopes of coming up with an adequate law to solve the problems. No solution presented itself, thus Bingham's plan.

It came late in 1908.

In the meantime, Joe Petrosino had been ill for a couple of months in the summer with a bout of bronchial pneumonia. His wife, Adelina, was pregnant and at 38 years old, there was a reasonable concern for her health. A relative of hers came to stay with the Petrosinos to help her through the birth. The detective was notified by the Italian consulate general that his government would present him with a gold watch in recognition of his help in the apprehension of Italian criminals "in flight from Italian justice." He accepted the award on October 20 presented by the consul general.

Bingham presented his special plan late in the year. It was to set up a Secret Service that would be responsible only to him, and Lieutenant Petrosino was to be put in charge. His aim was to turn this special force loose on the criminal element with literally no restraints and no authority except the commissioner himself. The board of aldermen, however, balked at the proposal and refused to appropriate the necessary funds. Their reason was given by the board chairman, Commissioner Redmond, who expressed the board's fear that "you could turn your secret service not only against the 'Black Hand,' but also in any other direction you saw fit."[2] One of the factors that helped promote Bingham's plan was a program presented by a criminologist who was an expert in Italian crimes, both in the U.S. and abroad. Emphasis was put on the deportation and prevention of immigration with Italy. Petrosino, of course, had urged improvement in this area, but the criminologist, who preferred not to be identified, supported Petrosino's thinking. His paper pointed out that of 10,662 persons tried in the United States in 1896, and 3,606 in Italy, 66 percent in Italy were convicted, whereas in the U.S. the conviction rate was only 1.3 percent. Since it is much easier to evade prosecution in America, the criminologist concluded, this is the reason for the increase in the immigration of Italian criminals to this country. All of this prior information, the criminologist's report and Petrosino's plan, led to the proposed trip to Italy by Petrosino and its plan of action.

The criminologist went so far as to say that he could provide names and instances of Sicilian gangs that have prevailed upon individuals to immigrate to America so that they may kill them with less danger of getting caught and prosecuted. Further, he outlined the reasons criminals come to America. One, as already discussed, is the ease with which it is possible to evade punishment here. It is easier to get ahold of weapons and explosives for criminal purposes. It is easier to hide in this country and the ease with which criminals get political protection was especially true in the Tammany Hall era. All of this played to the motives for sending someone to Italy to search out criminals to be deported and to prevent this level of undesirables from entering the country. In addition, there have been, according to this criminologist, more than 100 Italians that have been smuggled into the United States in the past month alone.

It was his recommendation that the police send to "Italy a trustworthy person who knows the local details of the underworld, the Italian criminal procedures, and the American immigration laws." Such a person obtaining the Italian judicial records of criminals completing their terms can lay the groundwork for the prevention of such individuals from immigrating to America. Petrosino's job had been laid out for him.

Bingham went ahead with his plans and sought funding from private sources. Named as sources were Andrew Carnegie and John D. Rockefeller among others, but this had never been confirmed. This took place in December 1908 and was a lead-in to the next phase of the plan, which was to send Petrosino on a mission to Italy. The Italian Squad would continue to operate under the direction of Lieutenant Gloster. As these plans were being formulated, Joseph Petrosino was entering a new phase of life, something he never had given thought to in the past. He was now a husband and on November 30, 1908, he became a father. The 12-pound baby girl was named Adelina Bianca Giuseppina and was baptized in St. Patrick's. The newest addition into his life, at nearly the age of 50, elated the tough detective and at the end of each day he hurried home to his wife and baby, the family life giving new meaning to his existence.

Petrosino, however, remained loyal to his work and accepted the new assignment, though with a good deal of reluctance. The overall purpose of his excursion was motivated by the need to prevent the saturation in New York City of the many murderers and extortionists who emigrated from the Italian peninsula and the island of Sicily. The plan to weaken the effectiveness of the Black Hand in the U.S. involved collecting evidence in Italy against men regarded as dangerous. The man selected for the mission would also recruit secret agents in Italy to aid in carrying out the overall plan. It had been determined earlier that in almost every case a man was arrested for a Black Hand crime in America he had also been convicted of a crime in Italy.

As these plans were unfolding, 1908 had proved to be a particularly horrifying period in the history of Black Hand atrocities. The death of a jewelry seller whose body was found in a trunk at the New York docks and an Italian banker named Louis Troja was bludgeoned to death at his business location were attributed but never proven to be the work of the Lupo-Morello gang. But, in Petrosino's view, they were not the only killers roaming the streets of New York. With the murder of "Diamond Sam" Sica, a gambler who was shot to death on a Manhattan street in 1908, the names of the Terranova family came across the police blotters. Nick and Ciro Terranova were also suspects in the death of a woman, a gangster's former girlfriend who had knowledge of one of the Morello assassinations.

The tandem of Italian Squad detectives Mike Mealli and Paul Simon-etti were joined by fellow detectives Antonio Vachris and Charles Corrao in an arrest of two suspects in the murder of Michaele Scudare on New Year's Dayin 1908. The arrests of junk dealer Francisco di Risa of 450 Carroll Street and his 17-year-old son, Giuseppe, were made in March. There was trouble between the men that came to a head, and the fatal shot was fired by the boy because he claimed that he thought the other man would kill his father. The two were arraigned at the Adams Street Court before Magistrate Dooley.

Vachris's Italian cops struck a blow against the kidnapping trade after little Vito Callia, the child of a barber at 17 McDougall Street, was taken from in front of his home and kept for a month. The father, though threatened, told his story to the police. The gang kidnapped the children of relatively poor people for ransom money and though the child was returned safely, Vachris and his men remembered the case with their eyes wide open until the chance came to nail the gang. A woman who had unwittingly been the ploy of the kidnappers in the Callia case, because she had taken care of the boy during his captivity, became the next victim of the criminals. The woman was living in fear as she obeyed the "certain Italians" who brought the boy to her house on East New York Avenue when she was told to feed him and care for him "but on no account to let him go out in the street."[3]

The leader of the band of kidnappers was in San Francisco at the time and wanted the woman in New York to care for other kidnapped children and told gang members to kidnap her and bring her to the Pacific Coast. She managed to inform the police and they were at her house when the gang members appeared. One of them, Francisco Furfare, got fifteen years in prison, the other two men each received 12½ years. The convictions put a hold on the kidnappers' activities and the Italian Squad was lauded for its efforts in the cases involved.

An unsolved murder case at about the same time reached a point in the investigation where police expected to be able to round up the men who murdered an Italian on Noll Street by inflicting multiple stab wounds. The same men killed Salvatore Marchinno and left his dismembered body in a lot in the Flatbush neighborhood.

It was also in the first decade of the 20th century that a new form of extracting money came to be a regular source of income to the Mafia and the Black Handers. "Protection" was easier than extortion. Gangsters merely had to offer their victims protection from themselves. If they paid, the perps needed to do nothing but collect. They reached everyone in the community from bankers to pushcart peddlers. Joe Valachi, the son of a vegetable seller from Naples, recalled the East Harlem area when he was growing up. "I remember my father had to pay a dollar a week for 'protection,' or else his pushcart would be wrecked."[4]

Bombings became an all-too-common occurrence. Even buildings close to NYPD headquarters at 300 Mulberry Street had been destroyed, just as the one on nearby Elizabeth Street had on March 2, which shook the headquarters building. In one case where the target was a banker, Giovanni Cozussi, living at 320 East 63rd Street, a Black Hander went to the roof of the four-story tenement, opened the skylight and dropped a bomb down the airshaft. The device exploded, wounding nine people. In response to this latest wave of violence and technique, Petrosino created the NYPD Bomb Squad, the first in the nation. The men were taught to identify certain types of explosives. They uncovered schemes whereby laborers were stealing sticks of dynamite from construction sites and selling them to Black Hand members. They learned of timers set to go off after the bombers had fled the scene. The bomb squad hired an expert to analyze devices that the squad uncovered.

On November 11, 1908, the Italian Squad raided a bomb-making location in Little Italy, confiscating 19 bombs and making five arrests. In the next three months there were eight bombings, a number of threatening extortion letters, and several murders thought to be the work of local gangs. As the crime rate elevated, Petrosino and his squad saw their workload increase immeasurably. It was also difficult to get convictions because witnesses still refused to testify in court. Petrosino became increasingly certain that the answer to much of the problem lay in the ability to deport known criminals and to prevent many from immigrating to the U.S. from Italy. Petrosino estimated there were at least 5,000 criminals who should have been deported.

Petrosino made many recommendations, most too impractical to be put into use. He suggested that more than one family living in an apartment should be banned to prevent overcrowding; he also suggested the banning of pushcarts "because they were used to transport bombs."[5] He wanted the criminal laws to be more stringent and immigration laws tightened up, and thought the Italian government should send records of criminals to make deportation proceedings more easily enforced. The only suggestion that Commissioner Bingham thought was doable—the recommendation to obtain documents from the Italian government—became the antecedent to Pertrosino's fatal trip and mission.

One such case further emphasized the importance of the upcoming plan to go to Italy and seek out criminals before they were able to flee to America. Petrosino and the bomb squad went after Pellegrino Mule, a Sicilian accused of setting off an explosion that injured twenty children. Inquiries to the Italian police provided information that Mule had been sentenced to life for murdering an informer. In Mule's house Petrosino discovered the tracings of an extortion letter. It was enough to deport Mule and break up his Black Hand gang. A man believed to be a major bomb maker named Pronzola Bonaventura was followed by Petrosino through Little Italy for days, hoping for some clues as to the actions of the suspect. Finally, Bonaventura entered the building of a landlord targeted by the Black Hand. Rushing into the building, Petrosino and his detectives caught Bonaventura in the act of lighting a fuse on a bomb. The result of a bloody fight was the arrest of the bomber.

In spite of their successes there were setbacks. The White Hand Society, formed in February 1908, was already proving to be ineffective. The 1,000 detectives they claimed to hire turned out to be a single one—and an ineffective one at that. Another fear that Petrosino had expressed was that the Black Hand would extend its violence to non–Italians as well. In early 1908 John D. Rockefeller, one of the richest men in the world, was revealed as a victim of the extortionists. At his estate in Pocantico Hills, New York, his workers had been attacked. His dismissal of all Italians working at his estate was praised by the press. But a number of states tried to attack the problem with stronger laws. New York and New Jersey increased the prison sentences for kidnapping and extortion. And even the famous Lloyd's of London began to insure businesses and individuals against attacks by the Society of the Black Hand.

Some of the newspapers turned on the Italian Squad and Petrosino. One paper screamed with the headline "Petrosino's Squad a Failure."[6] The squad however, had been effective. Over a four-year period they had made

2,500 arrests, 2,000 in Black Hand crimes, and had accomplished 850 convictions. The men were working 16-hour days and were getting results but the volume of Black Hand activity was so heavy that the task seemed endless. One of the things that made their jobs all the more difficult was the fact that crime had become better organized, more efficient and sophisticated. When Petrosino caught a Black Hand gang led by Francesco Santori, the police found notebooks that listed victims who paid protection money along with the names of associates and the amounts that each collected at regular intervals.

The old methods of detection by the police became less useful. Petrosino himself used to get by with simple disguises but eventually found that this method no longer worked because he was so easily recognizable on the streets of Little Italy. Obtaining convictions in the courts was harder and harder. Beside the perennial problem of witnesses too fearful to testify against these criminals, lawyers could apply more deliberate uses of the laws making it harder for prosecutors to get convictions. More and more, the idea of deporting criminals became a potential weapon for reducing the crime on the streets of the city.

It was in this environment that Bingham got the revenues for his secret service, named Petrosino to head it, and executed his plan to send the detective to Italy. The distinct aim of the mission was to stop the flow of criminals from Italy to America, something the Italian government could or would not do. In carefully checking the Italian criminal records, any individual who had served time in Italy could be deported from the U.S. under the Immigration Act of 1907, provided they had been in the country for less than three years. By collecting this information, U.S. authorities would be able to make note of these criminals as soon as they arrived—thus maintaining the three-year mandate—and be able to send them back to Italy immediately. The plan also called for a network of agents to be set up in America that would take notice of any Italian criminal who enters the country and turn their name over to the NYPD.

An example of the project's possibilities was made by author Stephen Talty. Giuseppe Profaci had served a term in prison in Palermo in 1920. After his release, he was allowed to immigrate to the United States where he founded the Colombo crime syndicate, which became one of the dominate crime families in the 1930s. Under the Bingham plan, Profaci would have never been allowed to reach America.

Joseph Petrosino was 48 years old in 1909, and had been on the police force for 26 years. His life was his family, a loving wife and a beautiful baby daughter. In spite of his reluctance, he agreed to make the trip, knowing that his success could break the backs of the Black Hand. But he also knew of the dangers, and the warnings from his friends and the squad members were the same: "Watch out for yourself." Lieutenant Vachris, the head of the Brooklyn unit of the Italian Squad, warned him. "Joe, you may be safe in the North," he told him, "but look out for yourself when you get down South. You know who is there." (He meant the Mafia.) Petrosino was cautioned not to make the trip by a priest friend at St. Patrick's for fear that he would not return. "Probably not," was the detective's response, "but it is my duty and I am going."[7]

The warnings and cautions from his friends were really not necessary. Petrosino was acutely aware of the dangers and of the threats that were directed toward him and in spite of his high profile, he was especially concerned for his wife and child. This was illustrated by an incident that Stephen Talty included in *The Black Hand.* One afternoon his niece was helping Adelina with the baby and had the child out for a walk when she saw Petrosino on the street.

"Uncle Joe," she called out to him. "Look, I have the baby."

He passed her by without a glance. Later as she carried the child up to the couple's apartment, Petrosino was waiting for her.

"Don't you ever," he said in a fury, "recognize me on the street when you have the child." She never made that mistake again.[8]

On February 9, 1909, Lieutenant Joseph Petrosino left New York for Genoa, Italy. He was not in the best of moods. It may be that his greatest regret was being separated from his wife and daughter for a long period of time. Perhaps there was anxiety over the constant cautions tended to him over the trip. Before leaving he signed over power of attorney to Adelina so she would have control over his affairs in the event of his death. Fellow detectives spread the word within the NYPD just before he left that he had taken ill and was advised by doctors to stop working for a while. At this point only his family, Commissioner Bingham and a few highly placed police officials knew of the trip.

In any case on February 9 he sailed for Italy. The ship was the steamship *Duca di Genova*, the first-class ticket purchased under the name Simone Velletri. Departure time was four o'clock and as the ship headed for the open sea Petrosino lingered at the rail, gazing at the diminishing shoreline.

Just one day before Petrosino landed in Genoa, the *New York Times* ran an article that detailed Bingham's plan for his secret service unit, that Petrosino would head it, and how it would be funded. The article incredibly hinted at Petrosino's whereabouts, in spite of the secretive nature of the trip to Italy. According to the *Times*, Petrosino "has received orders from the Commissioner to go ahead and wipe out the blackmailers and Black Hand gangs. Where he is just now is another secret at 300 Mulberry Street. He may be on his way to Europe and he may be right here in the city." When asked directly where Lt. Petrosino could be, Commissioner Bingham laughed and said, "Why, he may be on the ocean, bound for Europe, for all I know."[9]

His luggage consisted of two yellow leather suitcases, one of which contained his police revolver, a .38-caliber Smith & Wesson, and letters of introduction to the Italian minister of the interior and the head of Italy's police forces, Francesco Leonardi. He also carried lists of criminals he intended to get information about in order to initiate extradition proceedings, and a list of informers he intended to seek out once in Sicily. In addition to the other pressures upon him, Petrosino became seasick almost immediately and was confined to his cabin for several days. While the plan was shrouded in secrecy, there were some moments when Petrosino himself let a word here and there slip out. For instance, the ship's purser, Carlo Longobardi, said to him that he recognized the detective from a newspaper photo but assured him that "you can rely on my discretion." During a conversation Petrosino told Longobardi that he had "an important job to do in Italy."[10] He met some of the ship's other 192 passengers aboard the ship, but maintained his assumed identity. He was one of only fourteen passengers traveling first class. Shortly before leaving, Petrosino had broken up a gang of Sicilian criminals who were working a scam that resulted in forced prostitution. Sicilian accomplices sent the names of girls who wanted to leave their country to their American colleagues. The Americans sent letters from men who would like to have wives from their own country. After an exchange of letters and photographs, the suitors would propose marriage and send passage. Waiting for them at the dock would be the individuals who would force the girls into prostitution. The perpetrators were convicted and sent to prison, except for one who escaped prosecution. His name was Paolo Palazzotto, a 27-year-old Sicilian from Palermo. He had been arrested by detective Joseph Corrao of the Italian Squad and turned over to Petrosino. He was deported and was supposed to travel on the same ship as Petrosino was sailing.

His departure was delayed because he had to be hospitalized after a supposed beating by Petrosino. However, two other travelers, Leonardo Crimi and Domenico Saidone, were on board due to Petrosino. These undesirables would be among those suspected of the detective's murderer. Petrosino spent a good deal of time with Francesco Delli Bovi, although

76

he disappeared upon arriving in Genoa. Whether or not he revealed his true identity to Delli Bovi is unknown. He seemed to speak to a number of passengers on the trip and apparently maintained his assumed identity.

Among the criminal element in Sicily that Petrosino had left his mark upon was Vito Cascio Ferro, who, after returning to Palermo, became one of the most powerful Mafia figures on the island. There were countless potential assassins lurking in the corners of Palermo where Petrosino entered with courage and determination.

He probably needn't have been so careful to protect his identity, as the secret mission was revealed before he even arrived in Italy. In an interview with Police Commissioner Theodore Bingham published on February 20, the *New York Herald* reported, "As the first step in the work of the new Secret Service established by Commissioner Bingham, Lieutenant Joseph Petrosino has gone to Italy, specifically Sicily, in order to obtain important information bearing on Italian criminals residing in the United States and in particular in New York, where the police would like to initiate the deportation of many criminals."[11] Petrosino arrived in Genoa at 8:20 p.m. on February 21. He boarded the Paris-Rome express in Genoa and arrived in the Italian capital that evening.

It was Carnival in Rome and the city offices were closed so Petrosino visited the city. He wrote to Adelina, "I've seen St. Peter's, the Sistine Chapel and Michelangelo's Galleries, which are wonders of the world. At the sight of St. Peter's I was spellbound. It is beyond human imagination."[12] The next morning, on February 22, he attempted to see the ambassador, but the embassy was closed, as it was Washington's birthday. It gave the policeman the opportunity to do some more sightseeing and he did it with two friends who were newspaper correspondents, whom he met that morning on a Rome street. Later, in Palermo, the detective met an old family friend at the post office. While speaking with him, he noticed a man walking by, whom he was sure he recognized but couldn't place for the moment. His friend, named Cianfarra, noted that it seemed to trouble him. That night the two had dinner together and Petrosino was still concerned over the stranger and the feeling that he was being watched.

One more curious incident added to the suspect list of potential assassins. When in Rome Petrosino was surprised to see a man at the Hotel Angleterre whose face was familiar but whose name escaped him. He followed the man to a telegraph office and watched as he prepared to send a telegram. He was able to determine that the wire was being sent to Sicily. He was sure later that the man followed him to Palermo. On February 23, Petrosino visited the U.S. ambassador, Lloyd A. Griscom, who assured him that he would arrange for him to meet the Italian minister of the interior and the police chief. He passed this along to Bingham in his first letter to the commissioner a couple of days later.

That night he wrote a letter to his wife. He described all the sights he'd seen that day, but told her that he preferred New York. He closed with "Kiss my dear little girl for me. A kiss from your affectionate husband."[13] He met with the head of the police, Francesco Leonardi, the following day and presented him with the letter of introduction from Commissioner Bingham, but he didn't let Leonardi in on Bingham's plan for placing intelligence agents in Italy who would report back to the NYPD. The next morning he planned to take his leave of the Eternal City and cabled his brother Vincenzo in Padula of his arrival time the next afternoon. Vincenzo met him at the train station. When Petrosino saw that his brother had brought a cousin along, he chided him, reminding him that the trip was a secret. But Vincenzo showed him an article in the Italian paper *Il Pungolo,* which contained an article about Petrosino's secret mission including reasons and even some details of the trip. While it was a stupid move on Bingham's part, the question as to why seems to remain a mystery. Petacco suggests in his biography of Petrosino that the motive was political on Bingham's part and Talty hints at the same motivation while saying that even so "his recklessness is still almost incomprehensible."[14] Every newspaper in New York printed the story, as well as the European edition of the *New York Herald,* published in Paris. None of Petrosino's enemies were unaware of his presence in Italy.

The very next morning Petrosino left Padula by train for Naples, then took the mail boat to Palermo, Sicily. A passenger on the train, Valentino di Montesano, was a Mafioso who recognized Petrosino. There were also two members of the Black Hand who traveled to Italy at the same time as Petrosino. They were Carlo Costantino (alias Tomasso Petto) and Antonio Passananti, who had both been implicated in the 1903 barrel murder. Constantino, upon his arrival, sent a telegram to New York. It was a strange message, obviously in code, and it was addressed to Giuseppe Morello at 360 East 61st Street, New York. They also paid a visit to an old friend, Don Vito Cascio Ferro.

Upon his arrival in Palermo, Petrosino checked into the Hotel de France using another alias, Simone Valenti di Giudea. He visited the American consul, William A. Bishop, and informed him of his plans. Bishop expressed surprise at Petrosino's going to Sicily without even attempting to disguise his identity. "Perhaps a thousand criminals know you there. They hate you and may stab you, he said. Petrosino smiled as a man feeling sure of himself and did not mind the danger."[15] He opened a bank account at the Banca Commerciale and made a deposit of 2,000 Italian Lire for future use. He went to the courthouse in Palermo and began going through files. He searched out the paperwork for the criminals whose names he had on the list he brought with him. He took a carriage to a firm called A. Capra

Theodore Bingham was the police commissioner who let the press know of Petrosino's secret trip to Italy (Library of Congress).

and rented a typewriter still using a different alias for each transaction, he left a deposit of 10 lire and signed the receipt in the name of Salvatore Basilico. He indicated in a letter to his wife that he was disturbed over something but did not state what it was that upset him. He forwarded copies of penal certificates of several criminals on his list to Bingham, which would allow the commissioner to begin working on deporting procedures. He ate his meals at the Café Oreto and generally kept a low profile.

The next day, on February 28, he wrote to his wife what was to be his last letter, letting her know that he had arrived in Palermo. The following day he stayed in the hotel typing out copies of the penal certificates that he had examined at the court offices. He put them in an envelope and enclosed with them a letter to Bingham. He explained his later-than-planned arrival in Palermo was due to influenza, which had him in bed for several days. For the next few days he roamed through the neighboring towns as well as Palermo, sometimes in disguise, using different aliases and avoiding the local police. He did check in with ambassador Bishop on a daily basis and kept him informed of his activities.

On March 6 he made an appointment to meet with the police commissioner of Palermo, Baldassare Ceola, whose main role in Palermo was to eliminate Mafia infiltration. Corruption between the criminals and the police was commonplace; for that reason, rather than the position going to a Sicilian, Ceola had been brought in from Milan in the hopes that he would remain corruption free. Petrosino complained to the commissioner about the number of criminals that were immigrating to the United States. Ceola insisted that all passports were completely legal. Ceola remained cordial but there was a coldness between the two law enforcers over the issue. Petrosino would not tell him where he was staying. The commissioner offered protection for Petrosino while in Sicily but the detective declined.

Ceola introduced one of his commanders, Cavalier Poli, to work as closely with Petrosino as the American detective would allow. Poli sensed right away that Petrosino had no confidence in the Italian police. He realized also that the American was relying on a multitude of informants, some in very high places. Poli also cautioned his superior that because he spent much of his time in the worst areas of the city, he feared for his life. Petrosino was in the company of many different men, some identified, some not. Some were presumably informers, others contacts that Petrosino had from past encounters. He had meetings and encounters but no one revealed any contact they had with him after his death, so knowledge of much of his activities has not come to light. On March 11, he was noticed by two men as he walked along the streets of Palermo. One of them said to his companion, "This man is Petrosino, who came to die in Palermo."[16] He was Paolo Palazzotto, who was arrested for involvement in a prostitution ring and had been deported after receiving a beating from Petrosino.

Palazzotto's friend was Ernesto Militano. That night as Petrosino ate dinner at the Café Oreto, the two men sat at the bar and were joined by two others, Francesco Nono and Salvatore Seminara. Seminara had been arrested by Petrosino and been forced to leave the U.S. There were enemies of the policeman all around. Angelo Caruso had been knocked around during an arrest by Petrosino and hated the policeman. Vito Casio Ferro was 35 miles away in Burgio and was said to have left the house where he was staying on the night of March 11. That same evening Petrosino made a notation in his notebook: "Vito Ferro ... dreaded criminal."[17] Talty expressed his wonder at why he made this particular notation six years after he last encountered him.

Petrosino continued to roam about the city, often unarmed. Was he just confident in his ability to ward off any attackers or safe in the belief that his informants and the people he associated with would not betray him? This attitude seems inconsistent with the warnings he had received and his own consul regarding his fate. Thoughts that went through his mind these last days are not clear at all and one wonders how he regarded his fate.

The next morning, on March 12, Petrosino took the 9:30 a.m. train to Caltanissetta where he searched criminal files at the courthouse. He returned to Palermo early in the afternoon. He had an appointment with an unknown someone at 4 p.m. and returned to his hotel at 5 p.m. He did some work typing penal certificates that he had gotten that day in Caltanissetta and in his notebook of criminals added a name to the bottom of the list: "Vito Cascio Ferro, born in Sambuca Zabut, resident of Bisacquino, Province of Palermo, dreaded criminal."[18] Once again a hasty note about Ferro with no explanation available. It rained heavily early that evening and stopped about 7:30 p.m. Petrosino put on his hat and packed an umbrella and went to the Café Oreto for dinner.

Chapter Six

A Death in Sicily

The Piazza Marina in Palermo no longer had the magnificence of ancient times when Petrosino arrived there in March 1909. It had once been the seat of the Court of the Holy Inquisition during the Spanish rule but the palaces, Palazzo Partanna and Palazzo Chiaramonte, on two sides of the Garibaldi Gardens were crumbling. Both churches; the Church of San Giovannuzzo, at the corner of Corso Vittorio Emanuele, and San Giuseppe dei Miracoli, just opposite at the corner of Via Longarini, have been closed for years. They were to flank the Garibaldi Gardens. The gardens are a rectangular cluster of exotic plants surrounded by a high grille fence. In Petrosino's time it was a busy commercial center by day with a close proximity to the port. At night it was more sparsely populated, the lighting was poor and the gardens cast shadows.

On the right-hand side of the piazza was the Café Oreto, the restaurant where Petrosino took his meals while staying at the Hotel De France alongside the Palazzo Chiaramonte. This was one of the most elegant hotels in Palermo. That evening of March 12, 1909, at about 6 p.m. a violent electric storm broke out that lasted about an hour and a half. It was about 7:30 and the piazza was empty when Petrosino left the hotel for dinner. The streets were flooded with water and the skies were so black it seemed the rain would begin again. He sat at his usual table with his back to the wall. He ordered pasta with marinara sauce, fish, fried potatoes, cheese, peppers, fruit, and a half liter of a local wine. Two men joined him at the table. Talty said they sat with him through dinner, Petacco said the conversation was brief and the men left while Petrosino finished his dinner and paid the check, 2.70 lire. He left the café at 8:45. Instead of turning left to the hotel he walked straight ahead and followed the gate around the Garibaldi Gardens, apparently heading for a prearranged spot possibly to meet with the two men from the café.

He walked to the northwest corner of the piazza by 8:50 p.m. A man walking along the Via Vittorio Emanuele, a street behind the restaurant, heard two shots ring out. There actually were four shots altogether, three at one time then a single shot. The shots came from the corner by the church of San Giuseppe dei Miracoli across from the gardens. Petrosino had walked exactly 660 feet. The piazza was relatively deserted with the rain. There was a group of people waiting for a streetcar. Some people ran toward the shots, others went in the opposite direction. A sailor, 21-year-old Alberto Cardella of Ancona, off the naval ship *Calabria*, which was anchored in the port of Palermo, was the first person to reach the stricken Petrosino. Cardella saw two men fleeing the scene and then heard a carriage drive away. He stood by the body of a stocky man, an umbrella on the floor beside him and a large revolver. He was soon joined by the medical officer from his ship. Seeing that he could do nothing for him he left, instructing Cardella to stay by the body. It took 15 minutes for the police to arrive.

Meanwhile the streetlights illuminating the piazza went out sending the area in total darkness. It seemed the gas to the piazza had been cut. Someone came by with candles and they were lit by the eerie flickering light. Another 15 minutes went by before the piazza was lighted again. No one could identify the body at first. He was wearing a black suit, black shoes and a dark-gray overcoat. He wore a brown silk necktie around his neck and there was a gold watch on a gold chain in his vest pocket. He had been shot three times; in the right shoulder, in the right cheek and in the throat. They found a bullet in the fabric of his coat. Apparently he had been shot from the front at close range. The body was searched by a man named Consentino, an examiner on the staff of the public prosecutor. The deed was done. The great cop was gone.

Among the possessions they found on Petrosino were letters of introduction, the notebook containing the names of criminals, a number of business cards, an NYPD badge #285 and a scrap of paper with "6824" written on it. There was also a postcard of Palermo with Adelina's address written on it along with the note: "A kiss for you and my little girl, who has spent months far from her daddy."[1] As word of the detective's death spread, Commissioner Ceola, who was at the theater, left in the middle of the show and rushed to the scene of the crime. The police covered the area questioning anyone who may have seen or heard something. The nearby tram station provided witnesses. A ticket collector said he'd seen the shooter, but a fellow worker overheard and told him to be quiet. Another worker seemed to know something about the two men who ran away. He was taken to police headquarters where he decided he didn't see or hear anything after all. The questioning was futile. No one came forward with any substantial information.

Ceola knew what he had on his hands. He knew that this was the first American police officer to be killed on foreign soil in the line of duty. He knew as soon as he had been briefed that the murder had been meticulously planned. He wondered why Petrosino would go outside to meet two strangers, surmising that he must have trusted them, particularly since he was unarmed.

They found Petrosino's Smith & Wesson in his hotel room. Apparently he had been unarmed that night, as the gun found on the scene was not his. The first arrest the police made in the case was at two o'clock that morning and it was Paolo Palazzotto. He had been seen at the Café Oreto that evening and his name was on Petrosino's list along with his brothers Domenico and Michele, known Black Hand members from Brooklyn. Then came Ernesto Militano, one of the men seen with Palazzotto at the café, and his partner, Paolo Palazzotto. He had shaved off his moustache that morning, possibly to be harder to recognize and identify. Altogether they took into custody that night 140 suspects. Palazzotto was taken from his bed at 2 a.m., claiming he had been ill and was in bed all day. Tommaso Chiusa was a porter in a building at 8 Partinico. He testified that he had taken his little daughter to the Garibaldi Gardens, and he had recognized Carlo Constantino and Antonio Passananti sitting on a bench. He knew them and was surprised to see them in Palermo, thinking they were both still in America.

Within 48 hours, the list of suspects had been narrowed down to 15, all connected with the Mafia or the Black Hand.

Questioned about their apparent sudden decision to return to Sicily, they said it was to distance themselves from some moneylenders who were persisting in trying to collect loans. Both men, however, were known to have a good deal of money. An agent in Partinico (the town both men were from and had returned to) had gotten word that Cascio Ferro was waiting for their return and then upon arriving they went to see a noted Mafioso.

The police worked through the night trying to identify Petrosino's murderers. One man, Tommaso Chiusa, came forward to say he recognized Carlo Constantino and Antonio Passananti sitting on a bench in the piazza the previous morning. The police already knew that the two had recently reentered the country from America and also that upon their return they had gone to Bisacquino to visit Don Vito Cascio Ferro. The next day Passananti had disappeared, but they were able to question Constantino. Within 48 hours they rounded up 15 suspects who had recently come from America and were all connected to the Mafia and/or the Black Hand. They were not able to locate Passananti or Cascio Ferro. There were two mysterious telegrams, one Constantino had addressed to Giuseppe Morello in New York, which contained some sort of code: "I Lo Baido work Fontana." They found a reply from Morello in Constantino's pocket. It read: "Why cut his whiskers off?"[2] The police could not locate either Cascio Ferro or Antonio Passananti because both disappeared the day following the murder. A witness, however, said that he saw Cascio Ferro speaking to a man he identified as Pasquale Enea, who was a known crime figure. It was later revealed by Commissioner Bingham that Enea was an informant.

In New York, *The Herald* was the first paper to publish a story on the murder of Petrosino. A detective from headquarters called on Adelina Petrosino to give her the bad news. He told her that it was unconfirmed and hopefully it was not true. She was overcome with grief. Her brother Louis Saulino and his wife, who lived in the apartment upstairs, were soon with her. The family physician and a friend of Petrosino's for 25 years, Dr. R. Asselta, was called in. Deputy Commissioner Woods was called (Bingham was in Washington). He rushed to headquarters and they all waited, unable to believe until the cable from the consul William Bishop came at ten o'clock and confirmed the unthinkable. "Palermo, Italy, 12 March 1909 Petrosino killed revolver center city tonight. Killers unknown. Mar-

Petrosino's remains arrive at the widow's home on April 9, 1909 (Library of Congress).

tyr's death. Bishop, consul."³ Members of the Italian Squad gathered and gravely discussed the assassination of their chief.

There was a great deal of attention to the story in New York City and much publicity attached to it. Blame was directed on the Palermo police for not providing protection although Petrosino had refused it when it was offered. Theodore Roosevelt had only just completed his second term in the White House and was planning a long vacation; a yearlong safari in Africa. As he left a relative's house that morning he was accosted by a group of reporters. Thinking it was just routine, he said that he had no comments on anyone or anything. "Can't you say something," a reporter asked him, "about the assassination of Lt. Petrosino?" Roosevelt was shocked. He hadn't heard. After being told the story he said, "I can't say anything but to express my deepest regrets. Petrosino was a great man and a good man. I regret most sincerely the death of such a man as Joe Petrosino."⁴ Although Petrosino still had enemies among his NYPD brethren, overall he was highly respected by even those officers, and resentment, anger, and sadness were emotions that ran high in New York on March 13.

Newspapers called loudly and boldly for the elimination of the Black Hand. The *Washington Post* called for an end to all emigration from southern Italy. The *New York Times* blamed those Italians who would not name criminals when they witnessed a crime. An organization called the Society for the Protection of Immigrants called for warfare on the Black Hand through the organization of a private force to seek out and kill members of the Black Hand. The Mayor of New York George McClellan, Jr., and Commissioner Bingham issued a joint statement asking the board of aldermen to offer a reward for information leading to the capture of Petrosino's killers, also calling on the Secret Service to help in the investigation. They dispatched agents to search for the killers.

Alderman Tim Sullivan, who opposed Petrosino at every turn, called for the assassins to be brought to a speedy justice. An ordinance was passed ordering all knife and gun merchants to keep records of names, addresses and descriptions of people purchasing such weapons. It amounted to one of the first gun control measures in New York City. The New York State Assembly in Albany proposed a law making anyone convicted of blowing up a building or kidnapping a child to be punished with the electric chair.

The Italian Squad took action and began rounding up all suspicious characters in known Black Hand hangouts. They arrested 27 in a tavern on Monroe Street, charging them with disorderly conduct. They were trying to discourage meetings of large numbers of Italians. They raided billiard rooms and barbershops. Despite all this scrutiny no evidence regarding the Petrosino murder turned up. This type of activity leveled against Italians created the kind of ill feelings toward the law that resulted in a riot in the Italian section of Hoboken, New Jersey. Officers responding to the scene of an accident there were fired upon from tenement windows.

Detective Peter Angelo of Pittsburgh, an Italian and a close friend of Petrosino's since the two worked together on Black Hand cases in Angelo's city, said he was not surprised at Petrosino's death. He warned his friend several months before that his life was in danger, having learned that there were plots in the works. Superintendent of Police McQuaid ordered all suspected Italians be placed under arrest. Chicago's Acting Chief of Police Schuettier said his office was constantly on watch for Black Hand activity. "I knew Petrosino personally," he said, "and deeply regret his death. He was particularly valuable in just such exploits as the one which proved fatal to him."[5] The city of Pittsburgh had a large population of Sicilians and a strong criminal element among them. A vigorous crusade against Italian criminals had all but rid the city of them, but with the death of Petrosino, police were fearful that another wave of such crime would commence and police in Western Pennsylvania were put on special alert.

Petrosino's funeral mass was scheduled to be served in St. Patrick's Cathedral on Mott Street. Commissioner Bingham issued a denial to the rumor that a letter had been received threatening to blow up the church and the funeral throng. Father Kearney of St. Patrick's also denied the story saying, "I never received such a letter and the whole thing is absurd. I cannot understand where such ridiculous statements originate."[6]

Members of the Italian Squad left their assignments and gathered together. One of them, Rocco Cavone, wouldn't hear the news for weeks. He was on a ship bringing a murder suspect back from Buenos Aires. The mayor ordered the flags at city hall to be flown at half-mast for the next four days. The story was big news across the country and in the European capitals. The American consul took charge of the arrangements for transporting the body back to the United States, which was placed in a walnut coffin and guarded by Italian policemen followed by a train of local politicians and local notable individuals. The procession traveled to the pier where the coffin was draped in an American flag and loaded aboard the steamship *Slavonia*, a ship heading for the U.S. that Bishop had contracted to carry the body. The ship arrived in New York on April 9 and unloaded at Pier A on the West Side. President Taft had requested that Bishop travel to Washington to update him on the assassination. The consul did just that. From there a large gathering formed a procession as the bier was escorted to Petrosino's home at 233 Lafayette where Adelina was waiting.

A police band played "Nearer, My God, to Thee" and Verdi's "Requiem." Mrs. Petrosino was inconsolable. She kept asking to see her husband but the funeral director, Rocco Marasco, would not let her. He had discovered that the body was rapidly deteriorating. Though Professor Giacinto Vetere of the University of Naples had been hired to prepare the body, he was met with obstacles that prevented him from doing the task he was hired to do and no embalmment had been performed. The body was transferred to the headquarters of the Republican League where it lie in state, an honor guard in attendance and armed detectives on the roof scanning the crowd for Black Handers. Thousands of mourners filed past the casket. On April 12, the mayor declared a public holiday closing the city offices. As the coffin was carried to the hearse by pallbearers from Traffic Squad A, Adelina followed on the arm of her brother. It was estimated that a quarter of a million people lined the streets of Lower Manhattan amid mounted policemen, the police band, and eight Victorian coaches overflowing with flowers. The procession took a route along Lafayette to Broadway to Mercer, where at the Mercer Street station a unit of police officers stood at attention.

Among the mourners, a Chinese-American man spoke of how Petrosino had broken up a robbery in his store years before. "I'd be a dead man, but for Joe," he said.[7]

In the funeral procession, the hearse was followed by 1,000 mounted and foot police, 2,000 school children, 60 Italian associations in uniform and a crowd of about 200,000. It continued to Eighth Street to University Place to 12th Street where in passing Engine 72 the bell tolled, then up Fifth Avenue to 57th Street to the Queensboro Bridge. At the entrance to the bridge, Italian societies joined the procession and accompanied the body to Calvary Cemetery. Adelina nearly collapsed at the gravesite. "Joe, Joe," she cried, "my Giuseppe, come back to me! My God, can't I have my Giuseppe again?"[8]

When it was learned that the detective had died without leaving any money, $10,000 was raised for the widow and a thousand-dollar annual pension was awarded by the board of aldermen and the board of estimate. With threats from the Black Hand still evident against her and her daughter, Adelina moved in with her brother, Vincent, in a house at 623 Fifth Avenue in Brooklyn. She lived there until her death in 1957 at the age of 80. Their daughter Adelina would one day marry Michael J. Burke and have a daughter of her own, Susan Ann. Younger Adelina died on August 21, 2004.

The police commissioner in Palermo, Baldassare Ceola, had a difficult time in the weeks following the assassination of Petrosino. He was pressured to produce results in his investigation by the American consul Bishop, the ambassador Griscom, as well as the Italian authorities who fought the notion that Sicilian authorities were in league with the Mafia. There was even a rumor that the murder had been staged so that Petrosino could work undercover. It was prevalent enough so that Deputy Commissioner Woods had to publicly refute it. "I only wish it were true," he told reporters, "it really is not true. Petrosino is dead."[9] Bingham grew defensive about his role in revealing the detective's trip.

Ceola in Italy, meanwhile, worked to establish first the motive. He came up with three reasons for the crime: One was vengeance and accounted for the arrest of Palazzotto and other such undesirables from America. Another was to stop his plans to prevent Sicilians from immigrating to America and a third was to prevent the deportation of Black Hand individuals from the U.S. In the end he determined that all three reasons were probably correct and that they could be merged into one. There was no doubt as to motive and from what corner the killers would have come from: the Mafia or Black Hand. In spite of having hundreds of suspects with the same motive and coming from identical backgrounds, the authorities in both Italy and the United States could not compile enough evidence against anyone. Ceola received three anonymous letters naming all the potential assassins but for the first time suggesting that Cascio Ferro set the whole thing up.

The first letter was postmarked March 13, a few hours after the murder. The first two came from Manhattan, the third was postmarked Brooklyn. The first read as follows:

Illustrissimo signor Questore,

On you falls the responsibility for the murder of poor Petrosino, because you, knowing his lofty mission, never had him escorted by your subordinates.

That way a tremendous catastrophe would have been avoided. In any case, what's done is done. I only wanted to tell you that the organizers of this murder were: Giuseppe Morello, head of the "Black Hand." Giuseppe Fontana, murderer of Marquis di Notarbartolo. Ignazio Milone. Pietro Inzerillo, owner of the Star of Italy, a dive. And the two Terranova brothers, stepbrothers of Giuseppe Morello. All in the "Black hand," all very dangerous.

The job was turned over by them to their colleague, Vito Cascio Ferro of Bisaquino, whose photograph Petrosino always carried with him because he wanted to arrest him.

All this is as much as I can say. Secrecy and nothing but.

An Honest Sicilian

P.S. I have written another letter like this one to the Minister of the Interior.

What is interesting here is that Cascio Ferro was mentioned in connection with the murder for the first time. The second letter came three days later, to Ceola, and from the same writer:

Signor Questore,

I am confirming my registered letter of a few days ago. Note that the plot to murder poor Petrosino was made in New York and the orders were sent to Vito Cascio Ferro of Bisaquino and Ignazio Lupo of Palermo. These two criminals were implacable enemies of Petrosino and were the terror of New York.

The plot was worked out in New York and the chief organizers are: Giuseppe Morello, brother-in-law of Ignazio Lupo, Gioacchino Lima, also a brother-in-law of Morello, Ignazio Milone and the Terranova brothers. They are the most terrible killers in New York, having killed people even in broad daylight. The police know all these gentlemen well. They contributed fifty dollars each to send two killers to murder Petrosino, but it seems that at the last minute they changed their minds.

Pay attention to me: follow this road and you'll get to the goal. Don't accuse others. May I end in the poorhouse if I am not writing you the truth. Today in New York it is no mystery to anybody. Many members of the "Black Hand" are boasting about it.

An Honest Sicilian

In this letter the writer mentions two killers meaning Constantino and Passananti, so he must have heard rumors. The third letter was also anonymous and postmarked March 16, also from New York:

Signuri Questuri,

I am sorry about Petrosino's death because he was a too good guy, and therefore I want you to know that a certain Paolo Orlannu was a too much enemy of Petrosino he is the capo (chief) in the Mafia in Brooklyn while he was the chief of the Mafia of Tunis before. They sent him away from there and he came to Brooklyn and had his house at 32 Hopkins stritta [street]. He had him killed by two Partinicans who disappeared from Brooklyn because they went bankrupt and took away a lot of money. Petrosino was looking for them. They left all the wine in their store for this Paolo Orlannu and if you don't want to believe me write to Tunis and you'll see that it is the truth. You can write to Brooklyn for the two Partinicans whose names are A. Passananti and the other Carlo Costantino, Savannah 593, Husking, a.v.

An Honored Sicilian[10]

Piecing together the three letters with whatever else he knew, Ceola was able to figure out what happened, but all evidence was circumstantial and would probably be of little value in front of a jury. Cascio Ferro's story was that he was at the home of a friend, the Honorable De Michele Ferrantelli, who confirmed his alibi.

In Highland, New York, on the Hudson River, 50 miles north of the

Monument at Petrosino's gravesite at Calvary Cemetery in Queens, New York. Buried there are Lieutenant Petrosino; his wife, Adelana; daughter Adelana Petrosino Burke, and son-in-law Michael Burke (photograph courtesy Danny Ingellis).

city, Ignazio Lupo was engaged in the gang's counterfeiting operation when the news of Petrosino's death reached them. He turned to an accomplice, Zu Vincenzo, "Petrosino has been killed," he said. "It was successful!" He went on to express delight that the deed was done in Palermo. "The way it was planned, it never could have missed in Palermo. It is well he was fool enough to go there."[11] It seemed no one in the Black Hand community was taken by surprise by the news.

The conclusions that were being drawn by the police commissioner of Palermo were that Vito Cascio Ferro was the "brains" behind the murder and that Carlo Costantino and Antonino Passananti had pulled the triggers. Of the 15 principal suspects 13 had been arrested, Cascio Ferro was not to be found and Passananti had disappeared on the morning of the 12th, the day of the murder. Then, on April 3, Don Vito Cascio Ferro was arrested in Bisacquino after disembarking from a train and on the way to his house and taken to Palermo. He claimed he didn't know anyone was looking for him or he would have appeared of his own volition. His claim that he had spent the past nine days at the home of the Honorable De Michele in Burgio was later supported by De Michele, giving Don Vito an alibi.

Palermo Police Commissioner Baldassare Ceola conducted a thorough investigation. He was a professional law enforcement officer. Appointed commissioner in Milan in 1899, he was promoted to inspector general of public safety in 1905. His work against the Mafia since 1907, when he had been sent to Palermo, had borne fruit. Although Ceola believed his theories to be correct, just three months after the murder, on July 17, he received a dispatch from Rome relieving him of his duties and informing him formally that he was being placed in retirement. Ceola died on April 1, 1913. By coincidence the same date, July 17, saw the conclusion of the career of Theodore Bingham. As a result of his revealing Petrosino's mission to the press, he was removed, by order of the mayor of New York, from his post as police commissioner. Soon Cascio Ferro and all the other defendants were dismissed—some by bail, others on probation. It was not until two years later, on July 22, 1911, that a final decision—quashing all charges against all the suspects—was reached. Arrigo Petacco in *Joe Petrosino* found a copy of the order as handed down by the magistrates of the indictment section of the Palermo courts. All were set free for lack of evidence, yet it is clear, according to Petacco, that the evidence against at least three of the suspects was "quite substantial. Hence, one cannot understand how, in a case of such importance, the examining magistrates could have refused to send it to trial."[12]

In New York, good intentions were foiled. The New York assemblyman who had intended to introduce the bill making bombing a death penalty offense, withdrew his bill out of fear of the Black Hand. A benefit staged for Adelina by 35 vaudeville stars and organized by George M. Cohan fell far short of expectations. Performers reported that they received threatening letters. "At the last minute," said Cohan, "it began to be mysteriously whispered about that dire calamity would follow anyone having anything to do with the enterprise."[13] City officials, including the mayor who'd reserved tickets, failed to show up.

One hypothesis of the crime came from an unlikely source. In March 1911 while Giuseppe Morello was serving 25 years at the federal penitentiary in Atlanta, he asked to speak to Deputy Commissioner Flynn and tell him everything about Petrosino's murder. He said that Passananti and Constantino thought that Petrosino had come to Sicily to search for them. Both were wanted men in Italy and upon arrival there they turned to Vito Cascio Ferro for help. Morello claimed it was Don Vito who planned the murder and the trap. He allowed his own men to gain Petrosino's confidence and even promised the detective his own collaboration.

Morello even stated that on the night of March 12, it was Cascio Ferro that Petrosino was to meet in Piazza Marina and it was Don Vito who pulled the trigger. When somehow Morello's story got into the Italian newspapers in New York, Morello backed down refusing to sign a statement. There were other revelations over the years. Police headquarters in Palermo received about 3,000, one as late as 1967.

Is there a conclusion to the story of the murder of Joseph Petrosino? There may or may not be, for even some doubts may be cast upon the confession of Don Vito many years later. In prison Cascio Ferro stated it was he who had killed Joe Petrosino. "In my entire life I have killed only one person, and that I did disinterestedly," he said. "Petrosino was a courageous enemy; he did not deserve a dirty death at the hands of just any hired killer."[14] Petacco expressed the opinion that Cascio Ferro was the organizer of the crime and quite possibly the executioner as well. The news of Don Vito's confession did not reach America until July 6, 1942, while in the midst of World War II. Both the *New York Times* and *New York Sun* carried that the "Petrosino case" had indeed been finally solved. The war, Mussolini, and fascism prevented the story from being carried any further.

Of the other suspects arrested at the time of the murder, Antonio Passananti, who had disappeared on the morning of the murder, turned up in San Cipirello where he killed one man and wounded the man's two brothers. He was sentenced *in absentia* to 30 years on July 19, 1912. He turned himself in and was incarcerated until his release four years later in

August 1916. He was accused and arrested in 1926, 1933 and 1961. Then on March 6, 1969, an item in a newspaper said that "Antonio Passananti killed himself in his home in Partinico by shooting himself in the temple."[15] He was 90 years old.

Paolo Palazzotto died in 1959. Carlo Constantino, the other possible shooter along with Passananti, was born in Partinico on January 20, 1874. He had married and had three children. Arrested on March 19 in the Petrosino case, he was released on November 13. He moved around, living in Ravenna and Bardonecchia committing crimes until being sent to prison in Palermo. He was deported to Lampedusa, an island in the Mediterranean where the fascists sent political and criminal prisoners. He spent four years there then returned to Palermo and opened a feed warehouse. He died soon afterward in a mental hospital, riddled with syphilis.

Don Vito Cascio Ferro became noted as the greatest *capo* the Mafia ever had. He ruled over the western half of the island of Sicily, achieving a sort of royalty status. By 1924 the conflict between the Mafia and fascism was generating. Under Mussolini the fascists considered the Mafia as a threat to their own power. In May 1925 Don Vito was arrested for having ordered the murders of two men after having rebelled against the extortions of the Mafia. Released on bail, as the conflicts increased in intensity he was once again arrested in Agrigento and on July 6, 1930, sentenced to nine years in solitary confinement. Cascio Ferro was transferred to the penitentiary in Pozzuoli, his final days shrouded in some mystery. The story that prevails is that in the summer of 1943 fascism had collapsed and the Allied armies were moving north along the Italian peninsula. Inundated by the Allied bombing, prison authorities ordered the evacuation of the penitentiary. All were removed except one, who was forgotten in his cell. Don Vito Cascio Ferro died of thirst and terror in his cell in the abandoned penitentiary.

Once again we can ask if there is a conclusion to the Petrosino case. And once again, speculation takes a hand. In 2014 the Italian authorities announced the arrest of 95 members of the Palermo Mafia. Police recordings of some of the arrested men produced an unexpected revelation. Domenico Palazzotto is a descendant of the Sicilian mob boss Vito Cascio Ferro and was charged along with the others of extortion and association in a criminal network. Police said that during a wiretapped conversation Palazzotto boasted that his father's uncle, "whose name was Paolo Palazzotto, was responsible for the first policeman killed in Palermo. He murdered the first police officer to be killed in Palermo. He killed Joe Petrosino."[16]

The head of the Brooklyn Italian Squad and a friend of Petrosino's was Anthony Vachris. He wanted to seek revenge for his friend's murder and volunteered to go to Sicily. "I feel certain that I can land the gang responsible for the death of Petrosino," he told reporters and asked that the commissioner send him over.[17] He was granted permission and using the cover of John Simon, a Jewish businessman, he sailed for Liverpool but did not go alone. Not wanting to risk the same result, the NYPD sent along Detective Joseph Crowley, an Irish detective who spoke Italian. They sailed on April 12, 1909, and after arriving safely in England, boarded a ship for Italy. They traveled in Italy dressed as peasants and visited Rome, Genoa, and Naples in their investigation. They interviewed anyone they could find who had any relation to the case. They studied documents pertaining to criminals. Vachris wanted to go to Sicily since it seemed that was the only chance he had to find any worthwhile answers that lie in the island. Italian authorities, however, said such a trip was madness and meant certain death.

They persisted, however, and snuck into Sicily without the approval of the Italians but with the aid of American consul Bishop. They followed Petrosino's work on penal certificates and made great progress regarding

Petrosino Park at Kenmare and Lafayette streets in New York City (photograph courtesy Danny Ingellis).

information pertaining to men living illegally in New York. It was during their investigations in Sicily that the pair received a telegram informing them that Commissioner Bingham had been fired and they were ordered back to New York immediately. They returned on the *Regina d' Italia* arriving in America on August 11. On a positive note, Vachris and Crowley had completed Petrosino's work. They carried hundreds of penal certificates and a promise from the Italian authorities to send many more. They would be able to deport many Black Hand members. However, the new Commissioner William F. Baker, after a public announcement praising the work of the two detectives, privately instructed them not to talk to reporters about their mission. Baker, it was said, "had been raised from a lowly clerk to the very top of the department for no discernable reason apart from his loyalty to Tammany."[18] It was by Baker's orders that no arrests were made nor deportation proceedings begun. Instead Vachris was anchored to a desk and Crowley was demoted to the rank of sergeant, relieved of his duties as a detective and sent to walk a beat on St. Nicholas Avenue in the Bronx.

Vachris completed the paperwork on the penal certificates and then, while no action was taken toward deportation, was assigned to walk a beat on City Island. His new assignment meant a trip from his home in Bay Ridge, Brooklyn, each day of four hours. His shift ran from 5 p.m. to 1 a.m. and NYPD regulations prevented him from leaving until 8 a.m. so many nights he spent in the precinct house separated from his family for days at a time. The three-year expiration date was allowed to expire for hundreds of criminals. The NYPD under the new administration backed off from any investigation or action that stemmed from the Petrosino murder. Vachris had set up the program to deport 700 criminals from New York but no action was taken against any of them. The cover-up was traced to the office of Mayor McClellen. Incredibly it seemed that the motivation was political.

Both Petrosino and Bingham had believed that Black Hand criminals were being protected by high-up officials in city government. Bombings and kidnappings continued and the conviction rate for Black Hand crimes plummeted. The Black Hand had survived.

Chapter Seven

Enter the Great Caruso

With Petrosino gone, rumors persisted. Conspiracy theories abounded. One said that his enemies in the NYPD had set a trap for him. Why was he unguarded? Why had Bingham publicly revealed his secret mission? There was even a far-fetched idea that his family seems to have embraced: that Petrosino had faked his death in order to be able to work undercover uninhibited. This last theory was so prevalent that Deputy Commissioner Woods was forced to publicly retract it. Bingham sought to ease his part by saying of Petrosino, "he was eager to go, and looked upon it as a great opportunity."[1] He urged the secretary of state to push for new laws; to require all immigrants to carry identification cards, and to register with the police in the cities where they lived. He made foolish public statements about how dangerous the work of the Italian Squad was and how it was a surprise that they hadn't been all wiped out. The mistake of telling the newspapers about the mission could not be rectified.

There were hundreds of letters about the crime received by the police both in the United States and in Italy. Only the three sent to Ceola and shown in the previous chapter were considered to have any validity. Palermo and New York police blamed each other. Although retrospectively, blame was also put on congress for not strengthening immigration laws. Although the police in Palermo undoubtedly had those responsible in their hands after arresting Vito Cascio Ferro, Paolo Palazzotto and 13 others, the lack of evidence prevented any convictions in a court of law and all 15 were released.

In February 2013, the Palermo police heard a wiretap about the Petrosino murder while conducting an investigation into a drug ring. One suspect, Domenico Palazzotto, was heard to say that his father's uncle killed Petrosino. He said his family had been Mafiosi for decades and it was the American detective's actions against the Mafia that motivated the killing. But police dismissed the claim and any relationship between the two Palazzottos. It was, they said, a case of a thug trying to bask in the crime that his family had nothing to do with.

One of the most notorious underworld figures in the era was Ignazio Lupo. Known as "Lupo the Wolf," he was born in Palermo and immigrated to the United States around 1898. His full name was Ignazio Lupo Saietta and he worked in the dry-goods business from the age of 10. It was here at the store at 35 "Matarazzia," Palermo, during an argument, that Lupo shot a business rival named Salvatore Morello. In the legal proceedings against him, held on March 12, 1899, he was convicted of "a deliberate and willful murder" based upon the testimony of the clerks who worked in the store. However, Lupo had already fled the country, arriving in America in 1898 by way of Liverpool, Canada and Buffalo.

His first venture was a store in Manhattan on East 72nd Street with a cousin named Saietta, but after a dispute he moved his business to Brooklyn. He went back to Manhattan in 1901 with a small import store at 9 Prince Street and also ran a saloon across the street at 8 Prince Street. The saloon would soon become the headquarters and hangout for the Morello gang, with Giuseppe Morello owning the restaurant in the rear of the building. The next year Lupo's father, Rocco, arrived in New York and together they opened a retail grocery store on 39th Street between 9th and 10th avenues, also with his brother Giovanni Lupo. Tying in with Morello was the onset of the criminal career that would lead Lupo in and out of trouble for the rest of his life. Because he was one of the last men to see Giuseppe Catania alive before his murder in July 1902, he was a suspect in the crime. The two had traveled to Manhattan together to get some grocery stock. Both the police and the Secret Service worked on the case, and considered Lupo a prime suspect but they were never able to gain enough evidence to make the arrests.

Lupo was once again a suspect in the barrel murder in April 1903. Lupo was eventually arrested. Once again, the evidence was insufficient to convict. What became known as the Lupo-Morello gang went into counterfeiting and Lupo was again arrested in relation to a 1902 counterfeiting case. The charges would eventually be dropped. Following the barrel murder trial Lupo expanded his import business opening a new store at 210–214 Mott Street. It developed into a very impressive establishment. Lupo persisted in his criminal activities and was arrested again in January 1904, this time by Sergeant Antonio Vachris at a ferry house on Hamilton Avenue. He carried a revolver and was charged with carrying a concealed weapon. He was released after a short time.

His criminal relationship with Giuseppe Morello was further secured when he married Salvatrice Terranova, a sister of the Terranova brothers and stepsister to Morello. Lupo was arrested on May 7, 1906, on a kid-

Antonio Vachris took charge of the Italian Squad following the death of Joe Petrosino (Library of Congress).

napping charge, but the victim who identified Lupo backed off in court testimony and the "Wolf" escaped conviction yet one more time. Lupo claimed bankruptcy of his import business in November 1908. It was found that he had made $50,000 worth of purchases in the days before he went missing. The goods were later found on a transatlantic pier in New York. In a warehouse on Washington Street authorities further found 100 barrels of wine, and 98 bags of beans. Antonino Passananti, a member of the Morello gang, owned a wholesale wine business on Flushing Avenue, Brooklyn and had run his business into the ground. The receivers discovered willful fraud and called in the police.

In was subsequently found that Passananti had been paying large amounts of money to Lupo before both went into hiding. At this time in December 1908, an importer of wine and Italian produce, Salvatore Manzella, also went bankrupt. He testified that for over three years he had been the victim of extortion by Lupo, which caused him to lose his business. In January 1909, Lupo was in Ardonia, New York, under the alias Joseph La Presti staying with William Oddo. While there he traveled to Highland

99

to check up on the counterfeiting operation that was functioning there under the Morello-Lupo gang. On November 1, 1909, Lupo moved to a rented house in Bath Beach, Brooklyn, at 8804 Bay 16th Street, using the same alias. Arrested in the Manzella extortion, his accuser failed to appear at Lupo's arraignment and he was discharged. Dodging prosecution to date, Lupo's arrest history was prodigious.

"Lupo has a long career of a shadowy sort, and has much experience with the police, not only in this country, but in Italy as well."[2] Lupo was one of the many rounded up in the Petrosino murder case, as it was known that he was in Sicily some days before the crime took place, but once again the amount of evidence was insufficient for prosecution. One Saturday evening on January 8, 1910, Ignazio Lupo was arrested at his Bath Beach address along with a companion, Giuseppe Palermo. The arrests were made by Detectives Michael Mealli and Paul Simonetti of the Brooklyn Italian Squad under Lieutenant Vachris. Both suspects were indicted by a United States grand jury in New York County for counterfeiting.

Law enforcement agents from the Italian Squad to the Secret Service under Agent William Flynn were stymied at every turn when it came to the principals in the Morello-Lupo gang. From the barrel murder onward, although their criminal activities were massive, the police could never make any arrests stick. Lupo alone had been arrested 65 times without a single conviction. By the end of 1909 both men were still avoiding prosecution. Following the death of Petrosino, Flynn and his agents were still pursuing investigative work on the gang's counterfeiting operation. Authorities were constantly stymied by the reluctance of witnesses to testify against the gang. Flynn's approach was to obtain testimony from within the Morello family, though he found such evidence difficult to come by. Eventually he came upon Antonio Comito, learning in December 1909 that Comito had been one of the printers who worked for Morello's counterfeiting ring.

The farm in Highland, New York, where the phony money was produced was discovered through the diligent surveillance of Flynn's agents of gang members, and it was Lupo himself who led the feds directly to Highland. Satisfied that he had enough evidence, Flynn began to make arrests. Nick Terranova and Antonio Cecala were among them, but Morello was another story. After assigning his youngest agent, 17-year-old Thomas Callaghan, being the least known agent by the gang spotted Morello in Manhattan's Little Italy. Callaghan followed him to a tenement building and agents staked it out overnight. Several detectives from the Italian Squad joined the manhunt and on November 15, 1909, they entered Morello's apartment at 207 East 107th Street and apprehended Morello and one other Sicilian. Flynn had all his suspects with the exception of Lupo, who managed to avoid arrest for two months until he was located and traced to the Bath Beach house where he was arrested by Italian Squad detectives Mealli and Simonetti. Flynn believed that all the pieces were in place.

His confidence was based upon Comito's testimony so he went to work on the printer. The felons were confident of acquittal until the very first day of the trial when Comito took the stand and began to tell his story. Bail was set at unusually high figures, from $5,000 to $10,000. Unable to raise such amounts, they stayed in jail while awaiting trial. When Comito had come to work for Morello, his girlfriend Katrina accompanied him. Both were made to stay in Highland almost as prisoners so his loyalty to the gang was skittish at best. When Flynn convinced him to testify it was in exchange for protection, immunity from prosecution and enough money to make a fresh start in some state other than New York.

The trial began on January 26, 1910, with the defendants scrambling for alibis. Cecala claimed to be bedridden with illness and produced two witnesses to testify to that effect. The fact that the witnesses were his daughter and a friend allowed the prosecution the opportunity to successfully challenge them. The Morello plan was more difficult to counter. A doctor named Salvatore Romano swore that he tended the gang leader two or three times a week for articular rheumatism that gave him "severe pain and fever in his legs."[3] Flynn, however, stayed one step ahead of the defendant. He brought the testimony of eight of his operatives that proved that Morello was seen during the time in question in various places and was not, therefore, bedridden or housebound.

The trial that followed was held at the federal courthouse on Houston Street, under the jurisdiction of Judge Thomas Ray. The nine defendants, of course, included Lupo and Morello. There had been 14 convictions of minor gang members a few weeks before and a dozen others would be tried in the spring. Attempts were made to intimidate the court on the first two days. The Terranova brothers had sent a number of "Sicilian rabble" to fill the courtroom. Someone broke into a U.S. marshal's office and drove a stiletto into a wall. The next day a spectator made the death sign, hissing and sweeping his nails across his throat. But the no-nonsense Judge Ray had the hissing spectator ejected from the building.

The defendants faced a total of 548 felony charges, and clearly the most damaging evidence came from the printer Antonio Comito. Up until now Morello felt secure, certain that he would not be linked to the counterfeiting operation at Highland. Evidence had been hidden or destroyed. The plates were buried on the Oddo farm, the place where Lupo had stayed while hiding out from creditors in New York. Comito's first day of testimony convinced most reporters that Morello and Lupo were a lost cause. The desperation of the defendants was so evident when only hours after he made his first appearance on the stand there was a $2,500 price placed on the Calabrian's head.

There were 60 witnesses called in the trial, which lasted until February 19 with the jury deliberating just 45 minutes before bringing in a guilty verdict. Normally sentences in counterfeiting convictions were not so severe, and with time out for good behavior the norm would be about three years. So Lupo and Morello were still not overly fearful of long prison terms. But Judge Ray was aware of their past—the murders and other crimes—and came down hard on the entire list of defendants. For Giuseppe Morello a term of 25 years and a $1,000 fine. For Ignazio Lupo the same fine and a 30-year prison term. Dash, in *The First Family*, reports that Morello, upon hearing the sentence "dropped to the floor in a faint, then, half reviving, went into convulsions." Lupo "began sobbing as he stood before the judge."

There was an appeal in the case that was heard and dismissed in June 1911. It was inevitable that the Terranovas would plan to murder Comito but they never got to him. Flynn arranged for him to escape to a safe house on the Mexican border. Ultimately it was learned that he made it to South America and had become a successful businessman. It was later learned that the Terranova gang was gunning for Flynn, but as it turned out, William Flynn remained the head of the Secret Service until his retirement in 1917. He died of heart disease at age 60 on October 14, 1928.

Both Mealli and Simonetti, having made the significant bust of Lupo, would in two months become involved in another important case—the extortion of opera tenor Enrico Caruso.

The Society of the Black Hand stayed the course following the murder of Detective Lieutenant Joseph Petrosino in March 1909. In fact, other cops were targeted. In Chicago it was learned from a Sicilian captured by the police that three detectives were marked for death by the Black Hand Society months ago. Petrosino was the first victim. A second was Detective Gabriele Longobardi, called the "Petrosino of Chicago," who had been watched for weeks because of the suspected plot against his life. New York Italians came to Chicago and opened a little grocery store in the Italian quarter on the West Side. From this headquarters they hatched their plot against Longobardi. According to the Sicilian, "They learned his habits and his fearless nature and decided that the best way to get him was to trap him into a combat when he was unarmed."[4]

On the night of May 1, 1909, Longobardi noticed men prowling in his alley and went out unarmed to ask what they wanted. One man with a stiletto attacked him and another hit him in the head. The man with the stiletto struck at Longobardi's throat, but missed and cut the arteries in his left wrist. Thinking they had mortally wounded their target the Italians left the alley. Longobardi recovered from his wound.

The third detective to be targeted was John D'Antonio, head of the Italian detectives in New Orleans. A failed attempt was made on his life as well. Much of the extortions were committed by the gangs that infiltrated Manhattan. "Dopey Benny's" gang was on the Lower East Side, the "Hudson Dusters" ran the West Side and the piers, and below 14th Street was where the Jack Sirocco gang and the "Chick" Triggers were in control.

There was the case of a grocer on Spring Street who received a Black Hand letter with a monetary demand that included the words "Petrosino is dead, but the Black Hand lives on."[5] The grocer turned the letter over to the police. The tenement where he lived was set on fire. Residents ran to the roof to escape the flames. Men and women jumped from the roof. Nine people were killed, including two infants.

Fear of the Black Hand could not be contained. A detective in the Brooklyn squad named Salvatore Santoro, and his wife and children were evicted by his landlord a mere two weeks after Petrosino's death. The landlord admitted he feared his home would be blown up because a member of the Italian Squad lived there. Commissioner Bingham was driving past a dark alleyway in Manhattan when a shot rang out. The bullet "passed so close to [Bingham] that it was regarded as marvelous that he was not shot down."[6]

A number of arrests were made by Inspector McCafferty's men in the detective bureau of Black Hand suspects. A squad of men were sent out to blanket known dens of the most notorious blackmailers. Detectives Caputo and De Gilo raided a barbershop on Second Avenue and arrested 10 men, one of whom was a known Italian blackmailer. Detectives Botti and Carrao entered the rear door of a saloon "about midnight last night and arrested a company of Sicilians and charged them with disorderly conduct. None were recognized at Police Headquarters."[7] There were several kidnappings and murders of children, bombs were exploded in lower Manhattan and as some officials had feared "the Black Hand had become a permanent feature of life in a number of major cities, including New York."[8]

In May the *New York Times* reported that the American Consul at Palermo, Sicily, William H. Bishop, was threatened with death just after the assassination of Lt. Joseph Petrosino in that city. He moved to New York and the place was kept a secret. "It seems desirable on more than one account that members of the Black Hand in New York should not learn of his whereabouts."[9] Mr. Bishop also expressed the opinion that the murderers would not be caught. He said the Sicilian police are hampered by the fact that any Sicilian who could know anything will not divulge any pertinent information to the police.

When Antonio Comito had been arrested by the Secret Service in connection with the Lupo-Morello counterfeiting operation, he told the police of a conversation he had overheard some years earlier in an upstate farmhouse. It was on the night that Ignazio Lupo paid a visit to the others and announced that Petrosino had left for Italy that Comito said he heard of a plan to kill Petrosino for the first time. The men spoke of all the difficulties Petrosino had made for them. They drank a toast. "Here's a drink to our success here and a hope of death to him," said a man named Cecala.[10] The Secret Service believed Comito's story, as there was no reason not to. If true, the plan to kill Petrosino was hatched in America by Lupo and Morello, and Vito Cascio Ferro was the man who made the arrangements in Palermo.

In November 1909, the city elected Judge William J. Gaynor mayor of New York. The judge had a reputation that made him no friend of the police. Gaynor would be the 94th mayor of New York City and serve from 1910 to 1913. He had been a New York Supreme Court justice from 1893 to 1909. He was born in Oriskany, New York, on February 2, 1849, to Irish parents who were devout Roman Catholics. An early feeling for a vocation in the Christian church was lost after several years of study, so he went back home to Utica where his family had lived. His father arranged a position for him in a law firm and this would be his entry into the political arena.

On January 1, 1910, he took the oath of office after walking to city hall from his home at 20 Eighth Avenue in Park Slope, Brooklyn. He was a strict adherer of the Bill of Rights. H. L. Mencken said of him, "Scarcely a day went by that he did not denounce the police for their tyrannies. He turned loose hundreds of prisoners, raged and roared from the bench."[11] He was a product of Tammany Hall but broke loose once he took the oath of office. He was shot in the throat in an assassination attempt by James J. Gallagher, a discharged city employee, who died in a prison in Trenton, New Jersey. He recovered but three years later he suffered a heart attack and died while on board a ship sailing for Europe. Gaynor as mayor was, too, not a friend of the police. He limited their powers and argued against the use of their clubs; a Brooklyn patrolman was given a five-day suspension for using his club on a burglar who resisted arrest. Gaynor had a demoralizing effect on the police.

The irony of his rule was illustrated in the case involving Owney "the Killer" Madden, the leader of a gang in Hell's Kitchen. The police went to Madden's gang hangout to investigate a complaint and were met with gunfire when they tried to enter. Madden was arrested but released on bond. Gaynor had encouraged the public to come to his office personally if they had any complaint against the police. Madden took him up on it and registered a complaint with the mayor against the police who used their clubs on his gang. Incredibly the mayor sympathized and issued a general order prohibiting policemen from using their clubs except in defense of their lives. The Petrosino investigation gained no ground under his administration.

The population of New York City in 1909 was nearing five million and the police force had increased from 4,000 in 1897, Roosevelt's last year as head of the Police Commission, to 10,000. In April 1905 Patrolman Michael Mealli was transferred from Central Office to Headquarters Squad, Brooklyn, for duty in the detective bureau. In 1904 Mealli had joined the Italian Squad as one of its original members. Between some of the more daunting arrests that Mealli made were some less explosive. For instance, an article in the February 13, 1906, issue of *Brooklyn Daily Eagle* was headlined "RAN SHOW WITHOUT LICENSE. Says Detective of an Italian Saloon Keeper, Who Denies Guilt." Mealli arrested Andrew Esposito, who ran an establishment at 232 Prospect Street, for running a show without the necessary license. After witnessing a show in a large hall in the rear of the barroom with a stage Mealli made the arrest. Esposito pleaded not guilty in the Adams Street court but received a fine and was released.

Mealli and Simonetti had been described in a newspaper article as members of the Italian detective squad and "have made many important captures of 'Black Hand' men." Mealli was cited for excellent detective work in a general order of the New York Police Department on April 14, 1908. Mealli and Simonetti did make important arrests as detectives in the Italian Squad and one of them was the highest-profile case in the annals of the squad—that of the extortion by the Black Hand of opera star Enrico Caruso.

Caruso was born Errico Caruso on February 25, 1873, to Marcellino and Anna in Naples, Italy. The third of seven children, Caruso's two elder brothers died at ages two and seven. He was baptized "Errico" spelled with two *r's* in the Neapolitan custom, and called "Erri" by his parents and brother Giovanni. His baptism took place on February 26 at the Church of San Giovanni e Paolo next door to the house where he was born. The death of Caruso's siblings may have been "Neapolitan fever," the name for typhoid, cholera, dysentery and typhus. Naples at the time was a filthy city and people lived in squalor. The Carusos had a second-floor apartment on Via San Giovanniello. Later when Enrico was eight they moved to a house in Via Sant'Anna alle Paludi owned by Marcello's employer. Marcello was a mechanic and a good enough provider so that there was always food on the table. By age 10 Enrico had not had any schooling as yet, so it was decided that he be sent to the *Scuola sociale e serale*, run by Father Giuseppe Bronzetti, which made his mother happy as she thought it wrong that young Enrico would have no education.

Not unusual for a Neapolitan boy, Enrico wished to become a sailor and hung around the docks with his friends and swam in the Bay of Naples. In the house he was constantly singing and could be heard by the organist in the Santa Anna Church next door. "I was a sad trial for my parents," Caruso recalled. "I was very noisy and lively. I sang constantly and my voice was very piercing. I remember well how father would pound in the mornings on the bathroom door and shout to me to stop making so much noise. Still, I continued to exercise my voice."[12] When one day the organist asked Enrico to sing at the Sunday service, the boy was paid 10 centesimi (about two cents), the first money he ever earned for his voice.

On May 31, 1888, Enrico sang at a service at the Church of San Severino. His mother was gravely ill and the boy did not want to leave her bedside but he went as scheduled. His mother died during the services. It was a tragic blow to the boy who worshipped his mother. "My mother always believed in me," he remembered. "She called me *'tesor della famiglia'*: The treasure of the family."[13]

Caruso first left home when he responded to a military call when he was 20 years old. He spent the first eight days at the induction center in Rome. After that, while assigned to the Thirteenth Artillery Regiment he sang during off-duty hours in a drill hall. The commanding officer took him to meet a friend of his, Baron Costa, a music lover and a good pianist, and he invited the young singer to practice at his home during off-duty hours. Incredibly in Italian military law when there were more than one brother in a family, only one had to serve in the military. Enrico was summoned to the officer of the major once again and informed that he could not be a singer and a soldier. The commander had arranged for Enrico's brother Giovanni to take his place. He continued to study, to sing in church and in local venues.

Caruso remembered his official debut being the tenor role in an original opera called *L' Amico Francesco* by Domenico Morelli on March 15, 1895, at the Teatro Nuovo in Naples. He was paid 75 lire for four performances. He began to have a reputation and as it spread he was heard by important impresarios. His debut at La Scala in Milan began with a confrontation with the conductor Arturo Toscanini. Caruso made it a habit to sing at less than his strongest so as not to tax his voice in rehearsals. Toscanini was not happy about this and wanted to hear the full voice. The result was that Caruso's voice in the actual performance was not up to par. After that he was allowed to set his own methods. His reputation was growing. He debuted at Covent Garden in London as the Duke in *Rigoletto* in 1903 and the next season he made his first appearance in Paris.

He was engaged for a season at the Ezbekieh Gardens in Cairo, Egypt. He was adding major roles to his repertory: The Duke in *Rigoletto*, Canio in *Pagliacci*, Rodolfo in *La Boheme*, and Cavaradossi in *Tosca*. A review in the *Gazzetta Livornese* of July 9, 1897, praised the performance of both Enrico Caruso and his leading lady Ada Giachetti in *La Traviata* at the Teatro Goldoni in Livorno, Italy. It was the first time the two would perform together, Caruso as Alfredo and Ada as Violetta, and it would lead to a relationship that would last many years and through the birth of four sons, two of which died in childbirth. Ada was married with a young son and was not ready to break up that marriage to Gino Botti, so for a time the liaison between Ada and Enrico was keep secret.

On July 2, 1898, Ada gave birth to a son whom they named Rodolfo, and would thereafter call "Fofo." The couple moved in together and set up an apartment in Milan, the center of operatic activity in Italy. Ada continued to sing and she and Enrico made a Russian tour together. By the turn of the new century, Caruso had established himself as the great tenor he would always be regarded as. He was lauded at Covent Garden in London where he sang the role of the Duke in *Rigoletto*. It was at this time that he agreed to his first contract at the Metropolitan Opera—for the 1903–04 season. Following his London season and his G & T recordings, he was in constant demand internationally. He was gaining the wealth that would ultimately make him a ready target for the Black Hand. The Metropolitan deposited a 25,000-lire advance in his account on April 5, 1903. With it he bought a villa at Castello, eleven miles from Florence. It was at this Villa Le Panche that Enrico Caruso, Jr., was born on September 7, 1904. When in the United States, Ada was always referred to as Mrs. Caruso and few knew that the couple were not married.

On opening night at the Met on November 23, 1903, he sang in *Rigoletto* and received favorable reviews. In a front-page review on November 24 the *New York Times* said of Enrico, "He made a highly favorable impression and he went far to substantiate the reputation that had preceded him in this country."[14] His United States tour in 1906 included performances in the cities of Boston, Pittsburgh, Chicago, Omaha, Kansas City, Los Angeles and San Francisco. He played in *Lucia*, *Pagliacci* and *La Gioconda*. Following a performance of *Carmen* at the Grand Opera House on April 17, he returned to his hotel, took a bath, and went to sleep. He was awakened at 5:13 a.m. when he felt the bed move. It was April 18, 1906, the morning of the San Francisco earthquake.

Plaster fell from the walls and water began to gush into the room from broken pipes. There were electrical fires creating terrible odors. Caruso and his servant Martino carried two trunks down to the street and they observed the rubble all around them. An American gentleman offered them a ride in his car and they escaped San Francisco, spending the night camped on a hill just outside the city. In the morning they managed to board a ferry to Oakland and stayed there with friends.

Later in the year he appeared with and had an affair with his leading lady, Rina Giachetti, Ada's sister. Rina had been attracted to Enrico before he took up with her sister and the opportunity that presented itself was apparently too opportune to resist. It was, however, a brief affair, and he would not leave Ada or his two boys. He sang in *Aida*, *Tosca* and *Madama Butterfly* in London and then for a month in Belgium. Back in New York for the open-

Enrico Caruso performed in Rigoletto in his Metropolitan Opera debut in NYC in 1903 (Library of Congress).

ing of the new season in November, Caruso would have 18 seasons in the big city. After the 1907–08 Metropolitan Opera season he began an extensive tour of American and Canadian cities. At 34 he was a world-class celebrity and was treated as such everywhere he went. His reviews were always excellent and his records were enthusiastically received by his adoring public. On May 30, 1908, he gave a benefit concert at Royal Albert Hall for King Edward VII. He performed in Paris that summer and Covent Garden in London. On November 14 he inaugurated the Brooklyn Academy of Music with his performance in *Faust*. He now had an exclusive recording contract with Victor.

In the early spring of 1909 Caruso was having problems with his throat. He was also overweight and needed to diet and it was in January of that year that Ada appeared unexpectedly in New York. All of these events put an emotional strain on the great tenor. He canceled some concerts and sang in others when he should not have. He began to take rest breaks. He sang the role of Radames in *Aida* on April 7 when he had not performed since March 4. His physician forbade him to sing for six months. He sailed for England on April 14 worried about his health and his career. From there he left for Milan to consult the throat specialist Professor Temistocle Della Vedova. The result was an operation on his vocal cords in early June. The operation was performed by Della Vedova and it cost Caruso 60,000 lire, the equivalent of $12,000. To add to his emotional state he was outraged at the bill, refused to pay it and went to court over it where it was reduced by half, an amount that Caruso paid.

He was back on stage by late July. Satisfied that his voice had returned, he fulfilled an engagement at Albert Hall in London on September 18, singing "Celeste Aida," and "O'Paradiso," with five encores that included "Vesti la giubba." The critics were enthusiastic. He was once again the Great Caruso.

Enrico and Ada would ultimately separate after 11 years together. It was a shock to Enrico when she ran off with the chauffeur. Enrico Caruso, Jr., said, "I have been trying to solve the puzzle of my mother's conduct for seven decades, yet all I can do is sift and resift the facts."[15] It would be several years before Caruso would meet Dorothy Park Benjamin, early in 1918 and on August 20 of that year they would be married at Marble Collegiate Church in New York. A young, aristocratic American, she converted to Roman Catholicism early in 1919 to please Caruso and the couple were married again in the Chapel of the Blessed Virgin at St. Patrick's Cathedral in New York. His marriage took his family and friends by surprise, in part because of the difference in their ages; she was 25 years old when they married, while Enrico was 45. Dorothy's father was strongly set against the marriage, the difference in age and social standing being among several reasons. He disowned his daughter afterward both emotionally and legally. The next year the Carusos had a baby girl they named Gloria.

Eerily ironic both Caruso and Petrosino were the same age when they met their untimely deaths. It was on December 3, 1920, that the first of the incidents happened that was to make that month one of the worst in the tenor's life. At the Metropolitan in New York during the last act of *Samson et Dalila*, a piece of scenery swung loose and hit him in the left side just below the left kidney. The pain grew steadily worse, and five days later as he sang "Vesti la giubba" at the end of the first act of *Pagliacci* the pain was so agonizing that he nearly blacked out. He had to be helped from the stage as the curtain ended act one but he completed the performance.

In the fall of 1909, Caruso had a British tour, sang in Germany and then left for America for the '09–'10 season. In 1910 Caruso had money, fame and popularity. It was early that year that Enrico Caruso had an encounter with the Society of the Black Hand.

Chapter Eight

Caruso and the Black Hand

Since joining the New York City police force, Mike Mealli had worked with some of the great officers in NYPD history. In the Italian Squad he worked under the leadership of Joe Petrosino, Antonio Vachris and "Big" Mike Fiaschetti and with so many officers like Rocco Cavone, Charlie Corrao and Paolo Simonetti, who distinguished themselves through the long battles against the Black Hand. The newspapers of the period were rife with stunning stories of the seamiest side of New York society in the early days of the last century, and those tales were dominated by the Black Hand. On May 24, 1907, the *Brooklyn Daily Eagle* carried a bizarre story that followed the arrest of three Black Hand extortionists. The murder trial of Rocco Panagiro, Genaro Esposito and Francesco Como began on March 22 and from the first day it was evident that the district attorney's office had built a remarkably strong case against at least two of the defendants.

At the opening of the trial extraordinary precautions were taken in an effort to prevent trouble as County Detective Joseph Bagnarello was stationed in the corridor and searched every Italian who entered the courtroom. "Consequently," said the *Brooklyn Daily Eagle*, "the swarthy sons of Italy, present in scores at the trial, left their pistols and knives at home."[1] The man the defendants are accused of murdering is Gaetani Costa, a butcher at 32nd Street and Fourth Avenue. The prosecution was conducted by District Attorney Robert H. Elder who gave credit for the tight case the DA's office had built to others. "Without the aid of the police, especially Lieutenants Vachris and Murgath and Detectives Castagnino, Mealli and Sanguinetto, he would have been unable to develop the evidence which was so forceful."[2] According to the scenario the police put together, Costa was shot down in his shop during a visit by four men, three of whom were the indicted trio; the fourth, Antonio Nobilo, decided to turn state's evidence. Nobilo's testimony was that the four entered the shop and demanded money from Costa after having sent him threatening Black Hand letters. The butcher refused to pay and attacked the four, slashing Nobilo with a knife before being shot down. Nobilo, in a hospital

111

and thinking he was dying, confessed to a priest who convinced him to speak to the police. The victim's sister, Mrs. Carmilla Berte, said that Panagiro had made threats against Costa three years ago. Witnesses testified to hearing shots and seeing men run from the shop. They positively identified that the prisoners were the men exiting the butcher's establishment. A cashier who worked for Costa, Mrs. Charlotta Purceli, gave the police access to a safe that contained several threatening letters sent to Costa in February and March of that same year.

Nicholas Abdate, a cook, testified that he had known Esposito under the name of Giratelle, and that Esposito had spoken to him of the murder of a butcher in south Brooklyn. According to Abdate, Esposito told him that if "it hadn't been for him, the butcher would have killed them all."[3] After a single day of testimony it seemed impossible that the defendants could escape the electric chair. Apparently with this in mind, one of them, Rocco Panagiro, committed suicide in his cell at the Raymond Street Jail. At 4 a.m., a jailhouse guard found Panagiro awake and he spoke of his fear that he would be sentenced to the electric chair, and even if he escaped that fate he believed "the Italians" would kill him. On his next round at 4:45 a.m., the guard, William H. White, saw the bed on end and the prisoner hanging from his belt with which he formed a noose. The discovery was made about 15 minutes after Panagiro had killed himself. No sooner had the word of the suicide reached the principals in the trial that James W. Ridgway, counsel for the defense, changed the plea of his client Genaro Esposito. The morning of the second trial day, Ridgway consulted with District Attorney Clarke and with Mr. Elder and followed that with a visit to the private chambers of Justice Crane. It was then announced in the courtroom that Esposito, who said that his real name was Ciro Carguilo, wanted to change his plea to murder in the second degree. Realizing that he was certain to be condemned to death, by changing his plea, his sentence would be reduced to life imprisonment.

That left Como, the third defendant, to be disposed of. Elder, however, had little in the way of direct evidence against Como since he was not apparently directly concerned in the murder. Nobilo gave only circumstantial evidence against him. The defense attorney asked that the charges against his client be dismissed. Elder offered little opposition and Judge Crane directed the jury to acquit the defendant. Thus ended one of the most sensational of the Black Hand trials in the annals of New York City.

Early the next morning, Antonio Nobilo, the Black Hand gang member who had turned state's evidence and helped convict his partners, was taken from jail and brought to the office of the district attorney presumably to be released from custody. Nobilo, however, told the DA that he didn't want to leave the jail. He offered two reasons for his request: One, that he was penniless, and the other was far more important to him. He felt that by betraying the Society of the Black Hand, he would be marked for death. The only thing that societies like the Black Hand or the Mafia can do, in their estimation, to prevent treachery in the ranks is to make examples of those who go against them by causing certain death and it was this fear that now overtook Nobilo. When asked by reporters, Elder said, "Yes, Nobilo knows they will kill him if they can."[4] He then went on to speak of his great desire to rid Brooklyn of all members of the Black Hand.

At the onset of the new year, 1910, law enforcement in New York City took a giant leap forward when Flynn's federal agents corralled the Morello counterfeiting gang. At the same time detectives Mealli and Simonetti of the Brooklyn Italian Detective unit arrested "Lupo the Wolf," and the government went to court convicting two of the most notorious criminals in New York—both Lupo and Morello went off to Sing Sing.

Arthur Woods served as New York City deputy police commissioner from 1907 to 1909 and would take over as commissioner in April 1914. As deputy he was an ally to Joe Petrosino and his Italian Squad, and remained supportive of the unit following Petrosino's death in 1909. Woods was born in Boston in 1870 and graduated from Harvard University in 1892. He did postgraduate work at Harvard and the University of Berlin. Woods received a doctorate degree in law from Trinity College in Connecticut in 1910. Working as a reporter for the *New York Evening Sun* he came to the attention of Commissioner Thomas Bingham with his ideas for reforming the police system, which led to his appointment as deputy commissioner.

He reformed police training and introduced an official police academy modeled after London's Scotland Yard, teaching courses on law and sociology. He promoted better understanding and communication between the public and the police. During the war he would serve in the United States War Department achieving the rank of full colonel. He retired from public life in 1937 due to ill health and died on May 12, 1942, in Washington, D.C. He was 72 years old.

The onset of the 20th century was an era when the politicians literally mingled with the people. Timothy D. Sullivan was known as "Big Tim" for his physical size as well as for the power that he wielded during the first decade of the century. He was Irish Tammany Hall through and through and served as state assemblyman, congressman, and state senator. His influence far exceeded the various positions he held. The most important reason was his ability to deliver votes, not just for himself but for others to whom he chose to give his support. He did it by making himself a man of the people. He turned out the vote with free Christmas dinners and jobs on the city payroll. There were Labor Day "chowders" and boat rides to amusement parks. He offered vaudeville, sports and movies. All of these gratuities along with Sullivan's outgoing and gregarious personality kept the politician in the good graces of the voters. He kept a grip on the Irish constituency that was his but incorporated Jews and Italians to keep abreast of the shifting immigration patterns and maintain control over the ethnic variations in the city of New York.

Although he reached the entire city with his power and influence, his base of operation was Lower Manhattan from Canal Street to East 14th Street and along the Bowery. His biographer, in fact, titled his book *King of the Bowery*. His strength was with his Tammany Hall base, originally a political-fraternal order founded in 1789, and grown through the influx of Irish immigrants in the 1840s. The Irish dominated the party after the downfall of William M. "Boss" Tweed in 1871 with the Democratic Party until Tammany lost their influence around 1932. He grew up in the Five Points neighborhood of Manhattan, his parents were Irish immigrants and he won his first political race in 1886 for state assemblyman. He clashed with Theodore Roosevelt after the Republicans won city hall in 1895 over the support given by Tammany to gambling and prostitution. Along with vice the Democrats of Tammany were also guilty of paying off the police, with whose patronage they enjoyed control of much of the city's functions.

It was 1886 also when Timothy married Helen Fitzgerald and Sullivan began building one of New York's most powerful political machines. With headquarters at 207 Bowery, Big Tim and his organization controlled virtually all jobs and vice below 14th Street in Manhattan. He was Tammany's candidate for Congress in 1902 and despite a scathing critique in the *New York Times*, referring to him as one of the most disreputable politicians in Tammany, he won the election and went to Washington. Apparently tired of the nation's capital, he left Congress and ran for the state senate in 1908. Sullivan was undeniably an excellent businessman. He was involved in real estate and theatrical ventures. He was involved in such activities as Dreamland in Coney Island and boxing. Illegal at the time, Sullivan used his influence to get the New York state legislature to legalize the sport in 1896, though it was repealed four years later. In spite of all illegal activities he did support such progressive legislation as women's rights and gun control. He supported legislation that limited a woman's workweek to 54 hours and in 1911 he helped to pass the "Sullivan Act," a state law requiring a permit to own or carry a concealed weapon. This support came despite his contacts with such notable underworld figures of the time as Monk Eastman, Paul Kelly and Arnold Rothstein.

Sullivan contended that men used to "take off their coats and fight it out with their fists. But now they carry guns. Why, there are places where a man could rent a gun for twenty-five cents for a night and there are leaders of gangs [who] armed their entire gang with these guns."[5] He said he wanted to make it tough for a desperate man to carry a gun and believed the way to do this was to make it hard for him to get a gun. When countered by those who balked at the idea that a good man would not be able to get a gun, Sullivan responded by explaining that the would-be purchaser had merely to obtain a permit while the "desperate" man would be unable to get such a permit because a magistrate would investigate him before a permit would be issued. The police would also have a list of all men who had been issued a permit. He also changed the penalty for carrying concealed weapons from a misdemeanor to a felony. The Sullivan Act became law on May 29, 1911.

Big Tim became ill in the years that followed that resulted in depression and mental illness. He was committed to a sanitarium after being declared mentally incompetent in January 1913. He was treated there until he moved to his brother's house in the Eastchester section of the Bronx. He managed to leave the house in the early morning hours of August 31, 1913, and was hit and killed by a train by the Westchester freight yards. With the unidentified body in a coffin supplied by the city for burial on Hart's Island, a Potters' Field, it was seen nearly two weeks later by a patrolman who viewed the corpse and identified it as Big Tim Sullivan. About 20,000 mourners lined the streets as the funeral procession made its way from the Lower East Side across the Williamsburg Bridge to a final resting place in Calvary Cemetery in Queens.

It was widely known that during his political career, Sullivan was identified with illegal activities including prostitution, gambling and extortion. This would be his legacy.

Although the Black Hand remained active and deadly and continued to attempt to extort victims with money, New York was not all murder and mayhem. Everyday life carried on in mundane ways in the mid-teens. At Brooklyn's famous department store, Abraham & Straus, an ad in the *Brooklyn Daily Eagle* on March 24, 1916, hawked men's socks for 19 cents a pair and women's topcoats starting at $8.95. At the Colonnade Theater on Nostrand Avenue near Fulton Street, Mary Pickford was starring in

The Dawn of Tomorrow. The Parkview at 15th Street and Prospect Park West was showing Ethel Barrymore in *The Final Judgement.*

The Brooklyn cranks, those rapid baseball fans of the Superbas, reveled in a piece written by beat writer Thomas S. Rice announcing that "Nap Rucker Holds the Cubs and Superbas Win Handily." The date is Sunday, September 17, 1911, and Rice expounds in the vernacular of the era: "Hummel wended his way homeward,...and Rucker drove with all his might and main right at the unafraid Tinker, who grabbed the grounder and threw out Davidson at the plate."[6]

In March of 1910, the Black Hand made contact with the famed Italian opera star Enrico Caruso. In his biography of his father, Enrico Caruso, Jr.,

recalled a morning as he stood by while his father opened his mail. The conversation came around to threatening letters and the young Caruso wondered in his naiveté, who would send his father a threatening letter. The great tenor then pulled out a stack of mail that represented threatening letters he had received over the years. The one, he explained to his son that had caused him the most trouble was sent to him in New York in 1910 by the Black Hand, an Italian extortionist group. They demanded money and threatened to kill him if he did not pay. "For years I have received begging letters," Caruso told police, "but never before these deadly threats."[7]

He had received a similar letter a short time before demanding $2,000

Enrico Caruso, the Great Tenor, was an extortion victim of the Black Hand in 1910 (Library of Congress).

116

to which Caruso had acquiesced thinking it would be over and forgotten. But that was not to be. The letter that arrived early in 1910 now demanded $15,000. Realizing now what he was up against, he contacted the police and the letter was turned over to the Italian Squad in Manhattan under Lt. Arthur Gloster. The first of three letters was received by the singer at the Knickerbocker Hotel where he was living on Wednesday, March 2. A translation of the letter was published on March 6 in the *New York Times.* It read, "Senor Caruso: You to-morrow at the hour of 2 will be stopped by a boy and you must deliver $15,000. You think right to not say anything to nobody. C.D.M." It went on to instruct the tenor to put $15,000 in an envelope in his pocket. He was to stroll along 42nd Street until a man would approach him. The man would speak to him and he was to hand him the money. "If you do you will not be molested," the letter said.[8] There was a black cross, the sign of the Black Hand, under the signature.

The police instructed Caruso to follow the instructions and two detectives walked behind him as he took the walk on the evening of Thursday, March 3, but nobody approached him. There was speculation that the detectives may have walked too closely to the tenor and given away the plan. Inspector McCafferty turned the case over to Lieutenant Vachris, the man in charge of the Brooklyn Italian Squad. This brought two of Vachris's men into the case. They were detectives Mealli and Simonetti.

The second letter was written two days after the first; it was more threatening than the first and it read, "Senor Caruso: You yesterday went in the company of two policemen. The boy could not make salute. To-night, just at 11, you must leave in one bag the sum of $15,000 under the stairs where the factory is on the corner of Sackett and Van Brunt streets, Brooklyn. You think good and don't fail. If you fail, Saturday night will not pass that you will pay. La M. C. D. M." There was also a cross under the signature in this letter.[9] Caruso was scheduled for a performance of *La Gioconda* at the Brooklyn Academy of Music. He appeared for the performance and during the opera 43 policemen were stationed in the chorus, on the catwalk above the stage and in the galleries. They provided the tenor with a loaded revolver to carry on his person. He remained under police escort and two detectives were placed on duty outside his room.

The first letter was mailed from an Astoria, Queens, post office in Long Island City at 6:30 p.m. on March 1. The next one was postmarked from the Station W. Brooklyn post office, at 7 p.m. on March 3, in Williamsburg, with the payoff planned for Friday, March 4. The pickup of the $15,000 was now set for Friday night at the assigned location. A decoy package was prepared for the drop. At 9 p.m. Lieut. Gloster, along with Brooklyn Italian Squad detectives Simonetti and Mealli, and two of Gloster's own men from Manhattan, Scrivani and Mundo, arrived at the factory at the predetermined location of Sackett and Van Brunt streets. Caruso, however, had had enough of strolling the streets and thought the corner of Sackett and Van Brunt was "no place in the dead of night for a grand opera singer,"[10] so a representative went in his place.

Enrico Caruso, Jr., explains that Martino, his father's valet, volunteered for the dangerous assignment of delivering the money to the specified place in Brooklyn. "There was a police stakeout and the extortionists were caught," he said. "From that day on, Martino, whom I regarded as merely an excellent valet, was my hero."[11] Around 11 p.m. Antonio Mesiani came from the direction of Second Street, stopped in front of the factory and looked at the stoop in front of the factory, then walked on to Union Street. He made that walk past the building several times.

Simonetti stood guard a block away at the corner of DeGraw Street while the others hid by the factory. One newspaper reported that the decoy bundle of money had been placed there by a friend of Caruso.

At the corner of Union Street and 3rd Avenue Mesiani was joined by a second Black Hander, Antonio Cincotta, and a third man who was on the corner with Cincotta. The two came back to the factory and were about to pick up the decoy package when Cincotta saw the flash of a policeman's badge at the end of the block. He yelled a warning in Italian and the men ran away as fast as they could. Mesiani tore up the street toward Sackett but at the corner Detective Simonetti grabbed him. There was a struggle but Mesiani was subdued and handcuffed. A search yielded a revolver and a shotgun he carried under his coat. It was fully loaded with an 18-inch sawed-off barrel, the same type of weapon police said was used in shotgun murders on the east side. Meanwhile Cincotta fled to a saloon at the corner of Sackett and Van Brunt streets where Lieut. Gloster and Detectives Mealli and Mundo caught up with him and overpowered him. The arrests were made at about 11:45 p.m. The third man made his escape but Mealli said he knew who he was and would be able to apprehend him in time.

The two extortionists, Antonio Mesiani of 155 Columbia Street and Antonio Cincotta of 117 Columbia Street, were both held in Brooklyn as suspicious persons. Mesiani was charged additionally with possession of concealed weapons. Cincotta had a saloon at 150 Columbia Street in Brooklyn, a known hangout for members of the Lupo-Morello counterfeiting gang. Caruso refused to speak to reporters. The two men were held in $5,000 bail each at the Adams Street Court in Brooklyn. Both men pleaded not guilty! Both had police records. Cincotta had been arrested in

March 1909 on a murder charge for killing Giuseppe Genaro. He had also been implicated in the murder of the grocer Cantania, as well as being implicated in the killing of Lt. Petrosino. He had escaped to Italy just before the Petrosino murder.

On March 16 Caruso traveled by subway to Brooklyn guarded by detectives to testify against the two men who had been arrested. The tenor had shaved off his mustache and was not recognized by the people in the car. He had sung in Philadelphia the previous day but was ready when Lt. Gloster and his men arrived to escort him to the Adams Street court for his testimony. In addition to the police officers he was accompanied by his special counsel, Alfred Seligsberg, and Tullio Bogheri, a musical director from the Metropolitan Opera House. At the courthouse Caruso said of the Black Hand, "They scare me not," Caruso says, "ha!, ha!, to the Black Hand."[12]

Word had gotten out that the singer would appear at the court as the complainant and witness and it brought a large crowd to the courtroom. There was also a battery of cameras and a flood of reporters. The tenor told of receiving three Black Hand letters. Detectives Mealli and Simonetti also testified to making the arrests of the two suspects, Mesiani and Cincotta, at Sackett and Van Brunt streets in the vicinity of the place where Caruso had been directed in the letters to place the $15,000 demand. On May 17 according to Magistrate Tighe the case would be referred to the grand jury. At the office of the district attorney, Caruso's story was taken down in shorthand and typed into a three-page affidavit. His affidavit read as follows: "That between the 28th day of Febru-

Detective Michael Mealli was one of the arresting officers in the Caruso Black Hand case (author's collection).

119

ary 1910, and the fifth day of March 1910, at the Borough of Brooklyn, City of New York, county of Kings, Antonio Cincotto and Antonio Mesiani committed the crime of attempted extortion in that they, the said Antonio Cincotto and Antonio Mesiani, did at the time and place aforesaid, attempt to extort by means of threats, to wit, threats that the deponent would be injured in his person by them, they said Cincotto and Mesiani, the sum of $15,000 good and lawful money of the United States of the value of $15,000."[13]

He then went on to state the facts concerning the receipt of the Black Hand letters and the money lure offered to the alleged assassins in the case. Affidavits were taken also from Detectives Paul Simonetti and Michael Mealli of the Brooklyn Italian Squad, as well as Lieutenant Gloster and Detectives Mundo and Scrivani of the Manhattan Italian Force.

On March 25 the case was again in the news as both suspects were arraigned. Judge Fawcett announced upon the arraignment that the bail had been increased to $10,000 for each. Since neither one could furnish bail they were locked up in the Raymond Street Jail. The judge stated his reason: "I have information that the prisoners are about to leave the jurisdiction of the court."[14] It was also reported that the tenor had previously paid the blackmailers between $1,500 and $2,000; however, he was still in receipt of threatening letters. His son Enrico Curoso, Jr., recounts the story of a 1920 Black Hand letter threatening to kill his father, Dorothy and Gloria. The demand this time was $50,000. Dorothy explained in her own account that on the day the money was to be delivered, Caruso arranged a casual outing by car for Dorothy, Gloria, the nanny and himself. Instead of returning home, they met the Long Island train, which made an unscheduled stop as previously arranged by detectives and traveled to the city. They stayed in New York a few days until Caruso felt it was safe to return home. An Italian detective accompanied them to East Hampton and stayed to provide protection.[15]

Antonio Cincotta was considered by police to be a leader among the local Italian criminals. Almost anytime a crime was committed they looked him up and checked his movements. He had been a saloon keeper with an establishment at 80 Degraw Street in Brooklyn. Of late he had been working for a steamship company, his job was to keep the unruly dock workmen in line. Cincotta lived at 321 59th Street. Both Mesini and Cincotta were convicted at trial and sentenced to a prison term at Sing Sing Prison in Ossining, New York.

Cincotta was first arrested on November 20, 1896, on a homicide charge but was discharged after a hearing, then arrested again on June

25, 1897, for felonious assault but the complaint was withdrawn when the complainant refused to testify. He was again charged with homicide in the murder of a man named Gennario on October 14, 1909, but when the wife of the dead man withdrew her statement, he was once again released. Cincotta served time for the Caruso extortion at Sing Sing beginning in March 1911 but was released pending an appeal and a new trial was granted him. The celebrated Caruso case happened in 1910 when the tenor reported a Black Hand letter he had received to the police. The Italian Squad under Detective Arthur Gloster "and with detectives Michael Mealli and Paul Simonetti lay in wait for the blackmailers."[16]

On February 15, 1915, while walking along Union Street toward the waterfront accompanied by Francesco Ricciardi, Cincotta was shot and killed as they passed 23 Union Street. The two men had just left a motion picture theater at 55 Union Street and had just reached the front of 23 Union Street. According to Ricciardi a man approached them and fired three shots at Cincotta. One shot missed but the other two hit their mark. Cincotta staggered and fell to the pavement. An ambulance from Long Island College Hospital responded but Cincotta died 48 minutes after his admission, unable to reveal information about the gunman.

The killer was never identified. One author speculated that "mobsters friendly to Caruso imposed rough justice of their own, gunning him down in Brooklyn's Little Italy."[17] Mesini at 31 years old was arrested the previous year and discharged for lack of evidence. Detective Mealli was one of the officers soon at the site and determined that the killer escaped into a house at 25 Union Street and out through the back door.

In later years members of Detective Mealli's family would recall the gratitude of the great tenor. Mary Mele, Michael's sister-in-law, would tell her grandchildren of the baskets of cheer and the opera tickets that were delivered to the Mealli home from Caruso. Michael's daughter Teresa saved her dad's newsclips but often remarked how "my father did so much with the early Italian Squad that has never been recorded anywhere."[18]

In a two-month period in the early part of the year 1910 Mealli was involved in two major arrests, the Caruso extortionists and the notorious Ignazio Lupo. Both were significant arrests but the link between the two made for an even more significant story. After the Lupo trial and sentencing in February the mobster was finally put in prison but his people made an effort at an appeal. The police believed that the Black Handers were low on funds and in order to raise the huge attorney fees needed to file the appeal made the extortionist attempt on Caruso. Cincotta was known to be a close associate of Lupo. Police had no doubt that the plot was hatched in

Brooklyn where Lupo and other members of his gang had lived for years. Both men had been suspects in connection with the murder of Francisco Caruso whose dismembered body was found in a gunny sack in July 1902.

In a good number of cases Mike Mealli was teamed up with another Italian Squad detective named Paul Simonetti. Note that in both the Caruso extortion arrests and the Lupo collaring the arresting officers were Mealli and Simonetti. Paolo (Paul) Simonetti was born in New York City in 1879 and was appointed to the police force on March 5, 1903. Simonetti along with Mealli was chosen for the new Italian Squad under Joe Petrosino in 1904. Both detectives moved to the newly formed Brooklyn unit of the Italian Squad in 1907 and continued their association under Lieutenant Gloster following the death of Joe Petrosino in 1909. Simonetti remained an active member of the squad through the leadership of Antonio Vachris. His untimely resignation from the force came on September 11, 1917.

It seems he was reduced in the department for reasons unknown and finally resigned. After his resignation, Simonetti organized a detective agency which apparently led to more grief for the former Italian Squad detective. In a case his agency handled Simonetti was hired by Joseph DeMartini who was seeking a divorce from his wife, Nora, and wanted evidence against her. At the trial the detective testified that he discovered the wife in Canarsie with a man he did not know. However, this "unknown man" was Frank Russo, who worked for Simonetti and he had once before figured was a correspondent in another case that the agency had been involved in. Simonetti's lawyer pointed out that his record as a police officer should justify a suspended sentence for the perjury he had committed.

The judge, Justice Dike, commented on Simonetti's past record by saying he was a capable and fearless police officer for a long time, and "then something happened. I don't know what it was, but from then he began to slip. He was reduced in the department and finally resigned."[19] He went on to say that having been a public officer should have made him realize the gravity of his offense. Given the chance to recant the false testimony Simonetti refused, staying with the perjured statement. The judge sentenced him to serve not less than two nor more than five years in Sing Sing prison.

Shocked at the sentence, he was granted a week's stay to arrange his affairs. Simonetti was 42 years old, married with no children and lived at the time at 1970 52nd Street in Brooklyn. Sentenced on June 20, 1921, it appears that he was released on December 15, 1922, having served 18 months of his sentence.

It was estimated that much of the Black Hand funds had already gone into attorney fees from the trial of Lupo and the other counterfeiters. Law enforcers have recorded a total of 141 years' imprisonment imposed on defendants in the month of February alone. It was the men of Vachris's staff in Brooklyn, specifically detectives Mealli and Simonetti, who were credited with finding and arresting Lupo in January.

The evidence against Cincotta was scant so he was held on a charge of vagrancy. However, the charge was a temporary measure as Cincotta owned a liquor store at 117 Columbia Street and would soon dispel the vagrancy charge.

Even with Morello in prison the Terranova brothers, who were now running the gang, went looking for revenge upon those informants who had helped to put away Lupo and Morello. Sam Lucino was a counterfeiter who had given information to the Secret Service during its investigation of the Morello gang. Lucino was hit by two bullets near his home in Pitt-

ston, Pennsylvania, by a lone gunman. He was fortunate in that the bullets just grazed his scalp and the shooter ran away without making certain his victim was dead. Luigi Bono of Highland, New York, moved to Manhattan out of fear of the Morello hitmen in his hometown. He opened a grocery store on Houston Street and after some warning incident Bono began making his way home from work each night by traversing the roofs of buildings. It wasn't good enough. On November 11, 1911, his body was found on a roof where he had been struck by an axe. The police found a card on the body that said, "This man was Morello's enemy."[20]

In spite of this terror Flynn was able to maintain some of his informants, but

Detective Paul Simonetti, also a member of the Italian Squad, was also in on the arrest (author's collection).

123

what he had was not enough and he searched out additional individuals who could provide information on the workings of the criminal gangs. It came in October 1910. He was Salvatore Clemente who had served time for counterfeiting and had close ties to the Terranova brothers. Clemente was born in Sicily in 1866 and it seems that when he was picked up by the police earlier that year he had had his fill of prison life. This is what made the Sicilian cooperative. It was Clemente who let Flynn know about the farm in Highland where the counterfeiting was being done and where the plates were buried on the property, and also of the graves that had been dug on the same grounds.

His warning that his children were in danger alerted Flynn to that possibility as well as important information about who might be taking over or moving up in the organization now that Lupo and Morello were behind bars. Morello held on to his power at least until the June 1911 appeal was dismissed and then he turned the operation over to the Lomonte brothers, Tom and Fortunato. As they tried to rebuild the criminal empire, the early teen years were difficult ones. According to Dash in *The First Family* the war years took the emphasis away from crime in the newspapers and also the activities of the Secret Service. Flynn did get 45 convictions in 1910 and infighting among the gangs took a toll on personnel and their criminal activities. As the Mafia proliferated, Black Hand crime after 1912 tailed off.

The Italian Squad continued its work until about 1915. As the activities of the Italian Squad became less centralized detectives were assigned to similar duties with other units. Mike Mealli had been living at 11 Navy Street and was at this time working cases in Brooklyn. On October 10, 1910, at 295 Third Avenue near Carroll Street in Brooklyn, Antonio Lauro, the proprietor of a coffee house at that location, was charged in connection with the shooting of two men, Blazio Coppola and Aniello Grimaldi. Grimaldi was free on bail while awaiting a second trial for murder. Detectives Michael Mealli and Paul Simonetti made the arrest in the case.

Police Officer Lewis Stokes of the Bergen Street station was at the corner of Carroll Street and Third Avenue about midnight when he observed a crowd of Italians congregate in front of Lauro's restaurant. As he approached, he heard four shots ring out and a man dart from the crowd and run up Carroll Street. He gave chase to the man who was later identified as Lauro. The policeman also said he saw Lauro throw away a revolver. When it was recovered it was found that four chambers were empty. Other police arrived and the two wounded men were discovered inside the restaurant. No motive for the shooting was given but Detectives

Mealli and Simonetti took Grimaldi into custody, charged with the murder of Frank Massei two years previous. Massei was found in the back of a saloon he owned with a bullet wound in his left temple. The jury could not agree on a verdict.

In was in this period at the close of the first decade of the 20th century that violence and lawlessness remained a paramount fixture in the lives of the city of New York. The Black Hand still operated but the Mafia was taking hold, and gambling and gamblers were branching out from the Lower East Side into the Tenderloin section of Manhattan. Traffic also became a factor in governing the city. In 1910 the police had a 500-man traffic force that included patrols on bicycle, foot and horseback; the automobile was becoming a traffic factor. In April 1910 the auto came on the scene when the first murder related to the automobile was recorded in New York. Rifle fire from a passing Pierce-Arrow on Second Avenue killed a gang leader named Spanish Louie. No arrests were made but a new batch of names were added to the police records of criminal suspects whenever such crimes were committed in the future. Names like Big Jack Zelig, "Gyp the Blood" (Harry Horowitz), "Lefty Louie" (Louis Rosenberg), and "Whitey Lewis" (Jacob Siedenshner).

Rhinelander Waldo took over as police commissioner in 1911. Waldo and Mayor Gaynor agreed that a crackdown on gambling was needed, and where raids were conducted. A 40-year-old lieutenant named Charles Becker was selected to head the headquarter's squads, which were set up for this purpose. Becker was considered ruthless in the discharge of his duties, described as a "formidable looking man with huge arms and a fierce visage," his presence was not unlike either Joe Petrosino or Michael Mealli.[21] Known for his deals with the gamblers in short order Becker had an arrangement with Bald Jack Rose, a leading gambler. Becker traveled in circles uncommon for a police officer. A regular on the Broadway scene he hit the fashionable nightclubs around town, often with a buddy, Bat Masterson, the famous western hero and sports editor of the *Morning Telegram* who often entertained people with tales of his days in the Wild West.

Becker met and formed a relationship with a gambler named Herman Rosenthal but in time Rosenthal's relationship with the police, Becker and the gamblers turned sour. In part because Becker's press agent, Charles Pitt, shot and killed a man and went on trial for murder. Rosenthal refused to contribute to the fund that Becker was raising for the defense of Pitt. After that Rosenthal believed he was harassed when his establishment was raided and his gambling ventures interfered with by both police and gamblers. At 2 a.m. in front of the Metropole, Rosenthal was shot four times and killed. District Attorney Charles Whitman believed that Becker was implicated in the murder and set out to prove it.

The four gunmen escaped in a 1909 Packard that was later identified and the killers were arrested. Becker also went on trial for murder, prosecuted by Whitman, and was found guilty and sentenced to death in the electric chair. The sentence was carried out on July 30, 1915. At the last moment Becker's wife begged the newly elected governor to commute the sentence. He refused. The governor was Charles Whitman.

This was the atmosphere that was prevalent at the start of the second decade of the 20th century in New York City and the world in which Detectives Michael and Andrew Mealli would perform their duties.

Chapter Nine

The Terror of Evildoers

In the early 1900s George M. Cohan owned Broadway. Between 1909 and 1912 alone he ran 14 shows along the Great White Way, including revivals of huge hits *Little Johnny Jones* and *Forty-Five Minutes from Broadway*. The movies wouldn't talk until *The Jazz Singer* late in 1927, but silent films produced historic names. Charlie Chaplin began appearing in films at the Keystone Studios in 1914 and in 1913, a bus boy at Murray's on 42nd Street, who had just arrived from Castellaneta, Puglia, Italy, would soon be heard from—his name was Rudolph Valentino.

As the second decade of the 20th century began baseball was becoming enormously popular. The New York Giants played up in the Polo Grounds where an Irishman, John J. "Muggsy" McGraw, called "Little Napoleon," stormed and raged while leading his club to two National League pennants in 1911 and 1912, and New Yorkers worshipped the redoubtable Christy Mathewson. Brooklyn's National League entry played at old Washington Park located between First and Third streets and Fourth and Fifth avenues. A tradition was established in Brooklyn ... a losing one, but they had a hero also—a young left-handed pitcher named Nap Rucker. The New York Highlanders played at the highest point in Manhattan called Hilltop Park at 165–168 Street before anybody thought to call them the Yankees.

Gamblers infiltrated the ballparks and arenas—how could you keep them away? There were suggestions, innuendos, and accusations of games being fixed or thrown particularly at World Series time. None of the rumors were fortified, however, until the 1919 World Series when gambler Arnold Rothstein financed the infamous Black Sox Scandal—the Chicago White Sox tossing the series to the Cincinnati Reds. Gambling and the onset of Prohibition would, of course, greatly stimulate the coffers of the city's mob gangs.

The Italian Squad's highest-profile case was the extortion of Enrico Caruso and though it came after Petrosino's death the Italian Squad under Lt. Arthur Gloster continued to function, though at a more subdued level.

Detective Michael Mealli lived at 11 Navy Street in downtown Brooklyn. Those of his siblings that were born in Italy and his parents came from Sala Consilina, located in the province of Salerno. It was built originally in the Roman ages and known as Consillinum. With 12,635 inhabitants today it is the most populated town of Vallo di Diano. On December 2, 1916, according to the personal records of the NYPD, Mealli's address changed to 446 Sterling Place, also in Brooklyn. His assigned precinct was the 150 and then the 151. He was a detective since 1905 with the detective shield number 215. He had been on the force eight years.

It was about the time that he changed his address to Sterling Street that Michael married Annmarie, which took place on December 1, 1916. The couple had two children: Annamarie, born in 1918 and Teresa, born on July 25, 1922. There were to be four grandchildren, all boys: Paul and Michael to Teresa and Bill and Peter were the offspring of Annamarie.

Lt. Arthur Gloster functioned as acting commander of the Italian Squad following the death of Joe Petrosino. That was through 1909 and 1910 until the point that police commissioner Rhinelander Waldo ap-

Navy and Sand Street. The neighborhood in downtown Brooklyn where Detective Mealli lived (*Brooklyn Daily Eagle* photograph, Brooklyn Public Library).

pointed Lt. Antonio Vachris, who had been heading the Brooklyn division of the squad as commander of the entire squad, which he led until September 1911 when the commissioner abolished the squad altogether. It was at this point that Mealli and the other squad detectives were reassigned to cases similar to those they had handled as members of the Italian Squad. Mealli began to work out of the Sixth Detective Branch specializing in Black Hand and gang cases. Mealli had worked with Lt. Vachris in the years prior to Vachris's appointment as commander. On October 3, 1905, Vito Laduca, whom the Brooklyn squad identified as a leader of the Black Hand, was charged with abduction and was arrested in Baltimore where he had fled. Detectives Mealli and Vachris delivered the warrant and assisted by Baltimore Detective Bradley arrested Laduca for kidnapping seven-year-old Tony Mannino on August 4, 1904.

Laduca was wanted on two kidnapping charges, the other being the abduction of Tony Merendino, who was taken from his home at 556A 17th Street on September 23, 1905. Laduca remained a suspect in the barrel murder of Benedetto Madonia from three years before. The butcher had his shop at 16 Stanton Street. Also involved with Morello's counterfeiting ring, Laduca had been shadowed by Flynn's Secret Service. They learned that Laduca had sold his butcher shop and fled to Philadelphia and then to Baltimore where he was apprehended by Mealli and Vachris on the warrant issued for the Mannino kidnapping.

Upon their arrival in Brooklyn with their prisoner, Laduca was locked up at the Adams Street station and the convoluted kidnapping case would gradually unfold over the next few days. The seven-year-old Merendino, after being held for 12 days, was left in a Third Avenue L train in Manhattan the evening of October 5 and was turned over to the police at the East 57th Street station by subway employees. Little Tony told a harrowing story, part of which the police believed he was coached to relate but there was little doubt that his experience revealed that there were other captives being held in a ring of kidnappings by these same perpetrators. Salvatore Piconi was identified as another kidnapper and arrested by Captain Carson and Detective Corrao. Francesco Merendino, the boy's father, seemed reluctant to aid the police, apparently having made some sort of an arrangement with the kidnappers in exchange for his son's safe return.

Evidence in the case gathered by Captain Carson and Detective Sergeants Vachris, Mealli and Corrao pointed to a lavish plot of kidnapping in the Italian quarters of the city. It appeared that evidence against Laduca and Piconi would prove conclusive, although unable to speculate on the number of kidnappings of children held for ransom because the parents usually paid the ransom rather than report the crime to the police. In the case of Tony Merendino his return was due to police pressure, and with the help of the boy's father the kidnappers hoped to ward off prosecution. Captain Carson informed the press that he believed the capture of Laduca and Piconi would effectively break up the gang that had terrorized the families of the Italian community.

Rhinelander Waldo was the eighth police commissioner in the last ten years. At 34 years old the former army captain had been the fire commissioner under Mayor Gaynor. The mayor held strong convictions about law enforcement and he believed Waldo was the man to carry his policies through. It was in 1911 that the state legislature passed a bill sponsored by Big Tim Sullivan that carried his name and made it a felony to carry a gun without a permit, punishable by seven years imprisonment. It was in this same year that Waldo took over as commissioner. Generally considered to be inefficient and described as "hapless" by Lardner and Reppetto in their book *NYPD: A City and Its Police*, Waldo was dismissed by the successor to Mayor Gaynor, who died of a heart attack on September 10, 1913, aboard an ocean liner on route to Europe.

The Italian Squad continued to function in the first few years following Petrosino's death and continued to produce heroic, functional, efficient officers. One such officer was Acting Detective Sergeant Charles Corrao. Born in Palermo, Sicily, Corrao was appointed patrolman for the city of Brooklyn on January 8, 1896. At the consolidation of New York City in 1898 he became a NYPD patrolman. Being fluent in the Italian language he was transferred from the old 72nd precinct to the detective division in 1903, shield #131, and soon after became a member of the Italian Squad under Lt. Joseph Petrosino.

On September 15, 1911, Detective Corrao along with several other Italian Squad members traced Black Hand member Giovanni Rizzo to a tenement at 356 East 13th Street. Rizzo was being sought for a bombing that same morning on 12th Street. Corrao encountered Rizzo on the fifth floor of the building, who had ignited the fuse on a bomb. Corrao grabbed the bomb from Rizzo and defused it as Rizzo fled. There was a chase and shots fired before Rizzo was apprehended. Detective Corrao was awarded the Rhinelander Medal for Valor and on May 18, 1912, the first Medal of Honor, which was designed by Tiffany & Co., was awarded to him by the New York City Police Department for his valor in the episode that occurred on September 15, 1911. Sgt. Corrao was promoted to lieutenant on August 4, 1921, and passed away while still an active member of the force on December 8, 1934, at age 61.

The Corrao family certainly contributed to the war against crime in the city. Charles's brother Francis was a "brash, young prosecutor working his way into the borough's [Brooklyn] Democratic machine."[1] Francis Corrao was the youngest Italian lawyer ever to practice in the borough. His personality was that of a pioneer; he was flamboyant and sought to help achieve acceptance for the Italian people. He knew, of course, that the Black Hand had to be defeated. He was aware also, through his brother Charlie's work in the Italian Squad, that the job was not an easy one. He saw also that an Italian prosecutor who knew the language and the culture of the Italian people could go a long way toward prosecuting Black Hand members. He urged the Brooklyn district attorney to hire an Italian prosecutor. Then, on April 2, 1907, Corrao was given the position himself. With a healthy salary of $5,000 a year Francis was ready to join the fight.

Detective Charles Corrao of the Italian Squad was the first recipient of the NYPD Medal of Honor (photograph courtesy Christopher Begg).

Corrao was the first Italian district attorney in the country but he soon came to realize that his appointment was just a sop, as he was doing clerk's duties while the Black Hand continued to kill and maim Italian victims. "Every avenue and every door was shut to me," he complained. "Murder, assault, and robbery of Italians are looked upon by the District Attorney's office with the most cynical indifference."[2]

Yet law enforcement agencies persevered. On January 10, 1910, a huge breakthrough came when William Flynn and his Secret Service men broke the counterfeiting ring of the Morello-Lupo gang effectively ending that activity and putting away numbers of criminals who were also associated with Black Hand crimes. Sixteen were taken into custody on January 10 adding to the 20 who were rounded up last fall and were sent to Sing Sing for terms varying from one to seven years. The arrests climaxed a year of diligent police work by the agents under Flynn. It was called the most complete round-up of alleged counterfeiters ever made by the United States Secret Service Department. Authorities say that the gang was responsible for passing $50,000 in bogus money on the public. Just two days before Ignazio Lupo was arrested in Bath Beach by Detectives Mealli and Simonetti of the Italian Squad. Giuseppe Morello was in the Flynn arrests, now both of the most notorious criminals of the day were facing the criminal charges that would finally bring them down. All eight were held on $15,000 bail.

Nearly a year before Flynn's agents found a large number of two- and five-dollar counterfeit bills in circulation. The bills had been struck off from zinc plates, as opposed to the steel plates the government used to make the bills more identifiable as counterfeit by Secret Service men. The phony money was found in upstate cities and Philadelphia as well as the New York area. A tip the agents received in the summer of 1909 provided the clue that put Flynn and his men on the right track. They learned that a grocery store at 235 East 97th Street was used as a distributing place for the bogus money. Antonio Maloni, Antonio Cecala and Giuseppe Morello owned the store. A stakeout was set up in a room in a tenement across the street where two detectives watched the grocery store. They noted that there were men who would go into a rear room and they noted also that the same three upon emerging from the store "would look furtively around and stealthily disappear. One day the detectives, after being satisfied that these mysterious callers were going there to get the counterfeit money, swooped down on the three of them."[3]

The three proprietors of the store were selling the bad bills for 70 cents for each two-dollar bill and three dollars for the five-dollar bills. It took a vigilant surveillance of known members of the gang by agents to determine where the money was being produced. They found that supplies like ink and stationery were being sent to an address in Highland, New York. Authorities went to Highland and located the farmhouse where the work was done but were dismayed to find that the operation had moved out a week before. They traced two of the gang, Salvatore Cina and Vincenzo Giglio, to Poughkeepsie and located them in the Italian colony of that city and made the arrests. Agents learned also that the gang had buried the counterfeiting press and plates in the ground on the Highland Farm territory. It was with the arrests and the evidence that gave Flynn, at long last, the confidence to think he had a conviction coming.

New names continued to surface in the wake of the jailing of the counterfeiters. One was Giuseppe Masseria from Marsala, Sicily. Just 16 when he got to this country in 1903 his first conviction came four years later for burglary and extortion, for which he received a suspended sentence. A second burglary conviction in June 1913 got Masseria a 54-month sentence and when he got out he was in time for a new war that put him in position for a future role he would fill as "Joe the Boss." The struggle pitted the Cosa Nostra of East 107th Street against a Camorra gang led by Giosue Gallucci, who held control over the local "numbers" gambling racket. Another Camorrist, Aniello Prisco, killed Gallucci's bodyguard and was himself slain three months later. The blood count according to the *New York Times* reached 33 murders in East Harlem by May 1914.[4]

As war erupted in Europe there were five gangs on the warring street of the city. The Sicilian Morello gang was led by Toto D'Aquila. A smaller Harlem group was being run by Manfredi "Al" aka "Alfredo" Mineo. In Brooklyn the Castellammarese immigrant had Nicolo Schiro at the head. Pellegrino Morano was running the Coney Island bunch and Navy Street was jointly led by Leopoldo Lauritano and Alessandro Vollero. There was at times collaboration among gangs. The Lomonte brothers worked with both Morello group and with the Neapolitans until Fortunato Lomonte was murdered on May 23, 1914. Umberto Valenti was fingered as one of the killers acting on orders from Toto D'Aquila. Gaetano Lomonte managed to survive until October 13, 1915.

A 27-year-old sailor, Harney Halstead, off the tugboat *Annie W.* docked in Erie Basin was beaten and robbed on the night of January 16, 1912. Halstead was in front of 116 Hamilton Avenue when he was set upon by three men who began to beat him unmercifully. Theodore DiDonne of 355 Hamilton Avenue intervened on behalf of the sailor, but when the assailants turned on him he fled. DiDonne went to the Rapelye Street police station and Detectives George Friday and Michael Mealli hurried to the scene where the three men were still beating Halstead. They arrested one of the three, Bert Benson, while the other two escaped.

Halstead, however, failed to appear at the Butler Street court the following morning to testify against Benson. Benson, of 1236 Prospect Avenue, was accused of being one of the three men who robbed Halstead of a gold watch, chain and eight dollars in cash. The *Brooklyn Daily Eagle* reported that a "subpoena was gotten out for Halstead and his appearance will be secured tomorrow morning."[5] Police said the reason for his failure to appear was that sailors around Erie Basin are often held up and rarely report the crimes for fear of being beaten up by the gangs. Petrosino's concern of witnesses' fears and failures to testify in court was very real and very much remained a detriment to law enforcement in New York City.

During the years working under Lt. Petrosino in the Italian Squad, Mealli had built a reputation for himself with the result that by 1913 he had earned his own nickname. An article in the *Brooklyn Daily Eagle* dated March 24, 1913, may have been the first time it was used by the press. The captain and officers of the freight steamship *Istena* reported that Stefen Mutcless, acting as the ship's steward on the trip to New York from Buenos Aires, shot and killed himself. "The police of the Hamilton Avenue station were notified and Captain Conboy and Detective Michael Mealli, the *Italian Specialist*, went on board."[6] They expressed suspicions that the man had inflicted wounds by his own hand. It seems that the bullet had entered the back of the man's head and it was further learned that the steward had attacked the captain with a huge carving knife, cutting him and causing him to be taken to the Methodist Episcopal Hospital in Brooklyn. An ambulance had taken Mutcless to Long Island College Hospital where Dr. Gildersleeve explained that it would be impossible for him to have inflicted the injury that caused his death. Upon questioning other members of the crew, Mealli and Conboy were told that the steward attacked the captain on the bridge with a knife and stabbed him. According to some of the crew the captain fought off the steward, who then drew a revolver and shot himself in the head.

The captain was taken to the hospital and kept under the surveillance of a police officer. He was badly cut but hospital officials said he would recover. He remained under suspicion while police determined if the man had indeed committed suicide or if he was killed by another's hand. In the first two decades of the 20th century, the police learned to be tough with criminals and hardened to their task. Mealli would be involved in hundreds of cases, everything from murder to kidnapping and extortion. The body of a 19-year-old Italian, Joseph Tagliarini, was found at the Bergen Beach Rod and Gun Club at East 71st Street and Avenue N in Brooklyn, a deep gash in his throat and a bullet hole in his left temple. The body was identified by the victim's brother, Frederick, who was escorted to the morgue from the Flatbush police station by Detective Michael Mealli, who was assigned to the case. There was jewelry on the body, indicating that robbery was not the motive, and police suspected a gang slaying. A prescription found on the body in the name of Siegel set the police on the lookout for the mystery man. The hope was that he would shed some light on the tragedy.

Both Petrosino and Mealli seemed to be cut from the same mold.

Neither was adverse to charging bull like into a fray where there were criminals to apprehend. Detective Mealli, referred to as "the terror of evildoers, waded into a gang of bad men near the Navy Yard alone early today, and picking out two of the number, members of the Navy Street Gang, said they were wanted for assault and highway robbery. 'Come socially or in an ambulance,' the detective ordered. 'We'll go anywhere with you Mike; we don't want to start anything with you,' replied the gang leader."[7] Two of the men went with Mealli. Whether the gang leader's reply was made out of fear, respect, familiarity or a combination of one or more, is not clear, but indicates a familiarity between the detective and the gang members. Mealli had spent some years living on Navy Street and was in all probability known by most of the gang members. The question of any existing relationship beyond that of job-related encounters would come into question at a future time.

The complaint in this case was made by Harry Sigmund and Austin J. Daly, both foremen at a shoe factory who reported that they were assaulted and robbed one night on a city street. They claim to have been accosted by one of 10 men who were shooting craps on the sidewalk. The man asked for change of a five-dollar bill and when he took money from his pocket he was hit from behind and his money taken. Three other men jumped Sigmund and robbed him also. Descriptions of the assailants were provided by the two victims to Mealli and the detective arrested Harry Burke, who was out on bail in connection with a murder the previous year. The second man apprehended was not identified at the time of the arrest.

In the few years immediately following Petrosino's death, Black Hand crimes had not abated. A case that stood out during the years when Arthur Woods was commissioner began on May 13, 1915, a Wednesday. Mrs. Lonzo was in the bakery owned by her family on Bleecker Street waiting for her six-year-old son, Francesco, to return from school. She waited until long past the hour he should have come through the door. Her husband, also named Francesco, thought the boy might be out playing with friends. The family had never been threatened by the Black Hand. However, two years before, a four-year-old nephew had been kidnapped. The boy's father, Felippo di Fiore, resisted his brother-in-law's arguments against paying a ransom. He knew that doing so would endanger other members of the family. So di Fiore paid the ransom and never revealed the names of the men involved although he knew them well.

The parents of Francesco searched the neighborhood, calling at the homes of friends and classmates to no avail. At 8 p.m. that evening a letter slipped under the Lonzo door which read, "Dear Friend: Beware not to seek your son Francesco. He will be found in good hands, and we want the sum of $5,000 ... if this comes to the attention of the police, you will receive the body of your son by parcel post."[8] Francesco Lonzo, Sr., went immediately to the home of his brother-in-law and blamed him for the child's abduction. He demanded to know the names of the di Fiore kidnappers. Though he refused to reveal any names, he did accompany Lonzo to the MacDougal Street police station and spoke to the detective on duty. It was Italian Squad member Rocco Cavone who, like Mike Mealli, continued to work on Black Hand cases.

Woods ordered the detective unit to pull out all the stops. Lonzo and Cavone continually prodded di Fiore until the latter finally gave up the names. They were Nicolo Rotolo, who owned a bakery shop in the neighborhood, and the Zarcone brothers of Long Island. Cavone's men set up a surveillance on the bakery and followed everyone that went in or out. Detectives disguised as mailmen, deliverymen and others visited the homes of suspects. Two of the suspects found their way to a store owned by Francesco Macaluso, known by the police as a longtime associate of Giuseppe Morello and Antonio Lupo. A twist in the case came when the kidnappers began following Francesco Lonzo, Sr., and once he was aware of it, Cavone had to take special precautions whenever he met with the boy's father.

There were three more Black Hand letters and finally a $700 demand and instructions. Marked bills were delivered to the kidnappers and the boy was returned to his home a few days later. The investigation had gone on over a period of several weeks but in the end all suspects were arrested. All were convicted and received stiff sentences, making the extraordinary efforts in the case a milestone in the NYPD's handling of such cases. "It ended kidnapping in the Italian settlements in New York," wrote Frank Marshall White, "and was the beginning of the end of Black Hand crime."[9]

A photo of Mike Mealli reveals a tough face and a dominant jaw with glaring eyes and in some ways an uncanny similarity to Joe Petrosino. He approached his job head-on every day of his working life. One day in January 1914 he was walking along Van Brunt Street near Union when he saw three Italians acting in a suspicious manner. As he approached them the men ran into a fish store. Mealli followed them in and frisked them for weapons. On one, Carmine Migkilo, he found 13 envelopes containing three lottery policy slips, policy instruction sheets and four lottery books. Migkilo of Harrison, New Jersey, was believed to be the head of a gang of lottery sharks working among the Italians collecting money for a Newark, New Jersey, lottery. Mealli of the Hamilton Avenue station made the arrest and Migkilo was held without bail by Magistrate Voorhees for the grand jury.

A shooting at a saloon at 217 Hudson Avenue brought Detective Michael Mealli, "who has special training in Italian feud cases," to the crime scene.[10] John Christiano, the 20-year-old proprietor of the saloon, was shot in the abdomen and taken to Brooklyn Hospital where he was said to be dying, the victim of an ongoing gang feud. Christiano refused to say the name of his attacker. His brother Tony, known as "Happy," was shot in the abdomen a year ago at the Superbe Social Club at the same time that Dennis Callahan was shot and killed. "Happy" had gone to the club to kill Callahan but was shot by another man. "Happy" survived. Mealli was assisting in the investigation, which was thought to be caused over trouble with women.

One of the difficulties that Petrosino, Mealli and the other members of the Italian Squad had encountered since its formation in 1904 was the mindset of the police in the first decade of the 20th century. It was that they did not mind the crimes among the Italians as long as they confined their operations to themselves. "This class of mutilating murderer has confined his operations to those of his own nation and kin."[11] The crime that changed this thinking was the murder and mutilation of Rufus Dunham in January 1915. Dunham was a collector of installment payments for a furniture business and was, as one newspaper termed it, the first murder of its kind. Incidentally between the years from 1914 to about 1916 Michael Meilli was joined by his brother Andrew at the Sixth Detective Branch where they worked a number of cases together. There had been a previous case of the murder and mutilation of a Jewish peddler, but he was also an alien and the police didn't stray far from their attitude of lack of concern when this class of killers preyed on their own. The Dunham case was a shocker to the authorities because it was the first time that an American-born citizen had been killed in this fashion. The Dunham case, therefore, was the most significant one, and as it turned out was one of the first in which the brothers Mealli joined forces.

Boy skaters discovered a dissected torso, without head or limbs, embedded in ice in a pond at Bay 50th Street between Coney Island and Ulmer Park. Thirty detectives from the sixth branch detectives of the Poplar Street station house were assigned the case, among them the Mealli brothers. The body was identified as Rufus Dunham, 61 years old, of 732 Macon Street, Brooklyn. He and his wife were childless. Both from Massachusetts, Dunham was a native of Bedford and his wife of Stockbridge. He had been missing since December 19 when he left the Cowperthwait Co. store at Flatbush Avenue and Nevins Street in Brooklyn. His job was to take furniture collections from Italian families door-to-door in the

Red Hook section. The neighborhood was predominately Italian and the area had given police a good deal of trouble in the past. All the available Italian-speaking detectives spent the night visiting families that were on Dunham's list, the theory being that Dunham had been robbed and murdered while taking collections.

The victim had been employed at Cowperthwait for seven years; before that he was a cashier at the Astor House, and had formerly lived in New Haven, Connecticut. Detectives at this period in time maintained a list of all of the laundry businesses in the city. Each launderer had a unique mark, referred to as a laundry mark, identifying the owner's business. Thus the term "laundry list of things to do" refers to the practice of a detective reviewing the list in order to identify the particular launderer.

In attempting to identify the body, an old scar from an operation on the left side and a depression of the breast bone were noted. In perusing missing persons reports, the police noted the same marks mentioned in the description of Rufus Dunham. When detectives visited the home of Mrs. Dunham at the Macon Street address she was overcome at the news. A laundry mark on the collar of the shirt found on the body was used by the laundry that the Dunhams patronized. Mrs. Dunham verified the marks on the body as being the same as the police had identified. Captain John D. Coughlin stated, "we are handicapped by the absence of the head and limbs, of which no trace has been found so far, but I really think that our success in establishing the identity so soon, not 24 hours after the finding of the torso, is a point in favor of a speedy solution of the mystery of this man's death."[12]

The murder, it was learned, took place in front of 23 Union Street at 10:30 p.m. on Friday, January 1. The medical examiner concluded that the mutilation of Dunham's body was the work of one who possessed the skills of a butcher. The two parts of the torso were found wrapped in copies of the *Bollettino Della Sera*, an Italian newspaper, and also an English paper, both dated December 21. The bundles were bound by a cord with a knot used chiefly by butchers, according to the police. Amid the wrappings was a piece of cretonne (printed linen or cotton cloth), and the stamp on the material read "New York Mills" and then the letters "J.W."

In obtaining a list of the places that Dunham was to visit on December 19, detectives noted that his last visit was the residence of Salvatore Carmoie at 115 Harrison Street. He made the stop shortly after 11 a.m. His next stop at Degraw Street was never reached. The neighborhood where the crime was committed was the area of the old Cincotta gang. Antonio

Cincotta was one of the extortionists arrested by Detectives Mealli and Simonetti in the Enrico Caruso case five years before.

Police had obtained a description of men who were in a car near the scene where the torso was found at the edge of the pond. Detective Mealli and other officers made arrests for weapons possession that was a violation of the Sullivan Act of 1911, which required a license to possess firearms in the state of New York. Arrests were made for other crimes, some minor, in an attempt to put pressure on the Italian community in Red Hook in the hopes that someone would come forward with helpful information.

Three arrests were made in the search for the murderers of the Cowperthwait furniture collector, who police speculated was killed for the day's collections, probably not more than $25. In scouring the Red Hook section for clues as to the murderers' identities, Detectives Michael Mealli and George Priddy found three men in Florintino's wine shop at 468 Hicks Street who had huge revolvers in their possession. They were charged with violating the Sullivan Act. They were Salvatore DiBello of 177 Union Street, Pedro di Mario of 113½ Columbia Street, and Gregori de Lucca of 133 Columbia Street. The three were arrested and brought to the Amity Street station.

The significance of the crime was in its horror. Police who heretofore left the Italians to each other believed here that a line had been crossed and a new and a much healthier attitude would prevail in the future.

In July of 1915 Detective Mealli made a trip to Geneseo in upstate New York and met with Deputy Sheriff Patrick O'Leary, and presented a warrant for the arrest of Christofico Incarvario. The warrant charged Incarvario with murder in the first degree, alleging that he killed a man three years prior. It was alleged to have happened as a result of a quarrel and though police arrived on the scene shortly, Incarvario escaped and was not heard from for the next 18 months. At that time a quarrel ensued between him and another Italian in Cleveland. He shot and killed this fellow also. A policeman who tried to subdue the perpetrator received a gunshot wound by Incarvario but recovered.

Once more the killer escaped and kept out of sight until the NYPD received a tip that he was held up in the upstate community using the alias of Andrew Carl. Mealli, upon his arrival in Geneseo, proceeded to give Incarvario's description to Deputy Sheriff O'Leary and they concluded immediately that Carl and Incarvario was one and the same man. It seemed that the Italian had some trouble in the town a few months before and as a result was well-known to the deputy sheriff. It was learned by O'Leary that Incarvario, as Carl, had been employed by the Pennsylvania Railroad since the previous July and recently laid off. He learned also that the alleged murderer had secured employment on the new waterworks and was staying in nearby Nunda. Mealli arrived in Geneseo on Thursday and on Saturday he and O'Leary went to the place where the workers congregated. Both law enforcement agents approached the suspect and quickly handcuffed him and hurried him away. They were certain of his identity, Incarvario as Carl, and he was jailed for the night.

A resident of the community for the past 18 months ever since he had committed a murder in Cleveland, Incarvario had married a young woman of the village. His life was one of a hardworking individual and he had made a number of friends in the community. Then in February of that year he was arrested for shooting a man named Sam Capadonia in the shoulder one Sunday evening that month. When Deputy O'Leary arrested him a few hours later that night he found two revolvers, a razor and a large quantity of cartridges on his person. By the time the case came to trial witnesses would no longer come forward and both Incarvario and Capadonia were fined $100 for carrying concealed weapons and released. Incarvario was not carrying any weapons when Mealli and O'Leary arrested him that July day in 1915. The prisoner was escorted back to New York by Detective Mealli to stand trial for murder.

A case that involved Mealli indirectly occurred at 171 Prospect Street in Brooklyn, the home of two cousins, Lawrence Facella and Anthony Pettala. Pettala was the complainant when he alleged that he had been supporting Facella in idleness for a number of years and tried to end the tie by leaving the house. Facella attacked him with a loaded gun and was apprehended after a chase through the streets under the Brooklyn Bridge by three detectives of the Fulton Street station. Pettala, in fear, "made a telephone call to detective Michael Mealli of the Italian Bureau only to learn the detective's father had died last night and he was not on duty."[13] Facella was held in $2,500 bail and charged with felonious assault and violation of the Sullivan Act for weapons possession. The call to Mealli was not explained other than by the fact that he was known for his wide acquaintance among persons of the city, both politicians and other assorted individuals that he came in constant contact with as a detective.

The Grimaldi family, father Aniello and son Frank, had been involved in two separate shootings and Detective Mealli was assigned to all the Grimaldi cases. In a previous case a Grimaldi was the accused; this time, however, a Grimaldi was the victim. Frank was confined to Brooklyn Hospital with a bullet in his left hip and another in his right elbow. Aniello is the proprietor of a pool parlor at Hudson Avenue and Johnson Street in

Brooklyn where Frank was shot. Mealli's file on the Grimaldis was a bulky one as Frank was twice tried for murder and acquitted, as was Frank's brother Michael and his uncle.

It was in this period of time, probably early in 1915, that Mealli was assigned to the Sixth Detective Branch and worked his cases out of that unit. It was in December of that year that he was detailed on a case of suspicious fires set aboard steamships. Fire Marshal Thomas Brophy called Mealli in on a case in which he declared fires were set in a dozen different places in hold number three of the British steamship *Inchmoor*, anchored at the foot of Warren Street in Brooklyn. Eight hundred tons of sugar were destroyed on the vessel, which had been carrying sugar to French and British ports since the onset of the European war and was due to depart with 3,500 tons of the product on Tuesday, December 28. Vincent Wallace, a seaman aboard the vessel, discovered smoke coming from the hold and notified Captain Thomas Pye. The fire department was summoned and the blaze was extinguished after about two hours.

Because of the suspicious nature of the fire, Fire Marshal Brophy called in the police and Detective Mealli, whose job it was to attempt to connect the fire to other such recent fires on sugar ships. The *Inchmoor* had reached New York from Gibraltar a week ago and began loading sugar on Friday. The loading was being done by a firm of Italian stevedores. The *New York Press* printed the story on Monday, December 27. It was this nature of possible criminal activity that the detective squad was now engaged in due to the possible sabotage activities relating to the war in Europe.

Chapter Ten

The Brothers Mealli

The first two decades of the 20th century in NYC can be divided into two eras, the first defined by the reign of Lt. Detective Joseph Petrosino. Adversaries of the Italian Squad were the notorious Morello-Lupo gang and by 1910 the two were jailed and though others stepped in to take their place, these two were through as criminal disruptions in New York. Another thorn in society's side at this time was Paul Kelly. Kelly, whose real name was Paolo Vaccarello, ran the Five Points gang that controlled the territory of the Lower East Side from his headquarters at the New Brighton Saloon on Great Jones Street. A Neapolitan, Kelly had taken the Irish moniker as a bantamweight boxer when he was younger. Kelly supported and got support from Tammany politician Tim Sullivan. In the 1901 election the state senator wanted his man, a saloon keeper named Tom Foley, elected in an assembly race so Big Tim called on Kelly for help.

Kelly's hoodlums blocked the voting places keeping away all but the supporters of Foley, using blackjacks when needed to enforce Foley's election. To the north of Kelly's territory was the Monk Eastman Jewish gang. One night in the summer of 1903 some Five Pointers ventured into the Bowery to hold up a card game and an exchange of gunfire ensued. It took a number of policemen and a charge down Rivington Street with guns blazing to end the dispute that left three dead and seven wounded and twenty or so arrests. Although an ally of Morello, the gun battle with Eastman put Kelly in bad with Sullivan and Tammany and led to his being the target of an assassination attempt at the New Brighton. With the lights out and a blaze of gunfire in the dark Kelly was hit three times but not killed, but his bodyguard was. Lupo and Morello hid him out in a house on East 166th Street where he convalesced. Eventually he gave himself up and was charged with murder. But the case was dropped for lack of evidence.

Perhaps showing some good sense, he closed the New Brighton, and after trying a few new businesses stayed close to the Morello-Lupo gang and eventually became an official in the longshoreman's union.

The second decade of the century saw the demise of some gang leaders like Morello and Lupo and the rise of others who took their places. The Terranova brothers—Nick, Vince and Ciro—took over the Morello operation and Caspare Gallucci moved uptown into East Harlem. They fought each other for the next several years. Gallucci's specialty was the Italian lottery. He rigged the numbers so as to not have to pay any large sums. Since Italian-American newspapers were forbidden by law to print the winning numbers and papers from Italy didn't arrive until days after the event, and since most people never saw them only occasionally would Gallucci be called on a phony number. Gallucci's end came one night when he and his 20-year-old son were in a restaurant on 113th Street, Morello gunmen came in and shot Gallucci dead. They killed his son also.

Next the Neapolitan Camorras began to move in on the Morello gang leading to what has been referred to as the Mafia-Camorra War. In effect, the Manhattan Morello Sicilians and the Brooklyn Neapolitans in Coney Island and also the Navy Street gang in downtown Brooklyn.

There was also Giuseppe Costabile who had come from Calabria at the turn of the century. Forced back to Italy by criminal charges he returned in 1907 and continued Black Hand extortion activity. In one month of 1911 police attributed 13 bombings to him. He was finally nailed with a bomb under his coat and sent off to Sing Sing.

It was in the teen years that detective Michael Mealli found himself working cases with his brother, Lt. Detective Andrew Mealli, when both worked out of the Sixth Detective Bureau in Brooklyn. It was at the onset of the new decade, in November 1910, that the police department conducted a shake-up of all detective units in the city. It was announced that all branch detective bureaus would be abolished with the notable exception of the detective bureau in Brooklyn. The entire system would be under the charge of Deputy Commissioner William Flynn. The object was to beef up the Brooklyn force where 84 men from other precincts were ordered to the Brooklyn Detective Bureau on State Street. Men experienced with the kind of work done by Italian Squad detectives were the principal types that were required. The Mealli brothers remained in the Brooklyn unit and would continue to have the opportunity to work as partners in the future.

Although Brooklyn and Manhattan remained the locations where the core of Black Hand activity was most prevalent, there were incidents in Queens, the Bronx and even Staten Island. In March 1910 Manhattan Detective Thomas Moresco had been working for a month with Staten Island police on a Black Hand case. On March 26, at about 2 a.m., Moresco attempted to arrest one suspect when three others attacked him. He blew his whistle and was joined by Detectives O'Hanlon and Folliard. Folliard beat one man to the ground but not before he had fired three shots that fatally wounded Moresco. While O'Hanlon attended to the fallen detective Folliard chased the gunman and apprehended him on Montgomery Street. They were in the Tompkinsville section of Staten Island. The man's name was Thomas Krone, 38 years old. Two other members of the band were arrested. Moresco was taken to St. Vincent's Hospital where Dr. Maguire said that he would not live out the night. O'Hanlon later testified that he saw Krone with a smoking gun standing over the fallen detective.

It was not uncommon for the Italian immigrants to travel as a divided family unit. Often the man came first to America and secured work, saved money and then brought the rest of his family to this country. Furthermore the records of such trips are uncertain and could contain errors. In the case of Angelo Mele, there are five references to his transatlantic trips in the population census. The first on record was in 1883 as a 33-year-old. Records do not indicate whether he traveled alone but he could have come with daughter Caterina, who was 10 years old at the time. Her future husband, Chresnza Sarlo (Sarli), arrived about the same time. The couple were married on February 5, 1885, in Manhattan. Kate was just 12 years old. They had seven children and they always lived in close proximity to the Mele family, being neighbors on Navy Street and again on 35th Street beginning in the 1920s. Known affectionately as "Aunt Kate" to three generations, she died in 1965 at 92 years of age.

Angelo made another cross–Atlantic trip in 1893 when he apparently traveled by himself on the ship called the *Neustria* from Naples to New York. Records also indicate the death of son Paul on December 12, 1894, and the naturalization of Annamarie on March 8, 1894, in New York City. A 1909 arrival was recorded for Mele when once again he is listed as traveling alone, possibly to visit his father Paolo living in Italy, departing Naples on March 18 aboard the *America*. His arrival in America on April 28, 1902, on the *Nord America*, lists Angelo, his wife Annamaria, and his two youngest sons, Andrew and Nicolas, as traveling with him. It is also noted that his son Michael was living in New York and they planned to meet with him. The last of the trips was apparently on March 22, 1912, the record shows a brother Paolo in Italy. Angelo died on July 16, 1912.

To try to slip the pieces of the puzzle together, we first recognize that Andrew was born in Brooklyn, New York, in 1885, which meant that his parents were here at that time but apparently traveled back to Italy where Nicolas was born in 1889. Thus the 1902 return was as a family unit. Michael, born in New York City in 1876, would have remained in New York.

Nick Mele, grandson to Nicholas, recalled his granddad telling him that his father (Angelo) made numerous trips to Italy and back again. "I remember him telling me that he arrived in the United States at about age 11 or 12," Nick said.[1] In 1902 Nicolas was 12½ years old and Andrew was 17 years of age. To further testify to this timetable Nickolas Lapardo recalled his friendship with Angelo's son Andrew in Italy until Andrew was 17. Sometime between 1894 when Paul died at age 12 (buried in Green-Wood Cemetery in Brooklyn), and 1902, the family, except for Michael, were in Italy.

Michael and Annamarie Teta were wed on December 1, 1916, eventually raising their family in the home in which he died at 2040 63rd Street in Brooklyn. Draft registration records filled out by Nicolas and Michael verify the place of birth of both but there is no draft forms available for Andrew. Also, the birth records for the city of New York are not available before 1910.

Andrew married Maria Cavallo on August 4, 1907, in Brooklyn, New York. Both had their roots in Sala Consilina, Italy. Maria had 10 pregnancies, eight of which survived to adulthood. Michael, born in 1913, died in 1915. John was stillborn on June 24, 1929. Of the remaining eight children there were four boys and four girls. Two of the sons, Paul and Andrew, became members of the NYPD, Paul even wearing his father's shield #4005.

A story in the *New York Times* dated Monday, August 23, 1915, carried an interesting note for the family of Detective Mealli of Brooklyn. It said, "Detectives Michael Mealli and Andrew Mealli yesterday arrested at 16 North Portland Avenue, Brooklyn, Matteo Napolitano and Vincenzo Petrello of Pittsfield, Massachusetts, on a warrant charging them with the murder last March of Vincenzo Cresci in Pittsfield." The body was found in the woods just outside of Pittsfield. He had been shot in the

Detective Michael Mealli (author's collection).

back of the head. The Pittsfield police determined that the victim had last been seen in the company of three men, two of them were the ones that were arrested in Brooklyn.

In the few years that Mike was partnered with his brother, Andrew, they worked on the investigation of a number of Black Hand crimes. Andrew Mealli was appointed to the New York City Police Department as a patrolman on probation on August 23, 1911, and was issued patrolman shield number 4005. He served as a second-grade acting detective sergeant. He was elevated to second grade detective on January 30, 1925, and issued detective shield number 560. On June 22, 1931, a copy of general orders #20 shows an entry mentioning Detective Andrew Mealli's Departmental Recognition for Excellent Police Duty. On the night of March 27, 1931, at about midnight Detectives Andrew Mealli and Elliotte Holmes along with Lieutenant Andrew J. Sarosy arrested a hold-up man at 63 Reid Avenue, Brooklyn. The gunman was implicated in numerous other similar offenses.

The brothers joined forces in the arrest of Salvatore Scotto Lavino, a 27-year-old ship worker, on a charge of homicide. On the evening of March 23, 1916, Lavino stepped out of a theater at Pearl and Willoughby streets where the detectives made the arrest. The Meallis were joined by detective John Quinn. Lavino lived at 232 Van Brunt Street. He is alleged to have struck a fellow worker, Natale Castagliola, 48 years old, on the head with a hammer, fracturing his skull. The victim died at Methodist Episcopal Hospital. In the same month Mike Mealli was involved in a caper that was the remnants of the counterfeiting work that had been so prevalent under the Lupo-Morello gang. Mealli witnessed Giuseppe De Salvo try to hide a small package behind a lunch counter, a package which the detective then confiscated. The package contained 82 counterfeit half dollars. De Salvo, of 13 Hamilton Avenue, was then arrested by Mealli, charged with possessing counterfeit money. De Salvo was held on $5,000 bail.

It was the first anniversary of the execution of Charles Becker. The 1916 addition of the Ziegfeld Follies ran at the Amsterdam Theater at 214 West 42nd Street between Seventh and Eighth avenues. The stars were Fanny Brice, W. C. Fields, Will Rogers and Bert Williams. Through that summer the first major polio threat had reached epidemic proportions in New York City, most of the victims were children. By October when it began to abate, 9,000 cases had been recorded, about one-fourth of which had proved fatal. In that fall month the Brooklyn Robins took on the Boston Red Sox in the World Series with Boston winning in five games. In game two, a young left hander named Babe Ruth beat Brooklyn in 14 innings, 2–1.

In the years preceding the U.S. entering into World War I, federal agencies were almost nonexistent, the FBI was just at the toddling stage and the NYPD had the largest and most experienced detective branch in the country. In the New York area, German sabotage was a real terror threat and the NYPD played a major role in combating it. The United States supported the war effort in Europe by shipping supplies to European ports. German U-boats patrolled the seas in an effort to sink these supply ships. They attempted at times to prevent these shipments from ever leaving the U.S. ports. War materials manufactured in the northeastern states were sent to an island in New York harbor known as Black Tom for storage prior to transport to the Allied powers in Europe. The name of the island was such because from the air it supposedly resembled a black cat.

There were several attacks on homeland installations by German saboteurs in retaliation to the British naval blockade of Germany. On January 1, 1915, there was a fire in the Roebling Steel foundry in Trenton, New Jersey. After the Black Tom incident, on January 11, 1917, a fire took place at the Canadian Car and Foundry plant in Kingsland. These facilities had been contracted for goods to be sent to the Allies. In April 1917, the U.S. entered the war on the side of the Allies.

At 2:08 a.m. on the morning of July 30, 1916, an explosion of epic proportions rocked New York and Jersey City. It happened on Black Tom Island, which in reality is a peninsula jutting out from the Jersey shore opposite what was at the time called Bedloe's Island (now Liberty Island). The space between the island and the shoreline had been filled in creating the peninsula, now called Liberty Park in New Jersey. Jersey City firemen fought the blaze which began on a barge tied to Pier 7 of the National Storage Company, a subsidiary of the Lehigh Valley Railroad. The area was used as a work yard where the National Dock and Storage Company had warehouses.

The effects of the explosion were felt all over Manhattan and Brooklyn, with the shock felt as far south as Philadelphia. A half an hour later another even larger explosion followed. The view of the harbor showed spectacular fires blazing across the New Jersey waterfront. Immigrants held at Ellis Island were evacuated as pyrotechnics drifted across the bay and landed there. Some 500 people living on barges and houseboats in the harbor had to be evacuated. The Statue of Liberty sustained $100,000 in damages from the spray of shrapnel. Four people were killed in Jersey City as hundreds of policemen took to the streets. Reports the next morning revealed that two million tons of munitions waiting to be shipped to the

Allies and stored in 200 railcars and a bevy of barges on Black Tom Island had been detonated. German agents were suspected of causing the blasts. Damage was estimated at 20 million dollars. The death toll would rise as high as 50.

The blaze that started the disaster commenced aboard the deck of a barge and spread from there furiously. Thirteen warehouses belonging to the National Storage Company were completely destroyed. In them were 40,000 tons of sugar, valued at $3,400,000. The barges and freight cars at Black Tom were reportedly filled with over two million pounds of ammunition waiting to be shipped overseas. There was black power, TNT, dynamite and shrapnel among the munitions. The Johnson Barge alone held about 100,000 pounds of TNT. The eight guards on duty fled but not before one of them sounded the alarm alerting the Jersey City Fire Department. The fires set off exploding shrapnel shells and pieces of metal struck the building of the *Jersey Journal* at Journal Square. They hit the clock tower stopping the clock at 2:12 a.m. The Hudson Tubes (the PATH system under the Hudson River connecting Lower Manhattan with Hoboken and Jersey City) was jolted by the blast.

There was an information blackout due to a disruption in telephone service. Emergency vehicles responding to the alarm did so without full knowledge of the extent of the emergency. Windows were shattered in Lower Manhattan and as far the Times Square area. Repercussions from the explosions were felt along the Jersey line to Staten Island and Brooklyn.

At the end of the peninsula a crater 20 feet deep and 50 feet across was dug and found to be nearly filled with debris: parts of cars, trucks, containers of explosives and still smoldering long after the fires had died down. Cartridge shells flew over the water, some landing a mile from where they had exploded. Doctors and nurses from local hospitals rushed to the scene. A Dr. Botti ran through flinging debris and dragged out Patrolman James Daugherty who had lost much blood from a severed artery in his head, the result of having been struck by a shell. At City Hospital in Jersey City, it was reported that his chances of recovery were slim.

The damages in Jersey City were extensive. Windows were shattered throughout the city. At City Hospital all of the windows on the side facing Black Tom were broken and patients had to be moved toward the center of the building. In addition to the deaths, at least 75 persons were reported injured. There were 12 injuries from falling glass in Manhattan.

Since the 1870s the NYPD kept a careful eye on security threats, identifying foreigners with anarchist tendencies and watched places where such individuals were known to congregate. On August 1, 1914, the bomb squad was created and Acting Captain Thomas Tunney was put in charge. An organization known as "Brescia Circle" had sprung up—named after the anarchist Gaetano Brescia who had assassinated the king of Italy in 1901. In 1914 they were about 600 strong. To some extent the police had to also contend with the Irish, who in some cases had been allied with German terrorists because of their conflicts with the British. In July 1914 three members of the Brescia Circle were killed when a homemade bomb exploded while they were working on it. The police said the bomb was intended for the Rockefeller family in Tarrytown, New York. In October bombs were set off in St. Patrick's Cathedral in Manhattan. In March 1915 another attempt was made in bombing St. Patrick's and this time the NYPD was ready.

During the celebration of mass two men dressed as laborers entered the church, each with a lighted cigar in his hand that he concealed. One of the men took an object from his pocket, laid it on the floor and lit a fuse with his cigar. As he began to walk toward the door he was grabbed by a scrubwoman who was mopping a marble floor. An elderly man with a white beard extinguished the fuse and a tall man nabbed the second saboteur as he was leaving a pew. The scrubwoman was Detective Patrick Walsh, the white-bearded old man was Detective Sergeant George Barnitz, and the tall man who nailed the second suspect was Captain Tunney. The two men were charged with attempted bombing and were convicted and given substantial prison terms. It was Tunney's placing an undercover agent, Italian-speaking detective, Amedeo Polignani, into the Brescia Circle that was responsible for foiling the plot.

Though the NYPD and the Allied agents working to counter acts of sabotage had a degree of success, the Black Tom Island explosion was not prevented. The island was the major ammunition transfer point in the United States but security was faulty. After the workmen quit at 5 p.m. on July 29, the railroad cars and the barges loaded with ammunition were left unattended. There were six watchmen from the Lehigh Valley Railroad to guard the freight cars and four private detectives protecting the barges. Both detectives Mealli were part of the NYPD task force investigating the sabotage and the perpetration of the crime was put together in this manner.

Two of the private detectives were bribed allowing two German officers to row out to the island. They were met there by one of the workers, an Austrian. The three set off the explosion, which caused $14 million in damages. Although investigations were extensive, the saboteurs were never positively identified. But it was ultimately believed that the German officers were Kurt Jahnke and Lothar Witzke, and the Austrian worker was Michael Kristoff. Kristoff was a 23-year-old immigrant living with relatives in Bayonne and had been employed at the Tidewater Oil Company. It was claimed that he started the fires at Black Tom with incendiary devices for which he was paid $500. Kristoff died in a Staten Island hospital in 1928. Jahnke's career as a spy continued into World War II, while Witzke wound up in Mexico and was later caught sneaking back into the United States. This was in 1918 and though Witzke was sentenced to death it was never carried out. He went back to Germany after the war. The German government was ordered to pay reparations of $50 million to all claimants but the Nazi government prevented those payments being made during World War II. The case was reopened after the war with claims added to outstanding war debts and the last payment was made in 1979.

In 2016 on the 100th anniversary of the Black Tom explosion Liberty State Park along with the National Park Service and the Hudson County History Advocates hosted a commemorative program. Family members of two Jersey City responders killed during the explosion were in attendance. A panel marking the event was unveiled at the site.

Criminal activity during the war kept the police bomb squad and other units busy, but the detectives of the sixth branch bureau to which Mike Mealli was assigned also faced the crime on the streets every day. A meeting in Philadelphia between Navy Street leader Alessandro Vollero and the Camorra leadership under boss Ricco planned to hit the Morello gang with the idea of taking complete control of Manhattan. A plan was formulated. A *New York Times* story headline on September 8, 1916, proclaimed, "2 Die in Pistol Fight in Brooklyn Street." Johnson Street between Fleet Place and Hudson Avenue in Brooklyn was the scene of a pistol fight in the late afternoon of the previous day. Two men, Nicholas Terranova and Charles Ubriaco, both residents of the Italian colony in Harlem, were walking along Johnson Street when a fusillade of shots rang out striking both men. A beat policeman, Coon, of the Adams Street station heard the shots and as he hurried toward the scene he saw a large crowd pushing and shoving and shouting. He immediately called for help and the back-up arrived from Adams Street. They cleared the area around the crime scene. Vollero was arrested but released in 19 days for lack of evidence.

Detectives Frank Tierney and Andrew and Michael Mealli led the team of detectives first on the scene. They found Terranova lying in the street with six bullet wounds, Ubriaco was about 50 feet away with a bullet through his heart. Both were taken to Brooklyn Hospital where Dr. Rickey said that both had died almost instantly. Detectives found three witnesses to the shooting. It was Detective Mike Mealli who recognized one of the victims as Nick Terranova. He was later identified by a relative. That afternoon Mealli arrested Rocco Valenti, 21 years old, at a billiard hall near the scene of the shooting. Though he denied any knowledge of the crime a loaded revolver was found in his room at 313 Hudson Avenue, Brooklyn, and he was held for a hearing. "Detectives Mealli, Michael and Andrew, Grattano, and Pucciano, along with Morris Eckler, a finger print expert, made an investigation."[2]

Mealli was by this time establishing a strong reputation for his expertise. The press reported in this case that "According to Detective Michael Mealli, who is perhaps the man in the Police Department most familiar with the pedigree of Italians of this type."[3] The paper noted that Mealli, who as a longtime member of the Italian Squad, was able to identify Terranova, the stepson of Joe Morello and brother-in-law to Ignazio "Lupo the Wolf" Lupo. Mealli's work was highly regarded by his peers and superiors. He was credited with causing the arrest and conviction of Lupo and three other counterfeiters who had been responsible with flooding the Brooklyn area with bogus bills.

The investigation revealed that the two men had been lured to Brooklyn to be killed or had come seeking to kill someone else. In either case it was the result of a feud. In Terranova's pocket police found a letter in Italian of the typical "Black Hand" sort.

In October of that same year the brothers Mealli acted once again as a team when they arrested Francesco Crisuolo for having a revolver in his possession, a violation of the Sullivan Act. Crisuolo, 33 years of age, was arrested at King and Con-

Detective Andrew Mealli (author's collection).

over streets on the evening of October 19. The suspect was held on $2,000 bail for the grand jury when he appeared before Magistrate Dodd in the Fifth Avenue court. The detectives were working out of the sixth branch.

In the period of World War I as the Italian Squad lay dormant crime in New York City remained a challenge for the NYPD. Both brothers Mealli worked as sixth branch detectives in Brooklyn through the mid-teens and it was during this time that street gang crime proliferated. Logistics reports by the department revealed that the rapid increase in Brooklyn's population had not produced a comparable increase in police officers. It was pointed out that patrolmen were taken from Brooklyn and reassigned to Manhattan making the job of the officers more difficult in Brooklyn. The fixed plan of stationing a patrolman on a fixed post every two blocks or so is said to be an excellent idea provided there were enough officers to implement such a plan ... in Brooklyn there were not.

It happened also that as a cry was made for more police officers in the borough, a criminal society even older than the Mafia had developed in Italy as early as 1735. It was known even then by the name *"Camorra."* Newton, in *The Mafia at Apalachin, 1957,* tells us that some historians claim it was an "offshoot of the Spanish *Garduna,* a prison gang founded in 1417, then exported to Italy by wandering members."[4] In 1820 the first official mention was made of the Camorra when police records described a Camorra meeting. A network of clans, or families, the Camorra was similar in structure to the Cosa Nostra and other Mafia factions. At times these factions worked in conjunction with each other and in others they were warring factions.

The name began to be heard in the United States in union with the Mafia in the latter half of the 19th century. On January 9, 1895, the Boston police laid the blame for a razor-slashing murder of Pasquale Sacco on a "branch of the Mafia or the Camorra."[5] With the huge influx of Italian immigrants at the turn of the 19th century (between 1900 and 1920) there were 3.2 million Italian immigrants that landed in New York, tens of thousands in New York City, and as with the Black Hand and the Mafia, there were numbers of Camorra among them. Since 1892 a Mafia family existed in New York under the boss Giuseppe Morello, previously mentioned for his crimes and ultimate conviction and imprisonment. It was the three half-brothers of Morello from his widowed mother's second marriage—Ciro, Nicola and Vincenzo Terranova—who established the Brooklyn gang that rose to prominence in the mid-teen years of the 20th century.

A feud between two Camorra families, the Morello group and one led by Francesco Meli, fought for control of the Brooklyn dockyards.

Giuseppe Morello killed Meli on December 4, 1892, settling that particular feud at the time but new battles would erupt 20 years later. Between 1910 and 1915 there were 161 murders attributed to Black Hand crime but at least a portion of them were due to gang warfare. The corner of Oak and Milton Street in Little Italy became known as "Death's Corner" because of the number of victims slain at that location.

The years from 1911 to 1916 were formative years for the Italian gangs as they grew in strength and numbers. The Lomonte brothers took over control of the Morello gang along with the Terranovas. New names were introduced to the world of criminal activity in New York City following the jailing of Morello and Lupo. Among them was Joe DeMarco, his brother Salvatore and Giuseppe Verrazano. They ran the gambling empire for the Morello gang. The most unusual of the figures to ally with the crime family was a Neapolitan woman named Pasquarella Spinelli, described as "dumpy, mannish, square-faced, red-haired and nearly sixty years old."[6] She owned a large livery stable at 334 East 108th Street in Harlem. Known to the police as the head of a gang of horse thieves and extortionists, she also acted at times as an informant to the NYPD. She worked in conjunction with the Lomonte brothers and Nick Terranova, who ran the Morello horse stealing rackets and made use of Pasquarella's stable to hide the stolen animals. She benefited from the gang protection she received since it was estimated that at least 20 murders occurred in and around her property so that it came to be known as "Murder Stable." It was, however, not enough as Pasquarella was murdered. She was found shot in the head presumably by a pair of gunmen who hid on her premises and apparently had lurked in the shadows for quite some time waiting for her to return. Though there were a number of possible motives for the crime resulting from her activities with the gangs, her murder was never solved.

A business partner of hers, Luigi Lazzazzara, took over her property and since he was not on very good terms with the Terranova brothers, he wound up dead as well two years later when he was found stabbed through the heart on East 108th Street. The bloodletting continued as the gangs fought for control. Just three weeks after Pasquarella was killed Giuseppe Morello's son, Calogero, was also killed. Morello's son was only 17 when he was walking with a friend, Joe Paluzzo, along 120th Street as he was confronted by several men. Some shots rang out. The two Sicilians fired back killing one attacker. Both, however, were badly wounded and both died the next day. As was usually the case, motives were blurred. Some said Morello had been a police informant, others that he had been the victim of a gang territorial dispute.

153

The police informer Salvatore Clemente revealed the motive to Agent William Flynn shortly after. It was part of a vendetta tracing back to the murder of the barrel victim nine years earlier. The killer had been "Kid" Baker, a gang leader from the Upper East Side. The Terranova brothers swore vengeance and in the next few weeks Nick, the youngest of the brothers, killed two members of the Baker gang. Nick Terranova, 22 years old in 1912, began to emerge as the strongest of the leaders of the Morello gang. Giosue Gallucci was one more influential mob figure in New York. He had come here from Naples in 1892 and built a power base that by 1912 had gained him the title the "King of Little Italy." He controlled the ice business in the summer and the coal business in the winter. He dealt in a number of industries including olive oil, moneylending, and a bakery at 319 East 109th Street. While posing as a legitimate businessman, the King dabbled in racketeering and extortion. He ran the New York office of the Royal Italian Lottery that sold thousands of tickets every month in Harlem. He was as well politically active.

A Tammany Hall participant, he delivered thousands of immigrant votes to the political machine giving him immense power. There was a friendship between the Lomonte brothers and Gallucci but it did not extend to the Terranovas, Sicilians, and Gallucci, a Neapolitan. The rivalry climaxed in 1914 when Fortunato Lomonte was murdered in the open by three shots fired at point-blank range. It happened near the Murder Stable that was in the heart of the King's territory. The killer escaped and no one seemed to know who he was. Clemente's nose could turn up nothing. At times it is difficulty to keep track or make much sense of the struggles for power. Gallucci's brother Gennaro had been gunned down in 1909 in the Gallucci bakery. Though Gallucci managed to stay on top he nonetheless became immersed in a power struggle with a Black Hander named Aniello Prisco, a cripple who went by the name of Zopo the Gimp. He foolishly tried to extract tribute from the bakery and was predictably killed by a Gallucci bodyguard. He took two bullets in the head from Gallucci's nephew, John Russomano, at the bakery who was released after a plea of self-defense. Another Gallucci hood, Capalongo, set up the hit. A few months later, Russomano and Capalongo were both shot but survived. It was thought that the shooting was set up by Amadio Buonomo, a partner of "Zopo" Prisco. Buonomo was attacked on April 5, 1913, and died on the April 9 of his wounds.

Retaliations on the life of Gallucci were made. In 1913 he was shot twice and in a gun battle on First Avenue a year later he took another bullet. Another of his bodyguards was shot and killed by a sniper aiming at the King and he began to sense the inevitability of the revenge when he said to a reporter from the *New York Herald* in May 1915, "They will get me, I know that they will get me yet."[7] Just a few days later on May 17 at 10 o'clock in the evening he left the bakery and walked four doors down to a coffee shop owned by his son Luca. There were several men in the room and two walked in behind Gallucci. There were at least seven shots and both Gallucci and his son were fatally hit.

On October 12 that same year Tom Lomonte was on a street corner on 107th Street talking to a cousin when someone came up behind him and shot him three times, murdering him. A policeman heard the shots and pursued the gunman to a building at 102 East 109th Street. He ran into an apartment and tossed off his clothes and jumped into bed. The policeman followed him, dragged him out of bed and found a pistol under the bed. His name was Antonio Impoluzzo, a 17-year-old who had seemingly no connection to the victim. Impoluzzo went on trial in December, was found guilty, and executed in the electric chair. The police never learned of a motive.

The assumption on the detectives' part was that he had been a hired killer, but the police believed that whoever was behind the killing had in all probability ordered the hits on Fortunato Lomonte and Giosue Gallucci. That individual being in all likelihood one who wanted to restore the Morello gang to its former prominence.

The recent upturn in killings, bombings and blackmailings caused the police to order a cleanup of the New York gangs. Arrests were made under the Sullivan law on whatever charges could be formulated. All was in place for the events of the next few years and the Mafia-Camorra war would lay the groundwork for the climax of the career of Detective Michael Mealli.

Chapter Eleven

The Mafia-Camorra War

Black Hand crimes became more uncommon beginning around 1912. Crime was developing in a far more organized way and gangs sought increased power. The motives behind all the killings began with gangs or families trying to build strength and extended to revenge murders. Disputes over territory and control of rackets like gambling, drugs, food and basic utilities, accounted for more killings. In 1915 were the existence of several major Italian gangs in New York City. The Sicilian Morello gang was in Harlem, the Neapolitan Navy Street gang was headed by Leopoldo Lauritano and Alessandro Vollero, and then there was the Neapolitan Coney Island gang led by Pellegrino Morano. In Brooklyn there was a Sicilian gang headed by Cola Schiro and another Brooklyn gang led by Manfredi Mineo, and yet another Harlem gang behind Salvatore "Toto" D'Aquila.

Joseph DeMarco was a Sicilian gangster with major connections to the gambling world in Italian Harlem. At 5'6" with a medium build and very dark complexion, he was often seen wearing a blue suit with a diamond and sapphire scarf pin. He had been close with the Morello bunch as a result of their collaboration in a murder in July 1912. DeMarco had killed a doctor in New York because he became involved with DeMarco's girlfriend. Then he worked with Nick Terranova and Fortunato Lomonte to plan the girl's murder. He had a falling out with the Morello gang largely because he would not give the Terranova brothers a larger share of the gambling he controlled, which they believed was coming to them.

DeMarco tried to kill Nick Terranova but he failed. In April 1913 the Terranovas struck back. The first attempt on DeMarco was at 112th Street and First Avenue when he was shot in the neck from behind a fence. Although the wound was serious DeMarco's life was saved by surgeons in Harlem Hospital. A second attempt was made on his life in July 1914 while he was in a barbershop getting a shave. Two men fired at him with sawed-off shotguns. He was riddled by more than a dozen shots yet survived. In November 1915 he moved downtown opening up a restaurant at

163 West 49th Street. In addition he also opened several gambling rooms in the Mulberry Street area.

The target of both eliminating DeMarco and expanding their own operations were the gambling dens in Manhattan that were controlled by DeMarco. On June 24, 1916, the Sicilian Morello gang met with the Neapolitans of Navy Street and Coney Island. They met in Coney Island and planned the murder of Joe DeMarco. The three gangs all had a stake in DeMarco's death. In line with that they divvied up the gambling interests among themselves. They arranged to meet at a café on Navy Street owned by Leopoldo Lauritano. There they would make their plans to kill DeMarco. Aware that DeMarco would recognize any of the Morello bunch they obtained the services of Giuseppe Verrazano, a friend of DeMarco's, to set him up for the kill.

The plan was for Verrazano to sneak some Navy Street gunmen into DeMarco's James Street gambling den where he would secretly identify the target. The chosen one for the hit was John "The Painter" Fetto but on the appointed night he was late getting to the James Street location and DeMarco had already left by the time he arrived. On the morning of July 20, 1916, another meeting was held, again at the Navy Street café. In attendance were Louis the Wop; Nick Sassi, who was another DeMarco confidant who would assist in the crime; and Steve LaSalle and Ciro Terranova. They selected Lefty Esposito, Painter and Fetto as the gunmen. Sassi got the gunmen inside the James Street den and through the kitchen to a back room. DeMarco sat at a table with several other men playing cards. There were spectators around the table watching the card game. Verrazano was in the room to identify the target and Nick Sassi and Rocco Valenti waited outside to assist in the escape. However, Esposito and Pagano misinterpreted Verrazano's signal and shot and killed Charles Lombardi who was seated next to DeMarco by mistake. But Verrazano took it upon himself to complete the job and he killed DeMarco. The gunmen escaped through a window into Oliver Street.

Nothing seemed to derail the vicious nature of the crimes that these gangs perpetrated against each other. In October 1916 the brother of the slain Joseph DeMarco was himself found dead in a clump of weeds in a lot on Washington Avenue in Astoria. His skull had been crushed and his throat slit. Potentially the motive for his death was that he claimed he was about to tell the police what he knew of his brother's death and other numerous shootings. In the meantime Verrazano was in the process of opening a new gambling establishment, which did not sit well with the Navy Street gang and so they began to plot his death. On October 16

Charles Giordano of Staten Island made his plans to kill Verrazano. He along with four others including Ralph Daniello went to the Italian Gardens restaurant in the Occidental Hotel on Broome Street in Manhattan and located Verrazano. Two of them, Alphonso Sgroia and Mike Notaro, stood by the door shooting into the establishment and killing Verrazano. Both gunmen escaped.

It was an all-out war between the Morello gang of Harlem and the Brooklyn Camorra gang that included the Navy Street gang. The Navy Street gang got stronger because of having taken over the Morello businesses but the murders continued. George Esposito, a bodyguard to Gaetano del Gaudio, was killed on East 108th Street on November 8, 1916, and later that month on the 30th Gaetano himself was shot and killed while serving two men coffee in his restaurant at 2031 First Avenue, blasted by a shotgun placed against the window. Taken to the Flower Hospital, he claimed to know his killer but refused to identify him. When the Navy Street gang learned that Joseph "Chuck" Nazzaro, DeMarco's old friend,

The Navy Street Gang.

was seen talking to members of the Morello gang he was shot and killed in Yonkers.

The Neapolitan Camorras, like the Mafia, was an organized group of cutthroats that practiced crimes up to and including murder. It can be traced back to a 16th century Spanish secret society. In Italy during the 19th century Camorrists flamboyantly wore a multicolored sash flung over their shoulder and carried a cane with brass rings. There was a process of steps leading up to full membership beginning with the performances of services given them by members. If they did a satisfactory job, they might be invited to become a "picciotti"; in this regard they could be asked to carry out a murder, the accomplishment of which would grant them full fledged membership. There were rites and oaths and ceremonies connected with the rules of the organization. Often supported by businessmen, government officials and nobles, this kind of patronage would be emulated later in America.

The Camorras, like the Mafia, spread their venom to several states and by 1913 they had branches in much of the United States. It is uncertain exactly when they developed their operation in New York, but a number of Camorrists came into the city between 1900 and 1910. The Morellos, Sicilians, were based in Manhattan and Italian Harlem. The Camorras settled in Brooklyn where they formed two distinct gangs of Neapolitans but worked in conjunction with each other. One formed on Navy Street, the other in Coney Island. The first of them used a coffee shop at 133 Navy Street as headquarters and were led by Alessandro Vollero, a 30-year-old who had been born in 1889 in Gragnano, Italy, a small town near Naples. He arrived in New York in 1909 with his wife and children. Becoming involved with the street gangs that were aligned with the Camorra he eventually served as a lieutenant to gang boss Pellegrino Morano during the Mafia-Camorra War of 1916. Pellegrino Morano ran the Coney Island gang from the Santa Lucia restaurant. Pellegrino had a wife he left in Italy and lived in Manhattan with his mistress. Vollero was involved in the murders of Nick Terranova and Charles Ubriaco as revenge against the Morello bunch for their murder of his friend, Nicholas DelGardio.

The real name of Ralph Daniello was Alfonso Pepe, also known as "Ralph the Barber." He was born in 1866 in Pagani, Campania, in Italy. Arrested for attacking a woman in Italy and on suspicion of involvement in a murder, Daniello escaped from prison in 1906 and made his way to the French port of Le Havre. From there he sailed to New York and was illegally smuggled into the country. He became part of the Navy Yard group and took part in the ambush murders of Terranova and Ubriaco. It is chilling to read the Daniello testimony and his description of the casual way in which they planned and executed the crime. The plan was laid out at the home of Vollero at 61st Street. He mentioned that the murderers were told to flee through the same alley that Daniello had used when he shot Frank Grimaldi. Three men were given the assignment, one for each potential victim, and two others were to act in reserve and be stationed in a poolroom at Johnson Street and Hudson Avenue. They were to be prepared in case any more of the Morello gang should appear. He went on to explain that the guns were carefully examined to be sure that they were in good working condition and they left for the scene of the crime, while Vollero went to 215 Johnson Street to oversee that the plans were carried out.

After being acquitted of robbery and abduction charges, Daniello decided New York was not the safest place for him, so in May 1917 he and his girlfriend went to Reno, Nevada. In May the NYPD issued a warrant for his arrest for the murder of Louis DeMarro in Brooklyn on May 7. Daniello and his girlfriend were running low on funds so he wrote to the Camorra gang for help but was ignored by them. This would later affect his decision to tell the police all he knew of the crime syndicate. He was eventually arrested in Nevada and extradited back to New York. In 1913 he became involved in yet another gang type war of violence—the Labor Slugger Wars.

The Labor Sluggers Wars were a string of gang wars for the control of labor that lasted from 1911 to 1917. Industrialization led to the emergence of labor unions in the late 19th and early 20th century. Companies hired street gangs as strikebreakers. Unions would often hire labor sluggers as protection from the strike breakers. Two major gangs rose up in the early part of the wars, one led by "Dopey Benny" Fein, the other by "Joe the Greaser" Rosenzweig. A gunfight ensued on Grand and Forsyth streets in 1913. There were no casualties but one of the gang leaders, Philip Paul, was later killed by a Rosenzweig gunman. Later arrested and confessing to the crime, "Benny" Snyder testified against Rosenzweig. Fein ultimately testified against his own organization and an investigation led to the arrests of 11 gangsters and 23 union officials. Labor slugging lasted until 1927 when the fourth war of its kind ended one type of labor crime; from there and through the 1930s labor racketeering was divided among the National Crime Syndicate. Ralph Daniello took part in the first of the Labor Slugger Wars in 1913.

On the other side of the East River the Morello gang had been taken over by the three Terranova brothers after Morello went to prison. The middle brother was Ciro, born in Corleone, Sicily, in 1888. In 1893 young

Ciro came to New York with his family; his father, mother, four sisters, brothers Vincenzo and Nicolo, and met up with half-brother Giuseppe Morello who had come to the city six months earlier. Unable to find work, the family moved to Louisiana and then to Bryan, Texas, where they worked picking cotton. They moved back to New York in 1896. Ciro went to school and worked evenings and weekends in the family business, a plastering store. Ciro went to work eventually at a restaurant in the rear of a Prince Street saloon owned by his stepbrother Giuseppe.

Giuseppe had been implicated in the barrel murder of 1903 but was released due to lack of evidence. Ciro came by his nickname "the Artichoke King" by buying artichokes at six dollars a crate from California and selling them in New York for a 30–40 percent profit. His sales were good because he frightened vegetable sellers into buying them. One seller, Giuseppe Carulli, refused to be intimidated by Ciro. A few others joined him and were successful in standing up to the Artichoke King. Carulli built a successful business delivering to restaurants and hotels in the New York area.

Following the death of Nick Terranova the remaining brothers, Vincenzo and Ciro, were extremely cautious. They stayed close to their headquarters at East 116th Street. In fact Vollero and his Neapolitans became more determined to rid the city of the Morello members. They came up with a plan to smuggle a huge bomb into the basement of the Terranova's tenement and blow up the building with everyone in it. When that proved impractical they gave thought to the idea of poisoning their food. With this type of anxiety hovering over the Morellos the Camorra was able to make some headway into the Manhattan gambling operations of the Morello bunch. In January 1917 Vollero survived an ambush by the Mafia gang and spent several weeks in the hospital recovering from shotgun wounds. Vegetable sellers were informed that they would have to pay a tribute of $50 a railroad car to Navy Street for all the artichokes arriving in the city. They attempted to move in on the ice and coal trades as well.

The sellers balked because the amount was too high. They eventually settled on $25 per car. The same happened when Pellegrino Morano of the Coney Island Neapolitans muscled in on the Italian lotteries. His demand of $1,000 a week was simply beyond the gamblers' capacity to pay. After negotiation efforts they settled on $150 a week, a paltry sum compared to what they wanted.

As for Ciro Terranova he lived on, though he dodged a bullet when he was tried for the DeMarco shooting. As a result of the Daniello confessions both Ciro and his brother Vincenzo were arrested. Vincenzo along with several others were eventually released but Ciro was charged with ordering the gambler's murder. The trial began in February 1918 but was halted when the judge fell ill and was heard again several months later. Ciro's slick lawyer tied Daniello up on the stand making him admit that he and Terranova were of the same gang. This revelation took advantage of a law then on the books that said no man could be convicted solely on the evidence of an accomplice. Ciro was discharged from custody on June 6.

It is noted in a number of publications that Ciro's lowest point came about on December 7, 1929, when the board of directors of the Tepecano Democratic Club threw a banquet in honor of Judge H. Vitale at the Roman Gardens in the Bronx. Ciro Terranova was in attendance with six of his gunmen as well as numerous political figures and police officers. During Judge Vitale's speech at about 1:30 a.m., seven gunmen entered the room and stole money and jewelry from the guests, including a revolver from a

Ciro Terranova.

policeman. Within three hours all the stolen items had been returned. The story evolved into a scheme by Terranova to have the gunmen steal a contract that Ciro had signed to murder two men, Frankie Yale and Frankie Marlow. The underworld considered it a stupid move on the part of Ciro to have allowed such a document to exist let alone be circulated among the brethren. The robbery could not be hushed up and the bosses saw Ciro as a fool. It revealed Vitale's contacts with the underworld and he was removed from the bench in March 1930.

Antonio Paretti aka "Tony the Shoemaker," the Camorra leader who had taken part in the Torranova slaying, had fled to Italy to escape capture. He returned to New York in 1926 thinking witnesses against him would be gone. He, however, was convicted of first-degree murder and sentenced to death. Paretti was electrocuted on February 17, 1927, at the age of 35.

The beginning of the end for Ciro came on April 15, 1931, when he drove the killers to a hit on Giuseppe Masseria, another one of the mob bosses. After the killing it was said that Ciro was so unnerved that he could hardly drive the car and his reputation suffered as a result. He lived on for several more years until February 18, 1938, when he suffered a paralyzing stroke. He died two days later at Columbia Hospital, the only one of the three Terranova brothers to die in bed. All three lie in Calvary Cemetery in Queens, New York, not far from the grave of Joe Petrosino.

It was at about this time and into these circumstances that Ralph Daniello was making his threats about telling the police all he knew about the gang's operations. Daniello had fled to Reno after a shooting incident in May 1916 when he shot and killed the contact with whom he was fighting during an argument in a drug deal.. It may have been the eighth murder of his career. In Reno with his mistress, 16-year-old Amelia Valvo, he ran out of money. Vollero did not respond to any of Daniello's letters asking for money. He became increasingly bitter so that he next wrote a letter to the police. The Brooklyn Italian Squad knew that Ralph could give them some very valuable information.

By the end of November Daniello was back in Brooklyn ready to tell all he knew. After his return from Reno indictments were brought against him on the charges of murder, grand larceny and perjury. This coupled with his animosity toward his gang members led to Daneillo's confession at the office of DA Edward Swann. Over a period of 10 days he revealed the gang's activities of the previous 10 years. He confessed to the gang's involvement in the killings of both the DeMarco brothers, Nicholas Terranova, and Charles Ubriaco. He was arraigned on November 27, 1917, along with John Esposito, Alessandro Vollero, and Alphonso Sgroia. His confessions also led to the arrests of other members of the Navy Street gang. Material witnesses were Ciro Terranova, Vincenzo Terranova, and Nicholas Arra. All were held on $15,000 bail. On November 30 the grand jury handed down 12 indictments for the killing of Joseph DeMarco and Charles Lombardi.

His information led to the clearance of 23 unsolved murders. He described life as a Camorrist. According to Daniello he worked for a weekly pay of about $15 and for this sum he did whatever criminal activity the bosses deemed fit. Daniello had a score to settle and he went after the Neapolitan gangs with a vengeance. He identified Vollero and Morano as the leaders of the Camorra and named gunmen Tony Notaro and Tony the

Shoemaker as the killers of Nick Terranova and Giuseppe Verrazano. In all his testimony led to 21 indictments. His accusations against the gang included the murder of Giuseppe DeMarco and his brother Salvatore. The district attorney in charge of the case, Edward Swann, "expressed regret that certain parts of the confession of Daniello had been made public, and said he feared some of the suspected criminals were already trying to get away to Italy."[1] He also said that the police in New York and in other cities were cooperating with the district attorney's staff in the efforts to apprehend them.

The indictments that resulted from Daniello's testimony were the largest number of indictments in any one case that had ever been issued in Manhattan. Daniello also included in his testimony that most of the borough of Brooklyn's Italian police officers were taking bribes. He mentioned that he was in the wine shop of Vollero on Navy Street when he overheard a conversation between two members of the gang. "One of them," he declared, "said that he was about to contribute $50 to a fund of $100 that was to be given to Michael Mealli, a detective attached to the Sixth Branch Bureau."[2] It may or may not be true. One author wrote that following the killings of Terranova and Ubriaco the Camorrists "made regular protection payments to the local Italian detective, Michael Mealli, who was one of the first policemen on the scene and who conspicuously failed to turn in much in the way of evidence."[3] As part of his testimony against Mealli, Daniello also said, "Mealli never arrested any of us," in reference to the Navy Street gang. "He would come down there with a superior officer and wallop some of us, but that was it."[4] This was not, however, entirely true. Following the murders of Terranova and Ubriaco, Mealli located a gang member, Rocco Valenti, wanted in the shooting later that same afternoon in a billiard hall near the scene of the shooting and made the arrest.

There is little factual evidence to back up these charges other that the testimony of Daniello, which may be considered hearsay evidence and therefore not admissible. According to one writer, he also named the highly decorated detective Charles Corrao. "[Daniello] implicated not only Mike Mealli, but even such a storied officer as Charles Corrao [the subject of a recent and admiring profile in the *New York Times*], in efforts to protect the Neapolitans from retribution."[5]

Like so many of his Italian comrades Mealli lived for years in the heart of an Italian community. For him it was Navy Street in Brooklyn. It was incumbent upon the Italian detectives that they get to know the criminal element in the society as much as the honest and hardworking people among the immigrant population. He knew lots of people including criminals and murderers. It was said that he was commonly known for the wide acquaintances among all facets of the population he had nurtured through the years. In fact he was known "for his remarkable memory and had a wide acquaintance among the Brooklyn politicians."[6] It was also during this period of time that Detective Mealli was installed as acting captain. It should be pointed out, though not an excuse for taking money, if, in fact, he did, that his familiarity with the Navy Street gang gave him an advantage in the investigation of the dozens of criminal acts, which included such crimes as murder, attempted murder, robbery, arson, bombings and the like. Much of his success was attributed to his ability to recognize faces and identify criminals by name.

Since so many Italian policemen were known to take bribes it may be easy enough to believe that Mike Mealli was one of them. Evidence, however, came only in the form of the Daniello confession. Daniello's confession was made because of his attempt to get even with the Navy Street gang of which he was a part and whom he believed had not given him the money he requested while in Reno. In other words it was revenge. Could he have tossed Mealli or Corrao in the hopper along with Vollero and the other indicted? Possibly.

Further actions in the convoluted case occurred when Judge Isaac M. Kapper had taken ill causing a mistrial to be declared. Vollero was retried on March 4, convicted and sentenced to death at Sing Sing prison in Ossining, New York. However, his sentence was later commuted to life imprisonment. He served 14 years and on April 28, 1933, was released and sent back to his birthtown in Italy. Pellegrino Morano, head of the Coney Island faction, was convicted of murder in the second degree and sentenced to 20 years to life at Sing Sing. Another Navy Street gang member, Alphonso Sgroia, was sentenced to 12 years at Dannemora but after testifying against his fellow assassins was deported to Italy. Esposito and Notaro received sentences of six to 10 years for their participation in the murders. The trials dragged on for much of 1918 and into the early 1920s.

Charles Giordano, the saloon keeper from Tompkinsville, Staten Island, went on trial on April 27, 1918, for his part in plotting the killing of Giuseppe Verrazano in October 1916. Antonio Notaro and Ralph Daniello testified against Giordano.

Frank Fevrola was tried in April 1921 for the murder of Nazzaro. He was found guilty and sentenced to the death house at Sing Sing. His conviction was largely based upon his wife's testimony, but she withdrew it saying that she had been threatened and bribed by police. The judge denied any motion for retrial. Scheduled to die of on June 28, 1923, he received a reprieve that saved him until October 7 when the death penalty was carried out.

The outcome for the detectives was that "Corrao escaped apparently unscathed, the same could not be said of the unfortunate Mealli, who was reduced in rank and put back on the streets as a beat patrolman."[7] Mealli's demotion would seem to support his guilt in the matter, however, he was not subjected to a hearing or an investigation. Nor was he denied his pension upon retirement. It would appear that Daniello's testimony in regard to Mealli was hearsay and should not have been permissible. Further, the proceedings were declared a mistrial. His accuser, Ralph Daniello, a felon testifying against his own gang, received a suspended sentence because of the testimony he gave. Later on he was arrested for assaulting a man in Coney Island and was sentenced to five years in prison. Released in 1925 he was shot and killed in his saloon near Metuchen, New Jersey.

The 1918 trials following Daniello's confessions effectively demolished the Navy Street gang. It marked the end of the Camorra in New York, but the power of the crime families remained in the hands of the New York Mafia gangs.

On February 1, 1920, Giuseppe Morello was paroled from federal prison. Much had changed in the city and the world following the First World War. Prohibition opened up new avenues of revenues for the criminal element and new crime bosses emerged. Toto D'Aquila had taken over when Morello went to prison and he was still in control of the largest of New York's crime families. Still active among the crime bosses were Cola Schiro in the Bronx and Manfredi Mineo in Brooklyn. Others were making their way up the ranks of the Mafioso. Among them were Joe Masseria and Umberto Valenti in Manhattan's East Village. The Morello group had been weakened by the Camorra war but Ciro and Vincenzo Terranova, though not as dominant as their predecessors, remained in control.

The summer of 1920 also brought Ignazio Lupo back to New York City, apparently unsettling D'Aquila in part because of the reception granted to "the Clutch Hand" and "the Wolf" in New York in Harlem that summer. D'Aquila sensed a threat and saw the need to act on it. He denounced the two of them sometime in the summer of 1921, called them dangerous traitors and sentenced them to death. It would have included as well Umberto Valenti who struck up a positive relationship with Morello. Dash in *The First Family* suggests that Morello was indeed attempting to re-establish himself in his previous power position. Word apparently reached the potential victims and they chose to flee. After making their way to Newport News, Virginia, Morello and Lupo sailed for Italy. Lupo's parole was revoked in 1936 after the governor of New York made the request of President Roosevelt and he was sent back to prison.

Morello had been in the United States since 1892 and though he was still wanted in Italy on a counterfeiting charge from 1894 he apparently felt safer facing that possibility than trying to avoid a Mafia death sentence. Morello and Lupo arrived in Sicily around October 1921. For six months they remained in hiding in the Palermo area and sought the help of Nicola Gentile. Gentile's power spread throughout the U.S. as well as in Sicily. He was the underworld king in Pittsburgh as a result of his subduing the Camorra in that city. Though violent, as when he killed his own boss in order to take over as Mafia head in the city, Gentile was also noted as a negotiator, and it appears that this was the skill he utilized to solve the Morello-D'Aquila conflict.

The compromise that Gentile arranged had Morello renounce claims to leadership in the family, and to acknowledge D'Aquila as boss. With the death sentences revoked, the three—Morello, Lupo and Valenti—returned to the United States. Prohibition and the Volstead Act of 1919 increased the competitive fire of the gang wars in the city as there was now a new source of revenue that gave them reason for killing each other. Proceeds from prohibition dwarfed anything that the mobsters had seen before. Government accountants calculated that Al Capone, the notorious boss of the prohibition era, profited anywhere from $60–$100 million dollars a year. Morello's release from prison came in 1928 and two years later he was murdered.

Disputes between the gangs became an everyday occurrence. On May 8, 1922, Vincenzo Terranova was standing outside of an ice cream parlor on East 116th Street when a car pulled up alongside him. Two men fired from inside the vehicle with sawed-off shotguns hitting Terranova in the right shoulder, back and lungs, killing the 36-year-old. Another Morello family loss was Vincenzo Salemi, the husband of Lucia Terranova. Salemi was hit four times by bullets fired from a passing car on East 108th Street early in 1923. D'Aquila had his day on October 10, 1928, when he was gunned down in Brooklyn. A suspect was Joe Masseria, an up-and-comer who murdered Salvatore Mauro on December 29, 1920. Mauro was a bootlegger who worked with Umberto Valenti. Valenti retaliated by killing a Masseria ally, Vincent Terranova, on May 8, 1922. The very same day Masseria went after Valenti but missed and killed an associate, Silva Tagliagamba. Arrested not far from the shooting scene, Masseria was charged with the killing but never faced a trial. Valenti made two subsequent attempts at Massaria on August 4 and again on August 11, the second of which left Valenti dead. Joe the Boss wound up with two bullet holes in his hat and a reputation for being a hard man to kill.

Masseria was born in Sicily about 40 miles from Palermo, arriving in the United States in 1901. His criminal record began in 1907 with a conviction for burglary. He followed that up with a four-and-a-half-year stretch at Sing Sing for attempted robbery. His rise to influence began to accelerate after that and it resulted in his position second only to D'Aquila in power in New York. As the Italian Squad went out of existence in 1922 the criminal element was absorbed in the bootleg trade and continued that way through the 1920s. "Organized crime exists, in large part, to supply forbidden goods and services. Whenever anything is banned or rationed, criminals immediately fill the void."[8] Gambling, prostitution and extortion were the chief moneymakers to the underworld for years and then came Prohibition, a boon to the criminal element. The strength of the FBI was not fully formulated until the mid-thirties when they achieved full effectiveness.

Ciro Terranova remained a force through the twenties as did Toto D'Aquila; the latter maintained a secretive profile and he remained virtually unknown to the police through these years. He had never been convicted of a crime and came to local prominence only after Joe Masseria made the decision to remove D'Aquila in order to promote his own rise to future power. The killing of D'Aquila took place on October 10, 1928, after 18 years of being boss of bosses. He was ambushed on 13th Street after keeping a doctor appointment. D'Aquila was shot nine times by three assassins as he stood stranded by a car engine that had been tampered. Hit from point-blank range he died almost instantly. He had been so cloaked in anonymity that his murder was reported on page 20 of the *New York Times* where he was described as a "cheese importer." The lone witness was the owner of a nearby drugstore who described the scene in detail to the police upon their arrival. The next day, however, he completely changed his story, had seen nothing, and had nothing to say. This was the clue that indicated to authorities that the victim was someone more than a mere "cheese importer."

That left his presumed killer, Joe Masseria, as the last of the Mafia kingpins of the era. Joe the boss carried power to the extreme, attempting to harbor more of it than any of his predecessors. He reached out to Mafia families in Chicago and Detroit, something the New York Mafia had not done before. Opposition to Masseria led to the so-called "Castellammarese War." The term refers to the Brooklyn Mafioso from the port in Sicily, Castellammare del Golfo. The bloody power struggle lasted from

February 1930 to April 15, 1931. In opposition to Joe Masseria was Salvatore Maranzano, sent into battle to seize control of Mafia operations in the U.S. by the notorious Don Vito Cassioferro from his base in Sicily. Beneath the surface was the festering conflict between the old-line Sicilian Mafioso called the "Mustache Petes" for their old-world ways. One of their ways was refusing to do business with non–Italians, and the "Young Turks," a more "modern" approach which included a willingness to work with non–Italians.

Although the bad blood began festering as early as 1928, it was in February 1930 that the trees in the forest began being felled. In that month Masseria ordered the death of Gaspar Milazzo, a Castellammarese native who was president of the Detroit chapter of Unione Siciliana, reportedly because of a lack of support in a dispute. The same month his order was to eliminate an ally, Gaetano Reina. The supposed motive was to protect several secret allies. It backfired as the Reina family turned its support to Maranzano. On August 15 a key Masseria enforcer was killed at the Morello East Harlem office. Two weeks later the Masseria group killed Joseph Pinzolo, whom Masseria had appointed to take over the ice-distribution racket. Masseria ordered another Unione Siciliana hit in Chicago, Joe Aiello.

On November 5 a key member of Masseria's gang, Steve Ferrigno, was murdered. The tide was turning in Maranzano's favor and members of Masseria's gang were defecting. His allies made a deal with Maranzano—if Maranzano would end the war, they would betray Masseria. On April 15, 1931, while eating at the Nuova Villa Tammaro, a restaurant in Coney Island, Masseria was killed. This was the incident in which Ciro Terranova drove the getaway car but was too shaken up and had to be replaced behind the wheel. The Castellammarese war had ended.

Maranzano and his group were winners. The newly crowned total boss proposed to form the Five Families of New York, each as an autonomous entity with boss, underboss, capos, soldiers and associates. All but associates were to be full-blooded Italian Americans. Each would be beholden to Maranzano. Other cities were limited to one family per city with Maranzano declaring himself—*capo di tutti capi*—"boss of all bosses." Maranzano stood on top of the heap for barely five months. On September 10, 1931, he was shot and stabbed to death in his Manhattan office. The Young Turks assumed control over all criminal activities in New York City. There were additional changes made in the Mafia structure but in the end the real winners, the Young Turks, entered a new era of power and organization.

Our story officially ended in 1922 with the final disbanding of the Italian Squad, but the overlap of characters from year to year took us to the Castellammarese War. The principals who were in power before the outbreak of violence associated with it began to lose their lives—and their powers—after leaving the more modern group of mobsters familiar to the public from the 1930s on. Names like Luciano, Castellano, Capone, Anastasia, among them. All of them functioned after the disposal of the Black Hand had been complete and the Italian Squad had been permanently disbanded. They belong to another era, another story.

Chapter Twelve

The Italian Squad: Redux

The time was now passed. It was an era, an epoch, a period in history, one like any other. There was good and bad, rich and poor, joy and heartache, and people lived and died. The Italian Squad had its place and served a useful, positive role in the story of the NYPD and the history of the city of New York. Following the death of Lt. Detective Joseph Petrosino in March of 1909 the Italian Squad continued to function under Petrosino's friend and trusted lieutenant, Antonio Vachris. Vachris (Vacarezza) was the supervisor of the Italian Squad's Brooklyn division. It was in October 1907 that an announcement was made by Acting Captain Kuhne, the man in charge of the local detective service and of the formation of a new Italian Squad for Brooklyn and Queens. This decision was brought about because of the fine work done in the Ravenswood case just concluded by detectives Vachris, Mealli, Simonetti, Crowley and Ross. They arrested three Black Hand operators and caught them with the money they had just extorted.

When Captain Kuhne went to Manhattan the day after the arrests were made he suggested to Deputy Commissioner Woods that he thought it would be a good thing to have such a squad exclusively in Brooklyn. He was given authorization to go ahead with arrangements and a day later the squad was organized. Antonio Vachris was put in charge of the squad, for he was "active, fearless and energetic, and he has brains as well."[1] The Italian detectives who were assigned to the Brooklyn end of the department were first-grade detectives John Crowley, Paulo Simonetti and Michael Mealli. Other detectives of the central bureau were also placed on the new squad. They were Luigi Rossi (who called himself Ross), Salvatore Santoro, Francisco J. Lisante and James Peirano. The only non–Italian on the new squad was Crowley. He was Irish but he spoke and wrote the Italian language fluently.

The stated purpose of having such a squad is the same as when the original squad was formed in 1904: to have some organized system in handling Italian cases. Acting Captain Kuhne recognized that not speaking the language was a hindrance to his getting a hold on what amounted to dozens of Italian cases that came across his desk each month. Kuhne further noted that he was surprised when he first came to Brooklyn to find that there were so many Black Hand cases there. He noted also how often victims were afraid to speak out against their tormentors due to threats of arson, bombings and death. All of these circumstances were anticipated by Petrosino when he urged the department to set up the original Italian Squad.

According to Acting Captain Kuhne, the new squad would begin work "with a rogues gallery all to itself—a gallery of the criminal records and the pictures of Italian lawbreakers, confidence men, extortionists and kidnappers."[2] The new squad was organized on October 22, 1907, and went right to work. It was written on March 8, 1908, that the new Brooklyn squad since its formation had made "many arrests and secured more convictions than Petrosino has across the river, and has been a potent organization for the conservation of law and order among the Italians ever since."[3] Among the members of the new force were Paolo Simonetti and Giacomo Pierano, born in New York but whose parentage was from Liguria. There were Michael Mealli; Luigi Rossa from Salerno; Carlo Corrao, a Sicilian; and Salvatore Santoro who comes from Calabria. There was one Irishman, John R. Crowley, a six-footer from Cork who used to patrol the Hamilton Avenue district. He developed a likening for the Italians and learned their language and went to school to learn about them. He was one of the most fluent of men on the Italian force and was regarded by Vachris as one of his most dependable men.

Less than two years after the formation of the Brooklyn Squad under Vachris, Petrosino was shot and killed in Palermo, Sicily, and Vachris took over as head of the Manhattan squad. Antonio's parents were Italian but he was born in France in 1867. His family came to the United States when the boy was just three and settled in Brooklyn, New York, at 636 39th Street. At age 18 he married a woman named Raffela, who was slightly older, and the couple had a son, Charles, born in 1884. Vachris was naturalized as an American citizen in 1888. Vachris was described as a bull-necked, hard-knuckled man who did not know what fear was. He was threatened time and again over his career, but laughed off all of them.

Vachris would have come to the attention of the New York press for the first time when he was a 29-year-old detective with the Brooklyn police as he attempted to enforce a public decency law. It was a violation of section 675 of the penal code that Vachris enforced when, in July 1896, he arrested two "adult" entertainers in Coney Island. They were Adjie Costello of the *Streets of Cairo* show and Dora Denton of Bostock's Algerian Theater on Surf Avenue. Both were charged with performing a vulgar display known as the "coochie-coochie" dance. The dance, also known as the danse du ventre (belly dance) and the hootchy-kootchy, became a sensation when it was performed at Middle Eastern–themed exhibits of the 1893 Columbian Exposition in Chicago. It made its first Coney Island appearance at the Streets of Cairo two years later.

It was in December 1893 that "Clubber" Williams halted performances of the show at the Grand Central Palace at Lexington and 43rd Street in Manhattan. He first sat with a full house for three or four dancers before he stepped up on stage and ordered the show stopped. Following Vachris's action, another officer went out to Coney and arrested Fatima Slema, May Asher and Lou Mattin, dancers at Tilyou's Walk on West 16th Street. All five appeared before Judge John Lott Nostrand in the Coney Island police court on the morning of July 21, 1896. The charge against the latter three was dismissed since the arresting officer's statement did not agree with the written complaint. However, the attorney for Costello and Denton demanded trials by jury so that jurors might be able to see what the dance looked like.

The case against Costello, whom the newspapers referred to as a vivacious young Mexican, finally came to trial on August 7. Vachris was the first witness and when asked to describe the immoral movements, he found it hard to put into words. The judge asked him if could do the dance. When Vachris answered in the affirmative the Judge Nostrand instructed, "Well, then, you better show it to the jury."[4] Vachris stepped down from the witness chair, walked to the front of the jury box and proceeded to deliver his rendition of the coochie-coochie. The *New York Times* poked fun at the detective the following day. "Daintily clutching the skirts of his uniform coat, he began the first lazy movements of the dance. Backward he bent and forward. Now he stood on one foot, and now a mighty policeman's boot went toward the ceiling. Now he swayed to the right, now to the left, and in a trice he was almost on the floor, wriggling and twisting until he was red in the face."[5]

Upon completion of his demonstration the courtroom burst into applause. Though the jurors enjoyed Vachris' performance it took the all-male jury half a minute to issue a verdict of not guilty. Judge Nostrand, in dismissing the jury said, "If it had been left to me, I would have convicted the girl. I saw the dance myself, and I know that it is an immoral dance."[6]

In 1900 Vachris was promoted to sergeant. While facing the same anti–Italian prejudice that Petrosino was subjected to, in addition there was the system of political patronage that was in favor at the time. Republicans were largely in control and Vachris was a Democrat. He brought Police Commissioner John N. Partridge to court. Vachris argued that he had been doing detective sergeant work for years without the benefit of the appropriate title and pay. The court ruled in his favor. Shortly after the commissioner decided to reduce about a dozen detectives who had been drawing $2,000 a year in salary in the rank of detective sergeant to patrolmen. The maximum patrolman's salary was $1,400. It was specifically noted that "Antonio Vachris, the Italian, who is considered a very active person and who is now engaged in an endeavor to clarify the Catania mystery, would not be disturbed."[7]

Vachris spoke and understood several dialects of the Italian and Sicilian languages which, of course, made him a valuable member of the Italian force. He was assigned the case of the murder of Giuseppe Catania, a 40-year-old immigrant grocer. On July 23, 1902, some boys swimming at a cove off Bay Ridge found a body in a potato sack on the shore. His throat had been cut and his body was folded in half and stuffed in the sack. At first sight the mystery surrounding the killing was made deeper because there seemed to be no motive for the crime. He was thought to be a man with no enemies and not having done any wrongs to any persons who would react in this violent fashion. Investigation revealed that Catania had a business meeting with Ignazio Lupo, well-known to the police as a gang leader associated with the Morello gang.

The detectives further learned that Catania had recently been engaged in a dispute with a customer who owed him money. This man was identified as Vincenzo Trica. The debt that initiated the argument amounted to $14. Trica was taken into custody but detectives were unable to uncover any clues that would link him to the murder. The police came to believe that the crime was committed in another part of Brooklyn and dumped at the location that it was found, but once again their investigation could not corroborate any part of this story. They learned further that Catania had also betrayed two gangsters in Palermo, Sicily, before coming to America. There were four men who lived in the rear of Catania's store and police were only able to talk to two of them. The other two had disappeared.

New speculations arose, even among the Catania family, the idea that possibly this was an act of vendetta. Catania's son-in-law Dominigo Tutrone seemed to seriously consider this hypothesis. After his assurance that he had never known anyone to speak harshly of his father-in-law he reiterated the vengeance scenario. "There is something behind this. Vengeance, I believe. It's the kind of crime that would have been committed by a vendetta, and you know the Sicilians. They do not forget an injury."[8]

The importer that Catania had met with earlier in the day, Ignazio Lupo, was cause for suspicion but the police had no clues to involve him. The case was not solved but William Flynn, the Secret Service chief, had followed the case closely. The following year while investigating the barrel murder case in which Lupo was a suspect, Flynn urged that Lupo be charged with the Catania murder as well as the barrel victim. There had been a kidnapping of a young boy, Antonio Mannino, in 1904 (described earlier). A year later six-year-old Antonio Mareamiena was kidnapped. The Mannino and Mareamiena families were related. Vachris was on the case and noticed a common element between the two kidnappings. He remembered following a suspect in the Mannino case, named Vito Laduca. This same man visited the Mareamiena home after the kidnapping and offered to broker the safe return of the child.

He was arrested on September 30, 1905. The Mareamiena boy was returned to his family. The two families would provide no cooperation and there was no evidence to tie Laduca to the kidnappings without the testimony of the families. Laduca had been born in Carini, Sicily, and was an extortionist Black Hander in New York. He returned apparently with a pocketful of money to Carini in 1907, where he was shot and killed a year later.

Following the assassination of Joe Petrosino, Vachris thought he knew where at least some of the responsibility lied. Almost as soon as he heard the news he got three other detectives and rushed over to a Brooklyn saloon run by Erasmo Rubino. They arrested Rubino and his bartender Giuseppe Arturi for violation of the Sunday excise law. From there they went to 195 Johnson Avenue in time to see four men running from the house. Vachris chased one man across the backyard and grabbed Tassano Castranovi as he tried to scale a fence and beat him into submission. The other three surrendered without a fight. Armando Pietro, Vito Adragna, and Vito Vela along with Castranovi were held for having "knowledge of the recent assassination of a detective of worldwide repute." Officially the charge was being undesirable aliens and suspicious characters. Nothing, however, resulted from the arrests.

Soon after Vachris made the trip to Italy to collect Petrosino's records. While he was away Commissioner Bingham got himself in trouble. He created animosity with the Tammany Hall Democrats with his efforts to create a privately funded law enforcement agency that would answer only to him. The board of aldermen brought him up on charges and accused him of releasing information that led to the assassination of Petrosino through his telling the press about Petrosino going to Italy. Mayor George B. McClellan, Jr., relieved Bingham of his position and named William F. Baker in his place. The results of Vachris's mission produced 742 certificates of criminal activity by deportable aliens in the United States. Baker, however, made the entire mission moot when he ignored the criminal records that Vachris brought back. Four years went by and two more commissioner changes before the certificates would resurface. By then the three-year statutory limit that was put into the Immigration Act in 1907 had expired. Politics had outlasted common sense and justice.

During this period the effectiveness of the Italian Squad deteriorated with the influence of Tammany Hall. Detectives were assigned to other bureaus and generally assigned to areas within Italian colonies that had crimes similar to what they had been experiencing in the Squad. Vachris continued to work on such crimes as kidnapping, often in conjunction with Secret Service Agent William Flynn, who had taken leave from the service in order to temporarily take over the position of second deputy police commissioner. Vachris had lost his first wife in 1915 and remarried twice, in 1917 and again in 1921. He retired from the police force in 1919 and opened a private detective agency. Having lived in Brooklyn all his life, he moved to River Edge, New Jersey, to a community that had no police force of its own. He went about building one. When the community established a police department on October 6, 1930, Vachris served as its first police chief, which he held until his final retirement in 1933. On January 6, 1944, Antonio Vachris died at Hackensack hospital. He was 76 years old.

An era came to an end in 1915 but did not altogether disappear, as new names rose in the underworld of New York City. One was gambler Arnold Rothstein, known for his part in the fixing of the 1919 World Series when eight Chicago White Sox players were paid to throw the series. Facts ultimately indicated that Rothstein's role was to put up the money and remain on the sidelines, getting richer by betting on the underdog Cincinnati Reds. Another gambler to make his name known was an associate of Rothstein's, Nicky Arnstein, husband of Ziegfeld Follies star Fanny Brice. There was a redux of sorts beginning in 1917 under the leadership of Detective Michael Fiaschetti. Police Commissioner Arthur Woods officially re-formed the squad and named Fiaschetti as commander.

Born in Morolo, Italy, on January 8, 1882, Fiaschetti migrated with his parents to the United States and was raised in North Adams, Massachusetts. He joined the New York Police Department in 1904 when he was 22 years old. He was one of the early choices of Joseph Petrosino who was asked to join the fledgling Italian Squad. Following Petrosino's death in 1909 the squad remained active as a unit but in a more limited capacity. Their attention was directed to specific Black Hand crimes that involved bombings or extortions. Thus the work of the squad in the high-profile Enrico Caruso extortion case in 1910. Following the disbanding of the squad in 1915 detectives were assigned to other units but were kept within the scope of the crimes that they were most familiar with. Detectives like Mealli and Cavone, for example, worked with the sixth detective bureau.

Fiaschetti was the son of an Italian bandleader and was raised in a musical environment in North Adams. As a child, music appeared to be his destiny but as a 14-year-old in 1900 he saw an ad offering a $500 reward for information concerning an Italian fugitive. He asked questions and learned that the man was hiding in a small town in Vermont. He turned the information over to authorities and collected the reward. That defining moment put him on track for a future career as a detective. He moved to New York when he was 16, and at 18 began working as an informant for Joe Petrosino and the Italian Squad. Though not formally a member of the police force, he formed a close bond with the detective. He became a husband and father in the next few years but his wife died in 1907. A widower, he fell into depression. Petrosino convinced him to devote himself to police work as a stimulant to combat his depression.

Though a large and powerfully built man, Fiaschetti's approach to police work was not completely physical. "Psychology will catch more crooks than a mile of rubber hose," he wrote.[9] But with the gang killings and wars through the mid-teens and a rash of Black Hand bombings the new police commissioner, Richard Enright—the first time a career cop would hold that job—determined that the squad could once again provide a valuable aide to the Italian community. So in 1918 the Italian force was reestablished, with Detective Sergeant and now Acting Captain Fiaschetti put in charge. Ultimately, Enright expanded the squad to 150 men.

With the spread of Black Hand activities over the years to other American cities so, too, did the cooperation between police forces. A large and effective organized crime operation was established in Akron, Ohio. When Rosario Giuseppe Borgio arrived there in 1900 he opened a general-goods store with criminal operations in the two backrooms. He lived above the store amid an arsenal including shotguns, rifles, pistols, and submachine guns. Early in the second decade of the 20th century Borgio had control of the Black Hand operation that was aimed primarily at the growing Italian immigrant community. He enjoyed political protection for his gambling and prostitution rackets as well. For the most part Akron's police force remained honest, so that by early 1918 the Akron police began conducting raids on Borgio's gambling dens and brothels.

The vicious gangster decided to fight back by putting a $250 bounty on all of the city's police officers. Within a matter of days beginning on December 26, 1918, four officers were killed while on patrol. The first, Patrolman Robert Norris, was ambushed and killed, being shot several times in the back. Edward Costigan, Joe Hunt, and Gethin Richards were shot and killed a few days later. Akron police were baffled by the crimes since there seemed to be no facts to connect them nor any motive. They occurred in different sections of the city ruling out local gangs. Then Chief of Detectives Harry Welsh received an anonymous call from a woman who claimed one of the men responsible for the murders had gone to New York and could be identified by a scar on his hand.

Enter Lt. Michael "Big Mike" Fiaschetti. The Akron police contacted the NYPD looking for assistance in the case. It came to the desk of Lt. Fiaschetti and the Italian Squad went into action. The usual procedure was to contact informants and conduct surveillance of known criminals and their hangouts. The squad had a good deal of knowledge in these areas culled over the years and were aware of the ins and outs of the Italian community. A break came when Fiaschetti received a tip from an informant in January 1919 that a man fitting the description of one of the informants was seen at a pool hall. At the pool hall the following night he found the suspect, Tony Manfredi and another man, Pasquale Biondo. When he saw the scar on Manfredi's hand, Fiaschetti arrested the two of them.

An extradition order to return the two mobsters to Akron had Fiaschetti escorting them by train to Ohio. He sat in the lounge car with Manfredi and decided to take a stab at questioning him. After a few drinks Manfredi began to believe the detective's logic when he said that he would be killed to prevent his testifying at the trial. He admitted his and Biondo's guilt, and he also gave Fiaschetti information on Borgio's police bounty and other details of the organization. Both were convicted along with Borgio. Manfredi, because of his testimony, got 20 years' imprisonment. Borgio was convicted along with two of his lieutenants, Pasquale Biondo and his brother Lorenzo Biondo, of the Akron police murders. Borgio was sentenced to the electric chair and was executed on May 22, 1919. Lorenzo Biondo was sentenced to a life term in Ohio State Penitentiary. He was paroled by Governor George White on May 25, 1934, and fled to Italy.

However, with the Petrosino assassination in mind, Fiaschetti was assigned a partner, Irving O'Hara, who also served as bodyguard to the new commissioner in order to protect him from the fate that befell his predecessor. In 1921 Fiaschetti did as Petrosino had done and traveled to Italy in pursuit of a Camorra fugitive, a murder suspect named James Papaccio, for the death of John Pepi on March 7. While there, he also attempted to retrieve information on those suspected of being responsible for the death of Petrosino. He sailed to France aboard the *Rochambeau* then went by train to Rome. The Italian government assigned detectives to follow him in an effort to avert any replay of the previous incident but Fiaschetti, using the alias Don Pasquale, went undercover. In the guise of a thief looking to leave Italy, Fiaschetti got to know a Camorra member in Rome known as Don Gennaro. This relationship led to the Naples headquarters of Don Franco, whose business it was to smuggle Italian criminals to the United States.

It was through these contacts that Fiaschetti located his prey, Papaccio, and the Italian police apprehended him. Fiaschetti was responsible for leading the police to several other wanted men. Soon Don Franco became aware that an American detective was in Italy trying to infiltrate the Camorra. As they attempted to secure a description of the detective Fiaschetti decided it was time to head back home.

Back on the job in New York Fiaschetti was assigned a case of kidnapping. Black Handers had abducted a five-year-old boy, Giuseppe Verotta, from his home at 353 East 13th Street in Manhattan in May, and demanded a ransom of $2,500. The Verotta family was unable to pay such an amount and they turned the case over to the Italian Squad. A policewoman posed as a Verotta cousin and stayed inside the home to observe anyone who came to the door. After two weeks the police apprehended five men who surfaced as they bargained for a lesser ransom figure. Fiaschetti modestly explained how the arrest was made. "There wasn't any trouble," Fiaschetti recalled, "everything was nice and peaceful, guns poked in ribs, and a whack or two on the heads with batons, and we had our five prisoners."[10] Fiaschetti released a sixth suspect—who struck him as a clean-cut boy—who had accompanied the other five.

Salvatore Verotta, the boy's father, received an anonymous letter that read, "If you appear before the Grand Jury, you boy will be found in the river, and we will get that big Fiaschetti besides."[11] Eight days after the arrests, on June 11, the body of a dead boy was found on a Hudson River sandbar near Piermont, New York. The father, Salvatore, had to go through the agony of first identifying the boy's clothes and then the next morning viewing the mutilated body. The letter was described by the newspapers as "another startling feature of the boldness and cruelty of this gang of kidnappers and murderers who held the lad in bondage and terrorized the Verotta family with ransom demands and threats of violence."[12]

"Mrs. Verotta was in her home kneeling in prayer for the safe return of her son when news of the finding of the boy's body reached Police Headquarters."[13] Authorities believed the boy had been strangled two weeks before. Fiaschetti was angered when he learned that the killing took place while they were still negotiating a ransom. The detective was completely outraged when he learned from an informant that the murderer was the "clean-cut boy" he'd let go free. He went to the Tombs and got himself a broken baseball bat and confronted the five. "Yes, they told me everything they knew. In addition, they squealed on two other members of the kidnapping gang who were not among the five."[14] The other two were arrested and all seven were convicted and sentenced to the electric chair, although later the sentences were commuted to life imprisonment.

Michael Mealli and family. Daughters Annamarie (left) and Teresa (right) and wife Anna (courtesy Michael Romersa).

While still with the Italian Squad, Detective Sergeant Fiaschetti continued his work, highlighted by solving another major crime. He solved the murder of Camillo Caiozzo in the summer of 1921. Dubbed the "Good Killers" case, it was linked to a gang war between the Bonventre-Magaddino clan, known as the Good Killers, and the Boccellato clan that had committed dozens of murders in New York, New Jersey and Detroit, Michigan. Oddly, the Italian Squad began to fall out of favor at about this time. Tammany Hall politicians relied upon the immigrant vote, and often the underworld leaders who provided much of that support at times tried to curb police actions against what amounted to their constituents. Also the practice of beating confessions out of suspects and such strong-armed tactics that the police had used up to now was beginning to be frowned upon by many in law enforcement. The concept of the existence of an Italian Squad as prejudicial against Italian immigrants was taking hold. By its existence it seemed to imply that Italians were more prone to crime than other groups.

Fiaschetti was prone to violent outbursts and arrogance, which did not bode well for him in this newest climate. In one instance he was questioning a woman who was believed to be conspiring with a Black Hand extortionist against her husband. The husband happened to be an Italian American lawyer connected with Tammany Hall who tried to force his way into Fiaschetti's office during the interrogation. They got into an argument and the detective literally "kicked him out the door." Manhandling a local politician did not go well for Fiaschetti. The politician brought a formal complaint against him to the commissioner's office. It was announced by the press on August 26, 1922, that Detective Sgt. Michael Fiaschetti was demoted to the rank of patrolman by Police Commissioner Richard E. Enright. He was assigned to the Herbert Street station. The demotion carried a salary reduction from $3,300 a year to $2,280. As a further insult the Italian Squad was disbanded at the same time. While Fiaschetti declined to comment on the demotion, his friends were outspoken.

In their resentment of the commissioner's action, they "pointed out that the detective had solved some of the most important crimes which have confronted the department in recent years."[15] Fiaschetti had been decorated by foreign governments and by police departments in American cities. The city of Akron, Ohio, had awarded him two medals for his work in rounding up the murderers of four Akron policemen. Along with Fiaschetti's demotion, Commissioner Enright also disbanded the Italian Squad. All members were assigned to the bomb squad.

In an effort to avoid walking a beat, Fiaschetti used his influence to finagle a position in the district attorney's homicide bureau. But two years later he retired from the police force. He opened a private detective agency with an office at 401 Broadway and married his second wife, Jean Melillo. Fiaschetti was reasonably successful in this endeavor, but nevertheless did not hesitate when, in the early '30s Mayor Fiorello La Guardia appointed him as deputy commissioner of the department of markets in order that he might take part in the investigations of racketeering in New York's produce industry. In 1928 he wrote a book in Italy about his experiences in the Italian Squad called *The Man They Couldn't Escape*. It was released in the United States two years later under the title *You Gotta Be Rough: The Adventures of Detective Fiaschetti of the Italian Squad.*

But his time had passed. The federal Wickersham Commission in 1931 had condemned the third-degree tactics of the law enforcement agencies and even singled out Fiaschetti, quoting a passage from his book regarding the broken baseball bat story. His only child, Anna, died on November 15, 1936, after a long illness. She was just 25 years old. In 1938 he returned to private detective work, his agency, the International Detective Bureau, had an office at 401 Broadway and delivered lectures around the country. He spent time in the Army Reserves. Michael Fiaschetti died in the Brooklyn Veterans Administration Hospital on July 26, 1960. He was 78 years old.

There were other periods in NYPD history when special units were set up specifically to combat specific types of crime utilizing the methods of the old Italian Squad. Frank Gisondi was a sergeant in the '60s and the first officer to start a street crimes unit in the NYPD. Working out of Randall's Island officers assigned to this unit worked undercover in plain clothes, blending in with the populace much as the Italian Squad did. A perk of his job was the opportunity to work with actors Sylvester Stallone and Billy Dee Williams on the film *Nighthawks*. Sergeant Gisondi was a police officer for 30 years beginning in 1956. He passed away in 2004.

In 1978 a wave of mob hits induced the NYPD to create the Organized Crime Task Force, which was similar in nature to the old Italian Squad in that the concentration of the special unit was directed at organized crime in the city of New York. At the head of the task force was an uncommonly Joe Petrosino clone. Detective Joseph Coffey was called "one of the greatest detectives the NYPD ever had."[16] Dan Ingellis, a personal friend of this book's author and a photographer whose work has contributed to this volume, was a member of the NYPD in the 1970s. As a detective serving in the Staten Island district attorney's office, Ingellis's commanding officer was Lieutenant Jack Ferguson. It was through Lt. Ferguson that Ingellis met Joe Coffey. "He was one of the greatest experts on organized crime in New York City," Ingellis said. "A determined, efficient, investigator whose persistence paid off time and again with the successful conclusions to his department's probes into criminal activities."

His cases were legendary; the hunt for the Son of Sam serial killer, the Lufthansa heist at JFK Airport, the FALN terrorist bombing at Fraunces Tavern and the repeated arresting of crime boss John Gotti, among them. He arrested mob boss Paul Castellano in 1984.

Possessed of the instincts that were also instinctive traits of Joseph Petrosino and Michael Mealli, Coffey once surmised that a projected trip to Munich by Rizzo had mob implications while listening to a wiretap conversation of Vincent Rizzo, a Genovese family soldier. He got permission to follow Rizzo and ultimately uncovered an international scandal involving a corrupt Vatican banker.

Both Joseph Petrosino and Enrico Caruso died untimely deaths at the same age—48. Petrosino was killed in Palermo, Sicily, and Caruso died in Naples, Italy. Petrosino's legacy is written in stone in the history of New York City and the New York Police Department.

Patrolmen Andrew (left) and Paul Mele, sons of Detective Andrew Mealli (Catherine Ferri).

On December 11, 1920, Enrico Caruso performed *L'elisir d'amore* at the Brooklyn Academy of Music. It was during this performance that the tenor began hemorrhaging blood from the throat. A doctor was called and the rest of the performance canceled. Caruso insisted on singing *La forza del destino* two days later and then on the 16th, *Samson et Dalila*. Both programs were splendid. He prepared for a Christmas Eve performance of *La Juive*. His wife, Dorothy, tried to persuade him to cancel and rest. His comment was, "It's Christmas Eve, Doro. People want to be happy. Unless I am dead, they will hear me sing!"[17]

A shot of morphine was administered for the pain. Although a battery of doctors disagreed on the diagnosis, Dr. Erdmann considered surgery a matter of life and death, so he performed the operation on December 29. The news release called the condition suppurative pleurisy and announced that the operation was a success. Over the next few months Caruso's condition fluctuated and the New York papers carried almost daily updates. That spring Caruso left for Naples to rest for the summer. His attitude was positive. As he stood at the ship's railing he called out, "Goodbye America, my second home. I will be with you again soon, and will sing, and sing, and sing."[18] The Great Caruso never sang another note. He died at 9:07 on the morning of August 2, 1921, in Naples, Italy.

Andrew Mealli remained an active member of the NYPD until his death on July 7, 1936. He died at home at 1430 35th Street in Brooklyn at 10:45 a.m. of endocarditis, an infection of a heart valve that usually comes from bacteria spreading into the bloodstream from another part of the body, such as the mouth. We had been told in the family that he could have been cured with penicillin, which was not available to the general public until after World War II, but this seemed to be a bit of an exaggeration. However, it was confirmed to me by Staten Island cardiologist Dr. Thomas Vazzana that the family was indeed correct in saying that had antibiotics been available, he would in all probability have survived.

At the time of his death Mealli was a detective lieutenant assigned to the 18th division, 13th detective district out of the 88th precinct in Brooklyn since July 3, 1929. He was 51 when he died. Andrew and Maria had ten children, eight of which lived to adulthood. Two of Andrew's sons, Paul and Andrew, both had careers of 20 years or more with the NYPD. Paul even wore his dad's shield #4005.

When Michael Mealli joined the police force in 1902, it was in the same class as future Police Commissioner Lewis J. Valentine. Less than four months after he became a patrolman he was promoted to sergeant. While a member of the original Italian Squad, Mealli worked with Detective Joseph Petrosino, who headed the unit initially, and later worked with Lt. Antonio Vachris. Vachris headed up the Brooklyn unit and led the squad for a time after Petrosino's death. Mealli also worked many cases with John J. Sullivan, former deputy police commissioner, who at the time of Mealli's death in 1939 was the director of public safety at the New York World's Fair.

Noted for his work on the extortion case involving opera star Enrico Caruso—at which time he was responsible for directing the activities of the Italian Squad as acting captain—Mealli also was instrumental in the arrest and conviction of the notorious gangster and counterfeiter, Ignazio Lupo, known as "Lupo the Wolf." Mealli was highly respected by his brethren, known as "the man with the album brain." This is a reference to his ability to remember faces as illustrated by an incident in which he arrested a man on sight whose picture he had seen three years before. His obituary noted that "his memory for faces and his familiarity with underworld characters caused him to be greatly feared by criminals."[19]

After the Daniello confession and the trials of 1918 in which Daniello accused Mealli of taking bribe money from the Navy Street gang, Mealli was demoted to patrolman and put back on a beat. There was no suspension, no investigation. He retired shortly after on December 16, 1918. He received his police pension and went into business with his brother Nicolas. The Mealli Marine Detective Agency specialized in the protection of piers and vessels in New York Harbor. Most of the security officers he had working for him were former members of the NYPD. Michael Mealli died of a heart attack in his home at 2040 63rd Street in Brooklyn on July 24, 1939, at 3 a.m. He was 63.[20] His widow, Anna, never remarried. "I married a wonderful man," she told her children. "I married him for life."

Mealli's grandson, Michael Romersa, like the rest of our family, was never inundated with tales of the exploits of family members like Michael and Andrew, but he recalls his mother Teresa's declaration to him when he was a boy. "Your grandfather was a policeman," she told him, "a detective, and a good one!"[21] No mention was ever made by any family members to their children of the incident at the Daniello trial or its aftermath. "It was as if it just never happened," Romersa said.

The respect of his peers was never in doubt. Shortly before he died Mealli received a letter from an acquaintance, a judge of the Supreme Court of the State of New York, Lewis L. Fawcett. Judge Fawcett had presided over the extortion case of Enrico Caruso. The Judge's letter reads in part: "Your record in the Department speaks volumes for your devotion to duty and the deep interest you have ever manifested in the welfare of the public. You were a champion of law and order and rendered most efficient services in the protection of life and property in making the streets and highways and parks safe. You may be justly proud of your innumerable arrests of vicious criminals who were convicted. You were feared by the underworld and admired by honest people and all lovers of good government."

In a letter of response to Judge Fawcett, Mealli brought up the Caruso court case when he wrote: "This reminds me of an incident during the Caruso case when the late, cunning Antonio Cincotta attempted to lead the court to believe that he was suffering from a heart ailment and you took it upon yourself personally to visit the Raymond Street jail and put Mr. Cincotta through some physical exercises ... and then having your own personal physician examine him. That act, in itself, firmly convinced me of your fairness and desire to administer justice as it should be administered—and I have never forgotten the incident."

Giuseppe Morello was paroled from federal prison on February 1, 1920, having served exactly 10 years to the day. The boss of bosses was a Palermo man named Toto D'Aquila, in power since Morello's conviction. Most of the old leaders were dead. Lupo joined Morello in a return to New York representing a presence to D'Aquila. A rising power in the underworld was Umberto Valenti and when the New York Mafia called for the deaths of Morello and Lupo, they included Valenti. Having learned of the pronounced sentence, all three fled the country, leaving from the port of Newport News, Virginia. They were next seen in Sicily arriving in October 1921, where they hid out for six months. They took their troubles to Nicola Gentile, powerful in both the American and Sicilian Mafia. Operating out of Pittsburgh he fought the Camorra leadership, forcing their submission and rendering Gentile the most powerful figure in Pittsburgh's underworld.

He was willing to aid the Morello people. Acting as a negotiator Gentile effected a conciliation between D'Aquila and Morello, Lupo, and Valenti. The trio soon returned to the United States. A new climate existed among the fragile relationships of the families, and it was brought on by one act: prohibition. The Volstead Act of 1919 as the Eighteenth Amendment to the Constitution, prohibited the manufacture, distribution and retail of any alcoholic beverages. A federal agency called the Bureau of Prohibition was created to enforce the laws of prohibition with a unit of 2,000 members. One government official expressed the thought that the number needed for such an undertaking should be closer to half a million. The demand for alcohol was not deterred and the bars in New York

The grandsons: (left to right) author Andrew Mele is grandson of Andrew Mealli; Nickolas Mele is the grandson of Nicolo Mealli and Michael Romersa the grandson of Michael Mealli.

City doubled its numbers of speakeasies that went into operation. New sources of alcohol came from Canada or the Caribbean. The underworld developed bootleggers, smugglers and racketeers who got rich off the illegality of alcoholic beverages. A new and potent enemy of the law had been created and once again, government contributed to the cause. A new and prolific era had begun.

Statistics are often exaggerated or inaccurate, so when it is written that Petrosino's arrest total ran in the thousands and his squad helped to deport 500 criminals and Fiaschetti is credited with 1,000 arrests and having sent 12 to the electric chair, there may be some reason to take these figures with a grain of salt. The truth, however, may not be too far afield. The significance of the squad far exceeds the arrests and prosecutions that were accomplished, whatever the actual number. The immigrants who lived in squalor while trying to establish a new life for their families in a strange country needed to find support and comfort in the authorities that now reigned over their daily existence.

They found it in the men who possessed the courage and the fortitude, the toughness and the cunning, and—perhaps even more important—the ethnic pride to dedicate their lives to the salvation of their fellow countrymen. It was illustrated not just in the persons of Petrosino, Vachris and Fiaschetti, but in the Rocco Cavones, the Paul Simonettis and the Michael Meallis, all of whom put their own lives on the line in order to keep others safe. It was a period in history like any other, with its own heroes and villains, where good faced down evil. But it was also an era of the men of the Italian Squad, heroes of a memorable past.

Chapter Notes

Chapter One

1. Lardner, James and Thomas Reppetto. *NYPD: A City and Its Police.* New York: Henry Holt & Co., 2000.
2. Petacco, Arrigo. *Joe Petrosino.* New York: Macmillan, 1974.
3. Lardner, James and Thomas Reppetto. *NYPD: A City and Its Police.* New York: Henry Holt & Co., 2000.
4. Amfitheatrof, Erik. *The Children of Columbus.* Toronto: Little, Brown and Co., 1973.
5. *Ibid.*
6. Talty, Stephan. *The Black Hand.* New York: Houghton Mifflin Harcourt, 2017.
7. *Ibid.*
8. Tuohy, John William. *Joe Petrosino's War On the Mafia: The Mob Files Series.* Lexington, KY: CreateSpace, 2018.
9. Petacco, Arrigo. *Joe Petrosino.* New York: Macmillan, 1974.
10. Talty, Stephen. *The Black Hand.* New York: Houghton Mifflin Harcourt, 2017.
11. *Ibid.*
12. Petacco, Arrigo. *Joe Petrosino.* New York: Macmillan, 1974.
13. *Ibid.*
14. *Ibid.*
15. Storino, Pascal, Jr. The History of Policing in the City of New York, accessed 2018, http://nypdhistory.com.

Chapter Two

1. Newton, Michael. *The Mafia at Apalachin, 1957.* Jefferson, NC: McFarland & Co., 2012.
2. Petacco, Arrigo. *Joe Petrosino.* New York: MacMillan, 1974.
3. Storino, Pascal, Jr. "The Career of Italian Squad Detective Michael Mealli,"

The History of Policing in the City of New York (website), last modified September 4, 2018, http://nypdhistory.com.
4. Dickie, John. *Cosa Nostra.* New York: St. Martin's Press, 2004.
5. "Another Black Hand Bomb." *Brooklyn Daily Eagle.* December 17, 1906.
6. Lardner, James and Thomas Reppetto. *NYPD: A City and Its Police.* New York: Henry Holt & Co., 2000.
7. "Black Hand Desperado Shot by Banker Pati." *Brooklyn Daily Eagle.* March 8, 1908. Black, Jon—"The Black Hand," last modified 2014, https://www.gangrule.com/gangs/the-black-hand.
8. Petacco, Arrigo. *Joe Petrosino.* New York: MacMillan, 1974.
9. Talty, Stephen. *The Black Hand.* New York: Houghton Mifflin Harcourt, 2017.
10. *Ibid.*
11. Petacco, Arrigo. *Joe Petrosino.* New York: Macmillan, 1974.
12. Gambino, Richard. *Vendetta.* Toronto: Guernica, 1998.
13. *Ibid.*
14. Petacco, Arrigo. *Joe Petrosino.* New York: MacMillan, 1974.
15. "The Grisly Tale of Sicilian Lynchings." *Italian Tribune.* March 28, 2019.
16. *Ibid.*
17. *Ibid.*
18. Gambino, Richard. *Vendetta.* Toronto: Guernica, 1998.

Chapter Three

1. Black, Jon—"The Black Hand," last modified 2014, https://www.gangrule.com/gangs/the-black-hand.
2. Talty, Stephen. *The Black Hand.* New York: Houghton Mifflin Harcourt, 2017.

3. Petacco, Arrigo. *Joe Petrosino*. New York: Macmillan, 1974.
4. Talty, Stephen. *The Black Hand*. New York: Houghton Mifflin Harcourt, 2017.
5. "Sprang from a Coal Bin to Catch Black Hand Men. *Brooklyn Daily Eagle*. November 18, 1907.
6. Petacco, Arrigo. *Joe Petrosino*. New York: MacMillan, 1974.
7. Talty, Stephen. *The Black Hand*. New York: Houghton Mifflin Harcourt, 2017.

Chapter Four

1. *The New York Times*—April 30, 1905
2. Petacco, Arrigo. *Joe Petrosino*. New York: Macmillan, 1974.
3. *Ibid.*
4. Lardner, James and Thomas Reppetto. *NYPD: A City and Its Police*. New York: Henry Holt & Co., 2000.
5. Dash, Mike. *The First Family*. New York: Simon & Schuster, 2009.
6. Talty, Stephen. *The Black Hand*. New York: Houghton Mifflin Harcourt, 2017.
7. *Ibid.*
8. Barzini, Luigi. *The Italians*. New York: Atheneum, 1965.
9. Petacco, Arrigo. *Joe Petrosino*. New York: MacMillan, 1974.
10. *Ibid.*
11. Talty, Stephen. *The Black Hand*. New York: Houghton Mifflin Harcourt, 2017.
12. Dash, Mike. *The First Family*. New York: Simon & Schuster, 2009.
13. Talty, Stephen. *The Black Hand*. New York: Houghton Mifflin Harcourt, 2017.
14. *Ibid.*
15. *Ibid.*

Chapter Five

1. Petacco, Arrigo. *Joe Petrosino*. New York: Macmillan, 1974.
2. Talty, Stephen. *The Black Hand*. New York: Houghton Mifflin Harcourt, 2017.
3. "Italian Detectives Doing Effective Work." *Brooklyn Daily Eagle*. March 8, 1908.
4. Talty, Stephen. *The Black Hand*. New York: Houghton Mifflin Harcourt, 2017.
5. Dash, Mike. *The First Family*. New York: Simon & Schuster, 2009.
6. Talty, Stephen. *The Black Hand*. New York: Houghton Mifflin Harcourt, 2017.
7. *Ibid.*
8. *Ibid.*
9. "New Secret Service to Fight Black Hand." *New York Times*. February 20, 1909.
10. Petacco, Arrigo. *Joe Petrosino*. New York: Macmillan, 1974.
11. *Ibid.*
12. *Ibid.*
13. Talty, Stephen. *The Black Hand*. New York: Houghton Mifflin Harcourt, 2017.
14. *Ibid.*
15. *Ibid.*
16. Dash, Mike. *The First Family*. New York: Simon & Schuster, 2009.
17. *Ibid.*
18. *Ibid.*

Chapter Six

1. Petacco, Arrigo. *Joe Petrosino*. New York: MacMillan, 1974.
2. Dash, Mike. *The First Family*. New York: Simon & Schuster, 2009.
3. Talty, Stephen. *The Black Hand*. New York: Houghton Mifflin Harcourt, 2017.
4. *New York Times*. March 14, 1909.
5. "Petrosino a Terror to Criminal Bands." *New York Times*. March 14, 1909.
6. "Thousands Party at Petrosino's Bier." *New York Times*. April 11, 1909.
7. Talty, Stephen. *The Black Hand*. New York: Houghton Mifflin Harcourt, 2017.
8. *Ibid.*
9. *Ibid.*
10. Petacco, Arrigo. *Joe Petrosino*. New York: MacMillan, 1974.
11. *Ibid.*
12. *Ibid.*
13. *Ibid.*
14. Sauchelli, Dana and Sophia Rosenbaum. "Italian Police Solve 105-Year-Old NYPD Mob Detective's Murder," *New York Post* (website), June 23, 2014, https://nypost.com.
15. Talty, Stephen. *The Black Hand*. New York: Houghton Mifflin Harcourt, 2017.
16. *Ibid.*
17. *Ibid.*
18. *Ibid.*

Chapter Seven

1. "He Was Eager to Go." *New York Times*. March 14, 1909.
2. "Police Believe Lupo Is Dangerous Offender." *Brooklyn Daily Eagle*. January 10, 1910.
3. Dash, Mike. *The First Family*. New York: Simon & Schuster, 2009.
4. "Clue In Chicago to Petrosino Plot." *New York Times*. May 2, 1909.
5. Talty, Stephen. *The Black Hand*. New York: Houghton Mifflin Harcourt, 2017.
6. *Ibid.*
7. *Ibid.*
8. "Petrosino's Slayers Are Known in Italy." *New York Times*. April 4, 1909.
9. Talty, Stephen. *The Black Hand*. New York: Houghton Mifflin Harcourt, 2017.
10. "Why Petrosino's Slayers Will Escape." *New York Times*. May 11, 1909.
11. Talty, Stephen. *The Black Hand*. New York: Houghton Mifflin Harcourt, 2017.
12. Caruso, Enrico, Jr., and Andrew Farkas. *Enrico Caruso: My Father and My Family*. Portland, OR: Amadeus Press, 1990.
13. Talty, Stephen. *The Black Hand*. New York: Houghton Mifflin Harcourt, 2017.
14. "William J. Gaynor," Wikipedia, last modified September 19, 2019, https://en.wikipedia.org/wiki/William_Jay_Gaynor.
15. Caruso, Enrico, Jr., and Andrew Farkas. *Enrico Caruso: My father and My Family*. Portland, OR: Amadeus Press, 1990.

Chapter Eight

1. "Search All Italians at Court Room Door." *Brooklyn Daily Eagle*. May 23, 1907.
2. "Black Hand Suicide Ends Murder Case." *Brooklyn Daily Eagle*. May 24, 1907.
3. "Search All Italians at Court Room Door." *Brooklyn Daily Eagle*. May 23, 1907.
4. "Black Hand Informer Afraid to Leave Jail." *Brooklyn Daily Eagle*. May 25, 1907.
5. "Big Tim." *Brooklyn Daily Eagle*. September 17, 1911.
6. "Superbas Beat the Cubs." *Brooklyn Daily Eagle*. September 17, 1911.
7. "'Ha, Ha,' Caruso's Defi to Black Hand Threats." *Brooklyn Daily Eagle*. March 6, 1910.
8. Dash, Mike. *The First Family*. New York: Simon & Schuster, 2009.

9. "Hold Two in Big Plot Against Caruso's Life." *Brooklyn Daily Eagle*. March 5, 1910.
10. Caruso, Enrico, Jr. *Enrico Caruso: My Father and My Family*. Portland, OR: Amadeus Press, 1990.
11. "'Ha, Ha,' Caruso's Defi to Black Hand Threats." *Brooklyn Daily Eagle*. March 6, 1910.
12. "Two Italians Are Held." *Brooklyn Daily Eagle*. March 11, 1910.
13. "Caruso Pays Up to the Black Hand." *New York Times*. March 26, 1910.
14. *Ibid.*
15. Caruso, Dorothy. *Enrico Caruso: His life and Death*. New York: Simon & Schuster, 1945.
16. "Black Hand Leader Killed by Unknown." *Brooklyn Daily Eagle*. February 16, 1915.
17. Newton, Michael. *The Mafia at Apalachin, 1957*. Jefferson, NC: McFarland & Co., 2012.
18. Teresa Romersa (Michael Mealli's daughter), in discussion with the author, 1992.
19. "Simonetti Given 2 to 5 Years in Sing Sing Prison." *Brooklyn Daily Eagle*. June 20, 1921.
20. Dash, Mike. *The First Family*. New York: Simon & Schuster, 2009.
21. Lardner, James, and Thomas Reppetto. *NYPD: A City and Its Police*. New York: Henry Holt & Co., 2000.

Chapter Nine

1. Talty, Stephen. *The Black Hand*. New York: Houghton Mifflin Harcourt, 2017.
2. *Ibid.*
3. "Get Counterfeiters After Year Chase." *New York Times*. January 11, 1910.
4. "Sailor Robbed and Beaten." *Brooklyn Daily Eagle*. January 17, 1912.
5. "Insist Steward Shot Self." *Brooklyn Daily Eagle*. March 24, 1913.
6. "Locked Up for Assault and Highway Robbery." *Daily Standard Union: Brooklyn*. August 7, 1914.
7. Talty, Stephen. *The Black Hand*. New York: Houghton Mifflin Harcourt, 2017.
8. *Ibid.*
9. "'Happy's' Brother Shot and Is Believed Dying." *Standard Union*. July 22, 1914.
10. *Ibid.*

11. Storino, Pascal, Jr. "The Career of Italian Squad Detective Michael Mealli," The History of Policing in the City of New York, last modified September 4, 2018, http://nypdhistory.com.

12. *Ibid.*

13. "Arrested for Old Murder." *New York Times.* August 23, 1915.

Chapter Ten

1. Nick Mele (grandson of Nicholas Mealli and Michael Mealli), in discussion with the author December 2018.

2. "Double Murder Feud Outgrowth." *Brooklyn Daily Eagle.* September 8, 1916.

3. *Ibid.*

4. Newton, Michael. *The Mafia at Apalachin, 1957.* Jefferson, NC: McFarland & Co., 2012.

5. "Lured to Death in Vendetta Trap." *Daily Standard Union: Brooklyn.* September 8, 1916.

6. Dash, Mike. *The First Family.* New York: Simon & Schuster, 2009.

7. *Ibid.*

Chapter Eleven

1. "Indict Twelve in Murder Conspiracy. New York Times. December 1, 1917.

2. "Gunman Names Detective. *New York Times.* February 16, 1918.

3. Dash, Mike. *The First Family.* New York: Simon & Schuster, 2009.

4. "Says Murder Gang Collected Purse for a Detective." *New York Tribune.* February 16, 1918.

5. Dash, Mike. *The First Family.* New York: Simon & Schuster, 2009.

6. "Michael Mealli: Ex-Police Detective on Italian Squad—Succumbs at 63." *New York Times.* July 25, 1939.

7. Dash, Mike. *The First Family.* New York: Simon & Schuster, 2009.

8. Newton, Michael. *The Mafia at Apalachin, 1957.* Jefferson, NC: McFarland & Co., 2012.

Chapter Twelve

1. "Italian Squad, Now for Local Police Work." *Brooklyn Daily Eagle.* October 25, 1907.

2. *Ibid.*

3. "Italian Detectives Doing Effective Work. *Brooklyn Daily Eagle.* March 8, 1908.

4. "Vachris Danced in Court." *Brooklyn Daily Eagle.* August 8, 1896.

5. Hunt, Thomas. "The American Mafia: Bridges in Little Italy," Mafia History, http://mafiahistory.us.

6. "Vachris Danced in Court." *Brooklyn Daily Eagle.* August 7, 1896.

7. "Brooklyn Detectives Slated for Reduction." *Brooklyn Daily Eagle.* July 30, 1902.

8. "Old Vendetta in Sicily Behind Catania Killing." *Brooklyn Daily Eagle.* July 26, 1902.

9. Fiaschetti, Michael. *You Gotta Be Rough: The Adventures of Detective Fiaschetti of the Italian Squad As Told to Prosper Buranelli.* New York: Doubleday, 1930.

10. *Ibid.*

11. "Find Body in River Garbed in Clothes Verotta Boy Wore." *New York Times.* June 12, 1921.

12. "Body of Kidnapped Verotta Boy Is Taken from River." *Brooklyn Daily Eagle.* June 12, 1921.

13. Fiaschetti, Michael. *You Gotta Be Rough: The Adventures of Detective Fiaschetti of the Italian Squad As Told to Prosper Buranelli.* New York: Doubleday, 1930.

14. "Fiaschetti, Demoted, Is on Vacation; Deny He Quit Police Dept." *Brooklyn Daily Eagle.* August 26, 1922.

15. *Ibid.*

16. "Messing, Philip—Legendary NYPD Detective Dies at 77." *New York Post.* September 30, 2015.

17. Caruso, Enrico, Jr., and Andrew Farkas. *Enrico Caruso: My Father and My Family.* Portland, OR: Amadeus Press, 1990.

18. Caruso, Enrico, Jr., and Andrew Farkas. *Enrico Caruso: My Father and My Family.* Portland, OR: Amadeus Press, 1990.

19. "Michael Mealli, Detective, Dies." *Brooklyn Daily Eagle.* July 25, 1939.

20. *Ibid.*

21. Michael Romersa (Michael Mealli's grandson), in discussion with the author, March 1, 2019.

Bibliography

Amfitheatrof, Erik. *The Children of Columbus*. Boston: Little, Brown and Co., 1973.

Barzini, Luigi. *The Italians*. New York: Atheneum, 1965.

Brooklyn Daily Eagle

Caruso, Enrico, Jr. *My Father and My Family*. Portland, Oregon: Amadeus Press, 1997.

Dash, Mike. *The First Family*. New York: Simon & Schuster, 2009.

Gambino, Richard. *Vendetta*. Toronto: Guernica, 1998.

The New York Times

Newton, Michael. *The Mafia at Apalachin, 1957*. Jefferson, NC: McFarland & Co., 2012.

Petacco, Arrigo. *Joe Petrosino*. New York: Macmillan, 1974.

Reppetto, Thomas. *American Mafia*. New York: Henry Holt and Co., 2004.

Reppetto, Thomas, and Kames Lardner. *NYPD: A City and Its Police*. New York: Henry Holt and Company, 2000.

Romano, Anne T. *Italian Americans in Law Enforcement*. Bloomington, IN: Xlibris, 2010.

Talty, Stephen. *The Black Hand*. New York: Houghton Mifflin Harcourt, 2017.

Tuohy, John William. *Joe Petrosino's War on the Mafia: The Mob File Series*. Lexington, KY: CreateSpace, 2018.